Treasury of *Campbell's* Recipes

CRESCENT BOOKS

This edition was prepared by the Publications Center in coordination with the Creative Food Center and Communications Center, Campbell Soup Company, Campbell Place, Camden, NJ 08103-1799.

Managing Editor: Pat Teberg
Contributing Editors: Julia Malloy, Patricia A. Ward

Pictured on the front cover:
Barbecued Pork Spareribs (see recipe, page 114)
Fish Rolls with Asparagus (see recipe, page 166)
Layered Spinach Salad (see recipe, page 230)

Pictured on the back cover:
Gazpacho (see recipe, page 36)
Chicken Salad Croissants (see recipe, page 54)
Cheesecake Pie (see recipe, page 264)
Italian Mushroom Omelet (see recipe, page 62)

ISBN: 0-517-05258-X
Library of Congress Catalog Card Number: 90-83421

This edition published by:
Crescent Books
Distributed by Outlet Book Company, Inc.
A Random House Company
40 Englehard Ave.
Avenel, New Jersey 07001

Treasury of Campbell's Recipes

The Best From

Campbell's

Campbell Soup Company invites you to enjoy this treasury of more than 350 tried-and-true recipes ranging from taste-tempting appetizers to mouth-watering desserts. You'll recognize some of your family's favorites in this recipe collection: easy-does-it Classic Glorified Chicken, savory Green Bean Bake and deliciously moist Tomato Soup Spice Cake. Look, too, for a Greek-style pancake topped with crumbled feta, mushrooms and ripe olives; Blackened Chicken with a spicy New Orleans flavor; and garden-fresh Tortellini Salad glistening with a robust Dijon dressing. All the recipes in this cookbook have been updated for the way you cook and eat today. There are great-tasting recipes you can microwave, grill or cook conventionally on the range top or in the oven.

Whether your family prefers traditional meals or dares to try something different, you'll find lots of ideas just right for you. Each recipe uses one or more of the Campbell's family of quality, convenient-to-use products that will help you prepare delicious meals every day of the week without spending hours in your kitchen.

As you turn the pages of this cookbook, keep in mind that each and every recipe has been tested and approved by experienced home economists in Campbell Soup Company's Creative Food Center. That's why you can prepare all these recipes with complete confidence.

Campbell's Quality Products

You'll save lots of cooking time when you rely on Campbell's convenience products. For instance, cooking with Campbell's condensed soups is a sure-fire way to add a blend of flavors to any dish. The cream-style soups—celery, mushroom and chicken—are the start of foolproof sauces or gravies while the condensed broths make rich and flavorful bases for cooking.

Campbell's quality canned soups and dry soup recipe mixes also add convenience and flavor to many dishes. Try the soups as is or use as a shortcut for your own cooking needs.

Swanson clear ready to serve broth—another outstanding soup product that makes cooking easy—is available in two flavors, chicken and beef. Both are a great way to add rich flavor and convenience to most dishes.

Timesaving Swanson premium chunk chicken puts cooked chicken at your fingertips for refreshing salads and easy-to-fix sandwich fillings. It's also handy for making quick soups, potato toppers and pasta pour-overs.

Open Pit barbecue sauces add zesty flavor to many dishes and make delicious basting sauces for grilled or broiled foods. The sauces blend well with ingredients, too, when preparing tasty regional favorites, such as Sweet Georgia Barbecued Spareribs.

Look to Franco-American gravies to add silky smoothness to sauces and glazes. For perfect gravy every time, stir a can into the pan drippings of your favorite roast. No mess and no lumps.

You'll find picture-perfect Campbell's Fresh products in your supermarket's produce section. Juicy hydroponic tomatoes and tender butterhead lettuce, as well as several varieties of mushrooms, are available all year for your family's eating pleasure.

Also in the fresh produce section, discover Marie's refrigerated salad dressings. There's a wide variety of flavors including some reduced-calorie versions, too.

When you open a can, bottle or carton of V8 vegetable juice, you'll be ready to enjoy a delicious and nutritious blend of eight vegetable juices with no artificial colors or flavorings. V8 is naturally low in calories, a great source of vitamin A and a convenient-to-use ingredient for many recipes.

Popular Campbell's pork & beans in tomato sauce is the basis for many unique regional dishes, such as Cajun-Style Beans and Layered Spinach Salad. When you use these saucy plump beans in a recipe, you have all the homemade flavor of beans without the long hours of preparation.

Many of these recipes call for Vlasic pickles, relishes, peppers and sauerkraut. These condiments add extra zip each and every time you use them. Remember, too, that these products make fine accompaniments to many of your favorite dishes.

If you keep several packages of Mrs. Paul's frozen fish fillets on hand, you have the makings for many delicious timesaving main dishes that are sure to please. Mrs. Paul's frozen candied sweet potatoes are found in your grocer's freezer, too. Each package has its own seasoning packet, too.

Because Prego spaghetti sauce is already seasoned with basil, oregano and garlic, preparing homemade-tasting recipes is a snap. Each jar holds the makings of many of your favorite Italian-style dishes. As you turn these pages, you're sure to find some new recipes to add to your own recipe collection.

Lastly, you can depend on the quality of Pepperidge Farm frozen pastries, fresh breads, crackers and cookies time and again, whether served alone or as an ingredient in one of these recipes.

Microwaving Guidelines

Because microwave ovens vary, we suggest using these cooking guidelines so your microwaved recipes will be successful every time:

Microwave cooking times in this book are approximate. Numerous variables, such as the microwave oven's output wattage and the starting temperature, shape, type, amount and depth of the food, can affect cooking time. Use the cooking times as guidelines and check for doneness before adding more time. These recipes have been tested in 650- to 700-watt microwave ovens. Lower wattage ovens may require longer cooking times.

Grilling Basics

Many cooks are barbecuing and grilling all year around. For this reason, you'll find lots of recipes for cooking outdoors. In many cases, broiling directions give you a cooking alternative when the weather dampens your plans for outdoor meal preparation.

The grilling recipes in this book specify direct or indirect heat, coal temperature and whether covering is necessary. All foods were cooked 4 inches above the coals during recipe testing. Cooking times may vary when these conditions differ.

Most foods are grilled over direct heat, but some larger cuts of meat require slower cooking and we recommend indirect heat. In direct grilling, the hot coals are placed directly underneath the food and the grill rack. Burgers, steaks and fish are examples of foods often cooked by this method. In indirect grilling the coals are arranged around a drip pan and the food is placed on the grill rack over the pan. The pan catches the juices and fat that fall from the food and prevents flare-ups. Indirect grilling is the best way to get the smoky flavor of wood, such as mesquite, because the food must be covered during cooking. This method, for example, is used for ham, leg of lamb, beef roast and a whole chicken or turkey.

Grilling food at the right temperature is another key to successful barbecuing. Add more coals and wood chips to maintain the right temperature, but don't lift the grill cover more than necessary because it will slow the cooking process. Thinner foods cook better over hot coals than do larger cuts. To judge the coal temperature, hold your hand just above the grid—over the coals for direct heat and over the pan for indirect heat. Then start counting the seconds, "one Open Pit, two Open Pit, three Open Pit." If you need to withdraw your hand after two seconds, the coals are hot; after three seconds, they're medium-hot; after four seconds, they're medium and so on.

Appetizers &
Beverages

Herbed Mussels in Wine (page 8); Saucy Chicken Wings (page 8)

HERBED MUSSELS IN WINE

3 pounds mussels (about 5 to
  6 dozen)
2 tablespoons butter or margarine
⅓ cup chopped green onions
1 clove garlic, minced

¼ teaspoon dried Italian seasoning,
  crushed
¾ cup V8 vegetable juice
¼ cup Chablis or other dry white wine
Generous dash pepper

1. Discard any open mussels that do not close when tapped with fingers.*
Scrub mussels; clip off beards with kitchen shears.

2. In 4-quart saucepan over low heat, in hot butter, cook green onions, garlic
and Italian seasoning until onions are tender, stirring often. Add mussels,
V8 juice, wine and pepper. Heat to boiling; reduce heat to low. Cover; simmer
6 to 8 minutes or until mussels open, stirring occasionally. Discard any
mussels that do not open.

3. With slotted spoon, remove mussels from pan; remove and discard top
halves of shells. Arrange mussels on serving platter; pour sauce over
mussels. Makes about 5 dozen appetizers.

*To make sure raw mussels are safe to eat, tap on any open shells. If the
mussel closes its shell, it is alive and will be safe to eat after cooking.
Discard those that remain open. After cooking, discard any mussels with
closed shells, because they were not alive before cooking and are not safe
to eat.

SAUCY CHICKEN WINGS

2 pounds chicken wings (about
  10 wings)
1½ cups V8 vegetable juice
1 tablespoon soy sauce
2 cloves garlic, minced

1 teaspoon ground ginger or
  2 teaspoons grated fresh ginger
⅛ teaspoon sesame oil
2 tablespoons water
1 tablespoon cornstarch

1. Spray 10-inch nonstick skillet with vegetable cooking spray. Over medium
heat, cook chicken wings, half at a time, until browned on all sides. Spoon
off fat. Return wings to skillet. Add V8 juice, soy sauce, garlic, ginger and
sesame oil. Reduce heat to low. Cover; simmer 20 minutes. Uncover; simmer
10 minutes more or until wings are fork-tender.

2. Remove chicken to serving platter; keep warm. In cup, stir water into
cornstarch until smooth; gradually stir into V8 mixture. Cook until mixture
boils and thickens, stirring often. Serve sauce over wings. Makes about
10 appetizers.

MEXICAN-STYLE APPETIZER

1 can (11½ ounces) Campbell's
  condensed bean with bacon
  soup
1 package (1¼ ounces) taco
  seasoning mix
¼ teaspoon hot pepper sauce
1 cup sour cream
1 can (4 ounces) chopped green
  chilies, drained

½ cup sliced Vlasic pimento-stuffed
  Spanish olives
1 cup shredded longhorn cheese
  (4 ounces)
½ cup alfalfa sprouts
½ cup chopped Campbell's Fresh
  tomato

1. In small bowl, combine soup, taco seasoning mix and hot pepper sauce; stir until blended. On large serving plate, spread mixture into 6-inch round. Spread sides and top of bean mixture with sour cream to cover.

2. Layer chilies, olives, cheese, alfalfa sprouts and tomato on sour cream. Cover; refrigerate until serving time, at least 4 hours. Serve with tortilla chips for dipping. Makes 10 appetizers.

MUSHROOM QUESADILLAS

2 tablespoons butter or margarine
1 package (12 ounces) Campbell's
  Fresh mushrooms, coarsely
  chopped
2 green onions, sliced
4 flour tortillas (8-inch diameter)

1 cup shredded Monterey Jack
  cheese (4 ounces)
¼ cup canned chopped green chilies
2 tablespoons vegetable oil
Salsa
Sour cream

1. In 10-inch skillet over medium heat, in hot butter, cook mushrooms and green onions until mushrooms are tender and liquid is evaporated, stirring occasionally.

2. To make quesadillas: On half of each flour tortilla, layer ¼ of the cheese, green chilies and mushroom mixture. Fold tortilla in half; press edges firmly. Repeat with remaining tortillas.

3. Using paper towel, wipe out skillet. In skillet over medium heat, in 1 tablespoon hot oil, fry 2 quesadillas for 3 minutes, turning once. Using a turner; remove to paper towels to drain. Repeat with remaining oil and quesadillas. Serve immediately with salsa and sour cream.
Makes 4 appetizers.

OVEN-FRIED MUSHROOMS

½ cup all-purpose flour
½ teaspoon paprika
1 cup soft bread crumbs
½ cup grated Parmesan cheese
2 teaspoons dried basil or oregano
   leaves, crushed

2 eggs, slightly beaten
2 tablespoons milk
2 packages (8 ounces *each*)
   Campbell's Fresh mushrooms
¼ cup butter or margarine, melted
   Dipping Sauce (recipe follows)

1. Preheat oven to 450°F. Lightly grease 15- by 10-inch jelly-roll pan.

2. In plastic bag, combine flour and paprika. In another plastic bag, combine crumbs, cheese and basil. In small bowl, combine eggs and milk.

3. Shake mushrooms in flour mixture and dip in egg mixture. Shake in crumb mixture, pressing crumb mixture to mushrooms to coat.

4. Arrange mushrooms cap-side down on prepared jelly-roll pan. Drizzle with butter. Bake 10 minutes or until golden brown. Serve with Dipping Sauce. Makes about 24 appetizers.

DIPPING SAUCE: In small bowl, combine ¼ cup mayonnaise, 1 tablespoon Dijon-style mustard or prepared horseradish and 1 tablespoon chopped fresh parsley; mix well. Makes about ¼ cup.

Tip: To make ahead, coated mushrooms can be covered and refrigerated until baking time.

CHEESE-STUFFED VEGETABLES

1 can (10¾ ounces) Campbell's
   condensed cream of celery soup
1 package (8 ounces) cream
   cheese, softened
1 to 2 tablespoons lemon juice
1 clove garlic, minced
½ teaspoon dried savory leaves,
   crushed

¼ teaspoon pepper
   Cherry tomatoes, fresh snow peas
   or celery stalks (cut into 2-inch
   pieces)
   Chopped fresh parsley

1. In medium bowl with mixer at low speed, beat soup and cream cheese until well blended. Beat in lemon juice, garlic, savory and pepper. Cover; refrigerate until serving time, at least 4 hours.

2. Using a spoon or decorating tip, stuff vegetables with cheese mixture. Sprinkle with parsley. Makes about 2¼ cups filling or 36 appetizers.

Tip: To prepare cherry tomatoes for stuffing, slice off tops. Scoop out seeds and pulp with a small spoon or grapefruit knife. With a sharp knife, cut a decorative edge, if desired. To prepare pea pods for stuffing, make a slit in one long edge.

Oven-Fried Mushrooms

CHEESE WONTONS WITH CILANTRO SAUCE

¾ cup V8 vegetable juice
2 tablespoons chopped fresh
   cilantro or parsley
2 tablespoons chopped green onion
1 tablespoon vegetable oil
½ cup chopped onion
⅓ cup chopped sweet red pepper

2 teaspoons chili powder
1 can (4 ounces) chopped chilies
1 cup shredded Monterey Jack
   cheese (4 ounces)
25 Wonton wrappers
Oil for deep-fat frying

1. To make sauce: In small bowl, combine V8 juice, cilantro and green onion; set aside.

2. To make filling: In 8-inch skillet over medium heat, in 1 tablespoon hot oil, cook onion and red pepper with chili powder until onion is tender, stirring occasionally. Remove from heat; cool slightly. Stir in chilies and cheese.

3. Keep wonton wrappers covered with plastic wrap until ready to fill. Spoon about 1½ teaspoons filling into center of each wonton wrapper. Moisten edges of wontons with water; fold diagonally in half. Pinch edges to seal. Cover filled wontons with plastic wrap while working with remaining wonton wrappers.

4. In large saucepan or Dutch oven over medium-high heat, heat 1½ inches oil to 350°F. Adjust heat to maintain temperature. Cook wontons, 4 at a time, 1 to 2 minutes or until golden brown on both sides. Remove to paper towels to drain.

5. Serve warm with sauce for dipping. Makes 25 appetizers.

Note: Fried wontons can be wrapped and frozen. To reheat, preheat oven to 350°F. Place wontons on cookie sheet; bake 15 minutes or until crisp.

PIZZA FONDUE

½ cup finely chopped pepperoni
1 sweet red or green pepper,
   chopped
4 ounces cream cheese, cut into
   cubes

⅓ cup grated Parmesan cheese
1 jar (14 ounces) Prego spaghetti
   sauce (1¾ cups)

1. In 1½-quart microwave-safe casserole, combine pepperoni and pepper. Cover with lid; microwave on HIGH 3 minutes or until pepper is tender, stirring once during cooking.

2. Stir in cream cheese and Parmesan until smooth and well blended. Stir in spaghetti sauce. Cover; microwave on HIGH 5 minutes or until hot and bubbling, stirring once during cooking. Serve with cubed Italian bread for dipping. Makes about 3 cups.

Cheese Wontons with Cilantro Sauce

SOUTHWESTERN ZUCCHINI QUICHE

1 tablespoon butter or margarine
1 cup chopped Campbell's fresh
  mushrooms
1 cup chopped zucchini
½ cup chopped onion
¼ cup chopped sweet red pepper
1 clove garlic, minced
¼ teaspoon dried basil leaves,
  crushed
¼ teaspoon dried oregano leaves,
  crushed
1 tablespoon all-purpose flour
1 can (11 ounces) Campbell's
  condensed nacho cheese soup/
  dip
3 eggs, beaten
2 cups shredded Monterey Jack
  cheese (8 ounces)

1. Place butter in 10-inch microwave-safe pie plate. Cover; microwave on HIGH 20 seconds or until butter melts. Brush butter over bottom and side of pie plate; set aside.

2. In 2-quart microwave-safe casserole, combine mushrooms, zucchini, onion, red pepper, garlic, basil and oregano. Cover with lid; microwave on HIGH 4 minutes or until vegetables are tender, stirring once during cooking.

3. Stir in flour. Add soup, eggs and cheese, stirring until well blended. Pour into prepared pie plate.

4. Elevate pie plate on inverted pie plate or saucer if necessary. Microwave, uncovered, on HIGH 13 minutes or until center is nearly set, rotating plate 3 times during cooking. Let stand directly on countertop 10 minutes. Makes 12 appetizer servings or 4 main-dish servings.

SAUSAGE-STUFFED MUSHROOMS

2 packages (14 ounces *each*)
  Campbell's Fresh gourmet
  stuffing mushrooms (about 24)
½ pound Italian sausage, casing
  removed
¼ cup finely chopped onion
1 clove garlic, minced
¼ cup shredded provolone cheese
  (1 ounce)
¼ cup Italian-style fine dry bread
  crumbs
1 egg, slightly beaten
2 tablespoons butter or margarine,
  melted

1. To make stuffing: Remove stems from mushrooms; chop stems. In 10-inch skillet over medium heat, cook sausage, chopped stems, onion and garlic until sausage is browned and mushrooms are tender, stirring to separate sausage. Spoon off fat. Stir in cheese, bread crumbs and egg.

2. Lightly brush mushroom caps with melted butter; arrange on rack in broiler pan. Stuff each mushroom cap with about 2 teaspoons of the stuffing.

3. Broil 4 inches from heat 5 minutes or until hot. Makes about 24 appetizers.

SWEET AND SOUR FRANKS

1 can (10¾ ounces) Campbell's
   condensed tomato soup
¼ cup grape jelly
¼ cup vinegar
1 tablespoon prepared mustard

1 pound frankfurters, cut into 1-inch
   pieces
1 can (20 ounces) pineapple
   chunks, drained

1. In 2-quart saucepan over medium heat, heat soup, jelly, vinegar and mustard until jelly melts and mixture is very warm, stirring occasionally.

2. Add frankfurter pieces and pineapple chunks to sauce; heat through, stirring occasionally. Serve hot with wooden toothpicks or cocktail picks. Makes about 40 appetizers.

To microwave: In 3-quart microwave-safe casserole, combine soup, jelly, vinegar and mustard. Cover; microwave on HIGH 3 to 5 minutes until hot, stirring once during cooking. Add frankfurter pieces and pineapple chunks to casserole. Cover; microwave on HIGH 5 to 8 minutes or until heated through, stirring once during cooking. Serve hot with wooden toothpicks or cocktail picks.

ORIENTAL TURKEY PUFFS

½ pound ground turkey
1 cup chopped fresh or canned bean
   sprouts
½ cup coarsely chopped water
   chestnuts
⅓ cup chopped green onions
2 tablespoons soy sauce
½ teaspoon ground ginger
⅛ teaspoon hot pepper sauce

1 package (17¼ ounces) Pepperidge
   Farm frozen puff pastry sheets,
   thawed
1 egg
1 tablespoon milk
2 tablespoons sesame seed
   Oriental Dipping Sauce (see
   page 256)

1. In medium bowl, combine turkey, bean sprouts, water chestnuts, green onions, soy sauce, ginger and hot pepper sauce. Cover; refrigerate at least 2 hours.

2. Preheat oven to 450°F.

3. Roll each puff pastry sheet to 15- by 10-inch rectangle. Drop turkey mixture by tablespoonfuls about 2 inches apart onto 1 pastry sheet, making 24 mounds. Cover with remaining sheet of pastry. With sharp knife or pizza wheel, cut dough into 24 squares. Press edges of each square to seal. Arrange squares on ungreased cookie sheets.

4. In small bowl, beat egg and milk. Lightly brush pastry squares with egg mixture; sprinkle with sesame seed. Bake 12 minutes or until golden brown.

5. Meanwhile, prepare Oriental Dipping Sauce. Serve turkey puffs with sauce. Makes 24 appetizers.

BEAN DIP

1 can (16 ounces) Campbell's pork & beans in tomato sauce	¼ cup chopped green pepper
¾ cup shredded Monterey Jack cheese (3 ounces)	¼ cup chopped sweet red pepper
	1 tablespoon finely chopped onion
	1 or 2 Tortilla Cups* (recipe follows)

1. In small saucepan, coarsely mash beans with fork.

2. Stir in cheese, peppers and onion. Over medium-high heat, heat until cheese is melted, stirring often.

3. Spoon dip into Tortilla Cups. Serve with vegetables for dipping. Makes about 2 cups.

To microwave: In 1-quart microwave-safe casserole, mash beans; stir in cheese, peppers and onion. Cover; microwave on HIGH 3 minutes or until dip is hot and cheese is melted, stirring once during cooking.

TORTILLA CUPS: For each cup, brush both sides of 8-inch flour tortilla with melted butter. Place over inverted 2-cup glass measure. Microwave on HIGH 30 seconds. Press tortilla to side of measure. Microwave on HIGH 30 seconds more. Allow to cool on measure; remove carefully.

Note: For conventional preparation for Tortilla Cups, see page 92, Chili and Tortilla Cups.

*Tortilla cup will soften if dip remains in cup for a long period. To prevent this, fill custard cup with dip; place inside tortilla cup. Or, make two tortilla cups, filling each as needed.

ROASTED RED PEPPER DIP

1 jar (7 ounces) roasted red peppers	1½ cups sour cream
1 pouch Campbell's dry onion soup and recipe mix	Generous dash hot pepper sauce
	Red pepper rings for garnish

1. In covered blender or food processor, blend roasted peppers and their liquid until smooth.

2. In medium bowl, combine soup mix, sour cream, hot pepper sauce and pepper puree; mix well. Cover; refrigerate until serving time, at least 2 hours.

3. Garnish with red pepper rings. Serve with chips and fresh vegetables for dipping. Makes 2½ cups.

Bean Dip

BAKED NACHO DIP

1 round loaf bread (about 1 pound)
1 can (11 ounces) Campbell's
   condensed nacho cheese
   soup/dip
1 can (6½ ounces) tuna, drained
   and flaked

1 package (3 ounces) cream
   cheese, softened
½ cup chopped celery
Sliced Vlasic pitted ripe olives for
   garnish

1. Preheat oven to 350°F.

2. Slice top from bread; set aside. Pull out center of loaf, leaving ½-inch shell. Cut top and center part of loaf into 1-inch cubes for dipping; set aside. Place bread shell on cookie sheet.

3. In 2-quart saucepan, combine soup, tuna, cream cheese and celery. Over medium heat, heat through, stirring constantly.

4. Pour soup mixture into bread shell; cover loosely with foil. Bake 20 minutes or until bread is warm. Remove foil; top with olives. Serve with bread cubes for dipping. Makes about 2½ cups.

Tip: For a milder flavor, use an 8-ounce package of cream cheese for the 3-ounce package.

MINI REUBENS

20 slices party rye or pumpernickel
   bread, toasted
¼ pound thinly sliced cooked corned
   beef
¼ cup Marie's refrigerated regular or
   lite Thousand Island salad
   dressing

1 cup Vlasic sauerkraut, rinsed and
   drained
1 cup shredded Swiss cheese
   (4 ounces)

1. Arrange bread on 2 large microwave-safe plates lined with plain white paper towels. Top each bread slice with small piece of corned beef and some salad dressing, sauerkraut and Swiss cheese.

2. Microwave one plate at a time, uncovered, on HIGH 1 minute or until cheese is melted. Makes 20 appetizers.

Tip: Full-size slices of rye or pumpernickel bread can be used instead of party rye. Cut bread into festive shapes with a cookie cutter. Toast cutouts, then assemble sandwiches as directed.

Baked Nacho Dip

CHEESY MUSHROOM CANAPES

2 tablespoons butter or margarine
2 packages (8 ounces *each*)
 Campbell's Fresh mushrooms,
 finely chopped
2 tablespoons all-purpose flour
¼ teaspoon salt
⅛ teaspoon pepper

½ cup milk
1 cup shredded Swiss or Gruyère
 cheese (4 ounces), divided
Toasted party rye bread or
 crackers
Chopped fresh parsley for garnish

1. In 10-inch skillet over medium heat, in hot butter, cook mushrooms until tender and liquid is evaporated, stirring occasionally.

2. Stir in flour, salt and pepper until blended; cook 1 minute, stirring constantly. Gradually stir in milk. Cook until mixture boils and thickens, stirring often. Stir in ½ cup of the cheese.

3. Spread about 1 tablespoon of the mushroom mixture on each toast slice. Arrange on rack of broiler pan; sprinkle with remaining cheese.

4. Broil 4 inches from heat 3 minutes or until hot and bubbling. Garnish with parsley. Makes about 1½ cups mushroom mixture or 24 appetizers.

MINIATURE SHRIMP QUICHES

4 eggs
1 can (10¾ ounces) Campbell's
 condensed cream of celery soup
½ cup half-and-half
2 tablespoons grated Parmesan
 cheese

¼ teaspoon dried dill weed, crushed
 Pastry for 2-crust 9-inch pie
1 cup shredded Swiss cheese
 (4 ounces)
¾ cup chopped cooked shrimp
 Ground nutmeg

1. In medium bowl, beat eggs, soup, half-and-half, Parmesan and dill weed until smooth. Set aside.

2. Divide pastry in half. On floured surface, roll out ½ of the pastry to ⅛-inch thickness. Cut 9 rounds using 4-inch cookie cutter with scalloped edge. Line 3-inch muffin-pan cups with rounds. Repeat with remaining pastry.

3. Preheat oven to 425°F. In small bowl, combine Swiss cheese and shrimp. Divide mixture equally among shells.

4. Spoon about 2 tablespoons of the soup mixture into each prepared shell. Sprinkle with nutmeg.

5. Bake 20 to 25 minutes or until set. Cool in pans on wire racks 5 minutes. Remove from pans and serve. Makes 18 mini-quiches or appetizers.

MAKE-AHEAD HAM 'N' CHEESE CANAPES

1 can (11 ounces) Campbell's
condensed Cheddar cheese
soup
1 cup shredded sharp Cheddar
cheese (4 ounces)

½ pound ground cooked ham
1 clove garlic, minced
2 tablespoons chopped fresh parsley
Melba toast rounds
Paprika

1. In medium bowl, combine soup, cheese, ham, garlic and parsley; mix well. Spread mixture on melba toast and place on cookie sheets. Sprinkle with paprika.

2. Freeze canapes until firm. Wrap in foil or place frozen canapes in freezer bags for longer storage. Return to freezer.

3. To heat: Preheat oven to 375°F. Bake frozen appetizers 15 minutes or until golden brown. Makes about 80 appetizers.

CAPONATA

½ cup olive oil
1 medium eggplant, cut into ½-inch
cubes
1 medium onion, sliced and
separated into rings
½ cup sliced celery
1 clove garlic, minced

1 can (10¾ ounces) Campbell's
condensed tomato soup
1 bay leaf
½ teaspoon dried thyme leaves,
crushed
½ cup sliced Vlasic pitted ripe olives
1½ teaspoons vinegar

1. In 4-quart Dutch oven over medium heat, in hot oil, cook eggplant, onion, celery and garlic 10 minutes or until onion is tender, stirring occasionally.

2. Stir in soup, bay leaf and thyme. Reduce heat to low. Cover; simmer 15 minutes or until eggplant is tender. Remove from heat. Discard bay leaf.

3. Stir in olives and vinegar. Serve hot or cold with crusty bread. Makes about 4 cups.

Tip: Whether you serve hot or cold, caponata improves in flavor after chilling overnight.

To microwave: Reduce oil to ¼ cup. In 3-quart microwave-safe casserole, combine ¼ cup oil, eggplant, onion, celery and garlic. Cover; microwave on HIGH 6 to 8 minutes or until onion is tender and eggplant is translucent, stirring occasionally during cooking. Stir in soup, bay leaf and thyme. Cover; microwave on HIGH 6 to 8 minutes or until eggplant is tender, stirring occasionally during cooking. Discard bay leaf. Proceed as in step 3.

PICKLED PEPPER QUICHE

¼ pound bulk pork sausage
4 eggs
1 can (10¾ ounces) Campbell's
condensed cream of chicken
soup
½ cup half-and-half or milk
¼ cup chopped Vlasic mild pepper
rings

2 tablespoons chopped fresh parsley
¼ teaspoon paprika
1 baked piecrust (9-inch) in
microwave-safe pie plate
Vlasic mild pepper rings for
garnish
Carrot flowers for garnish
Fresh parsley sprigs for garnish

1. Crumble sausage into small microwave-safe bowl. Cover with plain white
paper towel; microwave on HIGH 5 minutes, stirring once during cooking to
separate meat. Drain on paper towels; set aside.

2. In large bowl, beat eggs, soup and half-and-half until smooth. Stir in
chopped pepper rings, parsley, paprika and sausage. Pour into baked
piecrust.

3. Elevate pie plate on inverted pie plate or a saucer. Microwave, uncovered,
on MEDIUM (50% power) 22 minutes or until center is nearly set, rotating
dish 3 times during cooking. Let stand directly on countertop 10 minutes.
Garnish with pepper rings, carrot flowers and parsley. Makes 12 appetizers.

DEVILED STUFFED EGGS

12 hard-cooked eggs
⅓ cup finely chopped Vlasic country
classic sweet gherkins
⅓ cup Marie's refrigerated buttermilk
spice ranch style salad dressing

2 tablespoons finely chopped onion
¼ teaspoon salt
Finely chopped Vlasic country
classic sweet gherkins for
garnish

1. Remove egg shells. Cut eggs in half lengthwise. Remove and chop egg
yolks. Dice 1 egg white.

2. To make filling: In medium bowl, combine yolks, diced egg white, ⅓ cup
gherkins, salad dressing, onion and salt; mix well.

3. Spoon about 1 tablespoon of the filling into each remaining egg white half.
Cover; refrigerate until serving time, at least 4 hours. Top stuffed eggs with
chopped gherkins. Makes 22 appetizers.

Pickled Pepper Quiche

CREAMY CHILI DIP

2 packages (8 ounces *each*) cream
  cheese or reduced-calorie
  cream cheese, softened
¾ cup V8 vegetable juice
1 can (4 ounces) chopped green
  chilies

½ cup chopped Vlasic pitted ripe
  olives
½ cup chopped sweet red pepper
2 teaspoons grated onion
¼ teaspoon hot pepper sauce
  Fresh cilantro for garnish

1. In medium bowl with mixer at medium speed, beat cream cheese until smooth.

2. Gradually beat in V8 juice until smooth and thoroughly blended.

3. Stir in chilies, olives, red pepper, onion and hot pepper sauce. Cover; refrigerate until serving time, at least 4 hours.

4. Garnish with fresh cilantro. Serve with fresh vegetables or chips for dipping. Makes 4 cups.

RATATOUILLE APPETIZER

¼ cup olive oil
1 large onion, chopped
2 cloves garlic, minced
1 teaspoon dried Italian seasoning,
  crushed
1 small eggplant, cut into ¼-inch
  cubes (about ¾ pound)

1 large sweet red pepper, cut into
  ¼-inch pieces
1 small zucchini, cut into ¼-inch
  cubes
¾ cup V8 vegetable juice

1. In 4-quart saucepan over medium heat, in hot oil, cook onion, garlic and Italian seasoning until onion is tender, stirring often. Stir in eggplant, red pepper and zucchini. Cook 10 minutes or until eggplant is tender, stirring often.

2. Stir in V8 juice; cook 3 minutes. Serve warm or chilled, with toasted French bread or pita bread wedges. Makes about 3½ cups.

Creamy Chili Dip;
Ratatouille Appetizer

CHICKEN LIVER PATE

2 packages (8 ounces *each*)
   Swanson frozen chicken livers
¼ cup water
1 pouch Campbell's dry onion soup
   and recipe mix
2 slices bacon, chopped
¼ cup butter or margarine, cut up
2 tablespoons brandy

½ teaspoon dry mustard
¼ teaspoon dried thyme leaves,
   crushed
¼ teaspoon pepper
Fresh parsley for garnish
Chopped hard-cooked egg for
   garnish

1. Remove frozen livers from boxes, but do not remove from pouches. Place in 2-quart microwave-safe casserole. Microwave, uncovered, on MEDIUM (50% power) 5 minutes, turning pouches over once during cooking. Let stand 5 minutes. Remove livers from pouches; place in same casserole.

2. Add water, soup mix and bacon. Cover with lid; microwave on HIGH 5 minutes, stirring twice during cooking. Cover; microwave on MEDIUM (50% power) 4 minutes more or until livers are no longer pink, stirring once during cooking.

3. In covered blender or food processor, blend liver mixture, butter, brandy, mustard, thyme and pepper until smooth.

4. Spoon mixture into 3-cup serving dish. Cover; refrigerate until serving time, at least 4 hours or overnight. Garnish with parsley and egg. Serve with crackers. Makes 3 cups.

PECAN MUSHROOM PATE

2 tablespoons butter or margarine
1 package (8 ounces) Campbell's
   Fresh mushrooms, chopped
2 tablespoons finely chopped onion
½ teaspoon salt

⅛ teaspoon coarsely ground pepper
1 cup coarsely chopped toasted
   pecans, divided
1 tablespoon heavy cream
1 tablespoon Madeira wine

1. In 10-inch skillet over medium heat, in hot butter, cook mushrooms and onion until onion is tender and liquid is evaporated, stirring occasionally. Stir in salt and pepper.

2. Reserve 1 tablespoon of the pecans. In covered blender or food processor, blend remaining pecans until paste is formed. Add mushroom mixture, cream and Madeira. Blend until smooth. Spoon into 2-cup serving dish. Garnish with reserved pecans. Cover; refrigerate until serving time, at least 2 hours. Serve with crackers and Vlasic gherkin pickles. Makes 1⅓ cups.

PARTY MEATBALLS

1 pound lean ground beef
1½ cups V8 vegetable juice, divided
½ cup chopped Campbell's Fresh mushrooms
⅓ cup Italian-seasoned fine dry bread crumbs
¼ cup finely chopped onion

1 egg, slightly beaten
½ teaspoon dried marjoram leaves, crushed
2 tablespoons vegetable oil
1 tablespoon cornstarch
1 tablespoon Worcestershire sauce

1. In large bowl, combine ground beef, ¼ cup of the V8 juice, mushrooms, bread crumbs, onion, egg and marjoram; mix well. Shape mixture into 36 small meatballs.

2. In 10-inch skillet over medium heat, in hot oil, cook meatballs, a few at a time, until browned. Remove to paper towels to drain. Spoon off fat; wipe out skillet with paper towel.

3. In small bowl, combine the remaining 1¼ cups V8 juice and cornstarch; mix well. Add to skillet with Worcestershire. Cook over low heat until mixture thickens, stirring constantly.

4. Return meatballs to skillet; stir to coat. Cover; simmer 15 minutes, stirring occasionally. Serve with wooden toothpicks or cocktail picks. Makes 36 appetizers.

SWEET AND SOUR MEATBALLS

1½ pounds ground beef
1 pouch Campbell's dry onion mushroom soup and recipe mix, divided
½ cup soft bread crumbs
¼ cup milk
1 egg, beaten

1 tablespoon soy sauce
1 cup water
½ cup red currant jelly
1 tablespoon vinegar
½ teaspoon grated orange peel
⅛ teaspoon ground ginger

1. Preheat oven to 375°F.

2. In large bowl, combine beef, 2 tablespoons of the soup mix, bread crumbs, milk, egg and soy sauce; mix well.

3. Shape mixture into 1-inch meatballs. Arrange meatballs ½ inch apart in 2 large shallow baking pans. Bake 15 minutes or until well browned. Spoon off fat.

4. Meanwhile, in 10-inch skillet, combine remaining soup mix with water, jelly, vinegar, orange peel and ginger. Over medium-high heat, heat to boiling, stirring often.

5. Add meatballs to skillet; stir to coat. Reduce heat to low; simmer 10 minutes. Serve with wooden toothpicks or cocktail picks. Makes 36 appetizers.

PARTY SCRAMBLE

½ cup butter or margarine, cut up
1 pouch Campbell's dry onion soup
   and recipe mix
2 cups unsalted peanuts
1 cup bite-size wheat cereal squares
1 cup bite-size corn cereal squares

1 package (6 ounces) Pepperidge
   Farm Cheddar cheese tiny
   goldfish crackers
1 package (5½ ounces) Pepperidge
   Farm pretzels, tiny goldfish
   crackers or 2 cups pretzel sticks

1. Place butter in 2-cup glass measure. Cover; microwave on HIGH 45 seconds or until melted. Stir in soup mix.

2. In 4-quart microwave-safe bowl, combine remaining ingredients. Pour butter mixture over cracker mixture; toss to coat well. Microwave, uncovered, on HIGH 5 minutes or until hot, stirring twice during heating.

3. Cool. Store mixture in airtight container. Makes about 10 cups.

Tip: If a 4-quart bowl doesn't fit in your microwave, divide the mixture in half. Microwave in two batches for 2½ minutes each.

ONION-BUTTERED POPCORN

½ cup butter or margarine, cut up
1 pouch Campbell's dry onion soup
   and recipe mix

4 quarts popped popcorn

1. Place butter in 2-cup glass measure. Cover; microwave on HIGH 45 seconds or until melted. Stir in soup mix.

2. Place popcorn in very large bowl. Pour butter mixture over popcorn; toss to coat well. Makes 16 cups or 8 servings.

Tip: This butter and onion soup mixture is also delicious served on bread, potatoes, vegetables and grilled meats or tossed with croutons.

Party Scramble

DOUBLE CHEESE PUFFS

1 cup water
½ cup butter or margarine
1 cup all-purpose flour
½ cup shredded Cheddar cheese
   (2 ounces)
4 eggs
1 package (8 ounces) cream
   cheese, softened

1 can (10¾ ounces) Campbell's
   condensed cream of celery soup
2 tablespoons crumbled blue cheese
1 tablespoon chopped fresh parsley
1 teaspoon Worcestershire sauce
Paprika

1. Preheat oven to 375°F. Grease 2 large cookie sheets.

2. To make puffs: In 2-quart saucepan over medium heat, heat water and
butter to boiling. Remove from heat. Add flour all at once. With wooden
spoon, vigorously stir until mixture forms a ball and leaves the side of pan.
Stir in Cheddar cheese. Add eggs, one at a time, beating until smooth after
each addition.

3. Drop mixture by heaping teaspoonfuls about 1½ inches apart onto
prepared cookie sheets. Bake 20 to 25 minutes or until lightly browned. Cool
on wire rack.

4. To make filling: In medium bowl with mixer at medium speed, beat cream
cheese and soup until smooth. Stir in blue cheese, parsley and
Worcestershire.

5. With sharp knife, remove tops from puffs. Spoon about 1 rounded
teaspoonful of the filling into each puff; replace top. Refrigerate until
serving time, at least 1 hour. Sprinkle puffs with paprika. Makes about
50 appetizers.

BACON-HORSERADISH DIP

1 pouch Campbell's dry onion soup
   and recipe mix
2 cups sour cream
5 slices bacon, crisp-cooked and
   crumbled

1 tablespoon prepared horseradish
1 teaspoon Dijon-style mustard
Cooked bacon curl for garnish

1. In medium bowl, combine soup mix, sour cream, crumbled bacon,
horseradish and mustard; mix well. Cover; chill until serving time, at least
2 hours.

2. Garnish with bacon curl. Serve with chips or crackers. Makes 2 cups.

CURRIED PEANUT DIP

1 pouch Campbell's dry onion soup
and recipe mix
1 cup sour cream
1 cup plain yogurt

¼ cup creamy peanut butter
2 teaspoons curry powder
Chopped peanuts for garnish
Sliced pears for garnish

1. In medium bowl, combine soup mix, sour cream, yogurt, peanut butter and curry powder; mix well. Cover; refrigerate until serving time, at least 2 hours.

2. Garnish with chopped peanuts and sliced pears. Serve with fresh vegetables and fruit for dipping. Makes 2¼ cups.

CREAMY BLUE CHEESE DIP

½ cup Marie's refrigerated regular or
lite blue cheese salad dressing
½ cup Marie's refrigerated regular or
lite sour cream and dill salad
dressing

2 tablespoons thinly sliced green
onion
1 teaspoon lemon juice

1. In small bowl, combine all ingredients; mix well.

2. Cover; refrigerate until serving time, at least 1 hour. Serve with fresh vegetables or crackers for dipping. Makes 1 cup.

LAYERED TEX-MEX DIP

1 can (16 ounces) Campbell's pork &
beans in tomato sauce
⅓ cup salsa
1 medium avocado
2 teaspoons lemon juice
1 clove garlic, minced
½ teaspoon ground cumin

¼ teaspoon salt
Sour cream for garnish
Sliced Vlasic pitted ripe olives for
garnish
Chopped Campbell's Fresh
tomatoes for garnish

1. In medium bowl, mash beans with fork. Stir in salsa. Spread in 8-inch glass pie plate.

2. In medium bowl, mash avocado. Stir in lemon juice, garlic, cumin and salt. Mound in center over beans. Cover; refrigerate until serving time, at least 2 hours.

3. To serve: Garnish dip with sour cream, olives and tomatoes. Serve with tortilla chips for dipping. Makes 3 cups.

MEXICALI SIPPER

4 cups V8 vegetable juice or no salt
   added V8 vegetable juice
1 Vlasic hot jalapeno pepper, seeded
2 sprigs fresh cilantro
1 tablespoon lemon juice

1 small ripe avocado, halved,
   seeded, peeled and sliced
Sweet red pepper rings for garnish
Green onion brushes for garnish

1. In covered blender or food processor, blend V8 juice, jalapeno pepper, cilantro, lemon juice and avocado until smooth.

2. To serve: Pour over ice cubes in 10-ounce glasses; garnish with red pepper rings and green onion brushes. Makes 4½ cups or 6 servings.

Note: To make green onion brushes, slice off the roots and tops of green onions. Leaving at least 3 inches in the center, make lengthwise cuts from center to ends at one or both ends to make a fringe; place in ice water for 15 minutes. The ends will curl to look like brushes.

HOT CURRIED V8

1 teaspoon butter or margarine
¼ cup finely chopped onion
½ teaspoon curry powder

1½ cups V8 vegetable juice or no salt
   added V8 vegetable juice
Alfalfa sprouts for garnish

1. In 1-quart saucepan over medium heat, in hot butter, cook onion and curry powder until onion is tender. Add V8 juice; heat to boiling.

2. In covered blender or food processor, blend hot mixture until smooth.

3. To serve: Pour into mugs; garnish with alfalfa sprouts. Makes 1½ cups or 2 servings.

SPARKLING V8

3 cups V8 vegetable juice or no salt
   added V8 vegetable juice
2 bottles (6½ ounces *each*)
   sparkling mineral water, chilled

Mint leaves for garnish

1. In 2-quart pitcher, combine V8 juice and sparkling mineral water; mix well.

2. To serve: Pour over ice cubes in 10-ounce glasses. Garnish with mint leaves. Makes 4¾ cups or 6 servings.

Clockwise from top: Mexicali Sipper;
Hot Curried V8; Sparkling V8

TROPICAL WHIRL

¾ cup V8 vegetable juice or no salt
    added V8 vegetable juice
¾ cup pineapple juice, chilled
½ cup diced canned peaches,
    drained

Dash ground ginger
Peach slices for garnish

1. In covered blender or food processor, blend all ingredients, except peach slices until smooth.

2. To serve: Pour into 8-ounce glasses; garnish with peach slices. Makes 2 cups or 3 servings.

SPICY WARMER

2 cups V8 vegetable juice
1 teaspoon Worcestershire sauce

½ teaspoon prepared horseradish
¼ teaspoon hot pepper sauce

In 4-cup glass measure, combine all ingredients; mix well. Cover with vented plastic wrap; microwave on HIGH 3 minutes or until boiling. Makes about 2 cups or 3 servings.

TONIC THYME

1½ cups V8 vegetable juice or no salt
    added V8 vegetable juice
1 tablespoon lime juice
⅛ teaspoon dried thyme leaves,
    crushed

¼ cup tonic water, chilled
Fresh thyme sprigs or lime
    wedges for garnish

1. In small pitcher, stir together V8 juice, lime juice and dried thyme. Add tonic water; stir.

2. To serve: Pour over ice cubes in 10-ounce glasses, garnish with fresh thyme. Makes 1¾ cups or 2 servings.

Soups & Sandwiches

Gazpacho (page 36); Chicken Salad Croissants (page 54)

GAZPACHO

3 cups V8 vegetable juice or no salt
added V8 vegetable juice
1 cup chopped, seeded and peeled
cucumber
½ cup chopped sweet red or green
pepper
¼ cup chopped onion

1 tablespoon olive or vegetable oil
1 tablespoon wine vinegar
1 clove garlic
⅛ teaspoon hot pepper sauce
Additional chopped vegetables for
garnish

1. In covered blender or food processor, combine ½ of each ingredient; blend until smooth. Transfer to bowl. Repeat procedure with remaining ingredients.

2. Cover; refrigerate until serving time, at least 6 hours.

3. To serve: Ladle into bowls; garnish with additional chopped vegetables. Makes 4¼ cups or 4 servings.

HOT GAZPACHO: Prepare as in step 1; pour into 2-quart saucepan. Over medium heat, heat thoroughly, stirring occasionally. Ladle into bowls; garnish with croutons.

MUSHROOM SPINACH VICHYSSOISE

1 tablespoon butter or margarine
1½ cups coarsely chopped Campbell's
Fresh mushrooms, divided
1 large leek, thinly sliced
1 medium potato, peeled and thinly
sliced
1 can (14½ ounces) Swanson clear
ready to serve chicken broth

½ cup milk
1 teaspoon lemon juice
⅛ teaspoon pepper
1 package (10 ounces) frozen
chopped spinach, thawed and
squeezed dry
½ cup half-and-half

1. In 3-quart saucepan over medium heat, in hot butter, cook ½ cup of the mushrooms and the leek until tender and liquid is evaporated, stirring occasionally. Stir in potato and broth; heat to boiling. Reduce heat to low. Cover; simmer 10 minutes or until potato is tender.

2. In covered blender or food processor, blend ½ of the soup mixture at a time until smooth. Return to saucepan with remaining mushrooms, milk, lemon juice and pepper.

3. Cook over medium heat until mushrooms are just tender, about 5 minutes. Stir in spinach. Cover; refrigerate until thoroughly chilled, at least 6 hours or overnight.

4. Stir in half-and-half just before serving. Makes 5 cups or 5 servings.

EGG DROP SOUP

2 cans (14½ ounces *each*) Swanson
   clear ready to serve chicken
   broth
1 tablespoon cornstarch
1 tablespoon rice wine vinegar or
   dry sherry

2 teaspoons soy sauce
½ cup cooked ham cut into thin strips
½ cup snow peas
3 green onions, sliced
2 eggs, beaten

1. In 2-quart microwave-safe casserole, combine broth, cornstarch, vinegar and soy sauce until smooth; stir in ham, snow peas and onions. Cover with lid; microwave on HIGH 10 minutes or until boiling, stirring twice during cooking.

2. With fork, stir broth in swirling motion. Without stirring, slowly pour eggs into swirling broth; then stir just until eggs are set in long strands. Makes about 4 cups or 4 servings.

SHIITAKE MARSALA SOUP

1 package (3.5 ounces) Campbell's
   Fresh shiitake mushrooms
2 tablespoons butter or margarine
¼ cup finely chopped onion

1 can (14½ ounces) Swanson clear
   ready to serve chicken broth
¼ cup dry Marsala wine
Chopped fresh parsley for garnish

1. Trim woody portions of mushroom stems and discard. Remove and chop stems; slice mushroom caps.

2. In 2-quart saucepan over medium heat, in hot butter, cook mushrooms and onion until tender, stirring occasionally.

3. Add broth and wine; heat to boiling. Reduce heat to low. Simmer 5 minutes. Garnish with parsley. Makes 2¼ cups or 2 servings.

CLEAR VEGETABLE SOUP

1 can (10¾ ounces) Campbell's
condensed chicken broth
1 soup can water
½ cup sliced carrot

½ cup sliced celery
¼ cup corkscrew macaroni, uncooked
1 teaspoon chopped fresh parsley

1. In 2-quart saucepan over high heat, heat broth, water, carrot and celery to boiling. Add macaroni. Reduce heat to low. Cover; simmer 20 minutes or until macaroni is tender.

2. Ladle soup into bowls; top with parsley. Makes about 3 cups or 3 servings.

HOT AND SOUR SOUP

¼ pound boneless pork loin or
chicken
1 package (3.5 ounces) Campbell's
Fresh shiitake mushrooms
2 cans (14½ ounces *each*) Swanson
clear ready to serve chicken
broth, divided
2 cups water
½ cup canned bamboo shoots cut
into matchstick-thin strips

2 tablespoons soy sauce
2 tablespoons rice wine vinegar
¼ teaspoon crushed red pepper
Generous dash sesame oil
2 tablespoons cornstarch
1 egg, well beaten
Thinly sliced green onions for
garnish

1. Freeze meat 30 minutes to firm for easier slicing. Slice across the grain into very thin slices.

2. Trim woody portions of mushroom stems and discard. Remove and chop stems; slice mushroom caps.

3. Reserve ¼ cup of the broth. In 4-quart Dutch oven over high heat, heat remaining broth, meat, mushrooms, water, bamboo shoots, soy sauce, vinegar, red pepper and sesame oil to boiling. Reduce heat to low. Simmer 20 minutes or until meat is fork-tender.

4. In cup, stir together reserved broth and cornstarch until smooth; gradually stir into soup mixture. Cook over medium heat until mixture boils and thickens, stirring often.

5. Slowly pour egg in a stream into soup while stirring. Remove from heat. Serve immediately. Garnish with green onions. Makes 6 cups or 6 servings.

Clear Vegetable Soup

GREEK LEMON SOUP

2 cans (14½ ounces *each*) Swanson clear ready to serve chicken broth
¼ cup orzo or regular long-grain rice, uncooked
2 eggs
2 tablespoons lemon juice
Thin lemon slices for garnish

1. In 2-quart microwave-safe casserole, combine broth and orzo. Cover with lid; microwave on HIGH 8 minutes or until boiling. Stir soup.

2. Cover; microwave on MEDIUM (50% power) 18 minutes or until orzo is tender, stirring once during cooking.

3. In small bowl, beat eggs with lemon juice. Slowly beat ½ cup of the hot soup into egg mixture. Return egg mixture to soup, stirring constantly until soup is slightly thickened. Garnish with lemon slices. Makes about 4 cups or 4 servings.

HARVEST BOWL SOUP

1 tablespoon olive oil
2 cups chopped onions
1½ cups thinly sliced carrots
1 cup thinly sliced celery
4 cloves garlic, minced
2 teaspoons dried Italian seasoning, crushed
3 cans (14½ ounces *each*) Swanson clear ready to serve chicken broth
3 cups V8 vegetable juice or no salt added V8 vegetable juice
¼ pound green beans, cut into pieces
1 bay leaf
⅛ teaspoon pepper
2 cans (16 ounces *each*) red or white kidney beans, drained
2 cups coarsely chopped zucchini or yellow squash

1. In 6-quart Dutch oven over medium heat, in hot oil, cook onions, carrots, celery, garlic and Italian seasoning until vegetables are tender, stirring often.

2. Stir in remaining ingredients, except kidney beans and zucchini. Heat to boiling; reduce heat to low. Cover; simmer 30 minutes.

3. Stir in kidney beans and zucchini. Cover; simmer 5 minutes more or until zucchini is tender. Discard bay leaf. Makes 14 cups or 14 servings.

CREAMY VEGETABLE BISQUE

2 tablespoons butter or margarine
1 cup carrots cut into matchstick-thin strips
1 cup sliced celery
½ cup chopped onion

1 can (10¾ ounces) Campbell's condensed cream of mushroom soup
1 soup can milk
⅛ teaspoon pepper
Grated Romano cheese

1. In 2-quart saucepan over medium heat, in hot butter, cook carrots, celery and onion 5 minutes or until vegetables are tender-crisp, stirring often.

2. Stir in soup, milk and pepper. Heat through. Ladle into bowls; top with cheese. Makes 3½ cups or 4 servings.

CREAMY CHICKEN BROCCOLI BISQUE

1 tablespoon butter or margarine
1 cup sliced Campbell's Fresh mushrooms
½ cup sweet red and green pepper strips
1 can (10¾ ounces) Campbell's condensed cream of chicken soup

1 soup can milk
1 package (10 ounces) frozen chopped broccoli
2 cups cubed cooked chicken or turkey
¼ teaspoon pepper
Generous dash ground nutmeg

1. In 3-quart saucepan over medium heat, in hot butter, cook mushrooms and pepper strips until vegetables are tender, stirring occasionally.

2. Stir in soup, milk, broccoli, chicken, pepper and nutmeg. Heat to boiling, stirring occasionally. Reduce heat to low. Cover; simmer 5 minutes or until broccoli is tender. Makes 5 cups or 4 servings.

MUSHROOM BISQUE

2 tablespoons butter or margarine
2 packages (8 ounces *each*)
 Campbell's Fresh mushrooms,
 sliced
⅓ cup finely chopped green onions
2 tablespoons all-purpose flour
½ cup water
2 cups half-and-half

½ teaspoon salt
¼ teaspoon ground nutmeg
⅛ teaspoon pepper
 Sliced Campbell's Fresh
 mushrooms, sautéed, for
 garnish
 Fresh marjoram sprig for garnish

1. In 3-quart saucepan over medium heat, in hot butter, cook mushrooms and onions until tender and liquid is evaporated, stirring occasionally. Reserve 1 cup mushroom mixture.

2. Stir flour into remaining mushrooms in saucepan until blended; cook 1 minute, stirring constantly. Gradually stir in water; cook until mixture boils and thickens, stirring often.

3. In covered blender or food processor, blend soup mixture until smooth.

4. Return blended mixture to saucepan; stir in reserved mushrooms, half-and-half, salt, nutmeg and pepper. Heat through, stirring occasionally. Garnish with sautéed mushrooms and marjoram sprig. Makes 4¼ cups or 4 servings.

CURRIED ZUCCHINI SOUP

1 tablespoon butter or margarine
2 cups coarsely chopped zucchini
2 tablespoons sliced green onion
1 teaspoon curry powder
1 can (10¾ ounces) Campbell's
 condensed cream of potato soup

1¾ cups milk
 Pepperidge Farm croutons for
 garnish

1. In 2-quart microwave-safe casserole, combine butter, zucchini, onion and curry powder. Cover with lid; microwave on HIGH 7 minutes or until zucchini is very tender, stirring once during cooking.

2. Stir soup into zucchini mixture. In covered blender or food processor, blend soup mixture until smooth. Return to casserole. Stir in milk.

3. Cover; refrigerate until serving time, at least 4 hours. Thin chilled soup to desired consistency with additional milk. Ladle into bowls and garnish with croutons. Makes about 4 cups or 4 servings.

Tip: To serve this soup hot, prepare as in steps 1 and 2. Cover; microwave on HIGH 4 minutes or until hot and bubbling.

Mushroom Bisque

APPLE-CHEESE SOUP

2 apples, peeled and chopped
1 tablespoon water
¼ teaspoon ground nutmeg
¼ teaspoon ground cinnamon
1 can (11 ounces) Campbell's condensed Cheddar cheese soup

¾ cup milk
Sour cream or plain yogurt for garnish
Ground nutmeg for garnish

1. In 2-quart microwave-safe casserole, combine apples, water, nutmeg and cinnamon. Cover with lid; microwave on HIGH 5 minutes or until apples are very tender, stirring once during cooking.

2. Stir soup into apple mixture. In covered blender or food processor, blend soup mixture until smooth. Return to casserole. Stir in milk. Cover; microwave on HIGH 3 minutes or until hot and bubbling. Garnish with sour cream and additional nutmeg. Makes about 3 cups or 4 servings.

LENTIL SOUP

3 slices bacon, diced
1 cup sliced celery
½ cup sliced carrot
3 cups water
1 pouch Campbell's dry onion mushroom soup and recipe mix

½ cup dry lentils
2 teaspoons chopped fresh parsley
¼ teaspoon grated lemon peel

1. In 2-quart saucepan over medium heat, cook bacon until crisp. Drain bacon on paper towels, reserving 1 tablespoon drippings in pan. Set bacon aside.

2. In same saucepan over medium heat, in hot bacon drippings, cook celery and carrot until tender, stirring often. Stir in water, soup mix and lentils. Heat to boiling.

3. Reduce heat to low. Cover; simmer 1 hour or until lentils are tender. Stir in parsley, lemon peel and reserved bacon. Makes about 3 cups or 3 servings.

SPEEDY POTATO CHOWDER

4 slices bacon, diced
½ cup chopped onion
1 can (10¾ ounces) Campbell's
    condensed cream of potato soup
¾ cup beer

¾ cup water
1 can (about 8 ounces) mixed
    vegetables
1 cup sliced frankfurters
2 tablespoons chopped fresh parsley

1. In 3-quart saucepan over medium heat, cook bacon until crisp. Drain bacon on paper towels, reserving 1 tablespoon drippings in pan.

2. In same saucepan over medium heat, in hot drippings, cook onion until tender, stirring occasionally. Stir in soup, beer and water until well mixed. Add mixed vegetables with their liquid, frankfurters, parsley and reserved bacon. Heat through, stirring occasionally. Makes about 4 cups or 4 servings.

To microwave: In 2-quart microwave-safe casserole, place bacon; cover with lid. Microwave on HIGH 3 to 4 minutes or until crisp, stirring once during cooking. With slotted spoon, remove bacon. Drain bacon on paper towels, reserving 1 tablespoon drippings in casserole. To drippings, add onion. Cover; microwave on HIGH 2 to 2½ minutes; or until tender, stirring once during cooking. Stir in soup, beer and water until well mixed. Add mixed vegetables with their liquid, frankfurters, parsley and reserved bacon. Cover; microwave on HIGH 8 to 10 minutes until heated through, stirring occasionally during cooking.

SKILLET SHRIMP BISQUE

¼ cup butter or margarine
1 cup sliced Campbell's Fresh
    mushrooms
2 tablespoons chopped chives
1 clove garlic, minced
3 tablespoons all-purpose flour
1 can (10½ ounces) Campbell's
    condensed chicken broth

1 pound medium shrimp, shelled
    and deveined
½ cup Chablis or other dry white wine
½ cup heavy cream
1 tablespoon chopped fresh parsley
    Fresh dill sprigs for garnish

1. In 10-inch skillet over medium heat, in hot butter, cook mushrooms, chives and garlic until vegetables are tender, stirring occasionally. Stir in flour until smooth. Gradually stir in chicken broth. Heat to boiling, stirring constantly.

2. Add shrimp. Reduce heat to low. Cover; simmer about 5 minutes or until shrimp are pink and opaque. Stir in wine, cream and parsley; heat through. Ladle into bowls; garnish with dill sprigs. Makes 4½ cups or 6 servings.

BAVARIAN PEA SOUP

1 tablespoon butter or margarine
½ cup shredded cabbage
¼ teaspoon caraway seed
1 can (19 ounces) Campbell's Home
   Cookin' split pea with ham or
   Chunky split pea 'n ham soup

Pumpernickel bread, torn into
   pieces
Shredded Swiss cheese

1. In 1-quart microwave-safe casserole, combine butter, cabbage and caraway. Cover with lid; microwave on HIGH 3 minutes or until cabbage is tender, stirring once during cooking.

2. Stir in soup. Cover; microwave on HIGH 4 minutes or until heated through, stirring once during cooking.

3. Pour soup into 2 microwave-safe soup bowls; top with bread and cheese. Microwave, uncovered, on HIGH 1 minute or until cheese is melted. Makes 2 servings.

ONION SOUP AU GRATIN

2 tablespoons vegetable oil
1 tablespoon butter or margarine
1 pound onions, sliced (4 cups)
¼ teaspoon sugar
2 cans (10½ ounces *each*)
   Campbell's condensed beef
   broth (bouillon)

2 soup cans water
6 slices French bread, toasted
2 cups shredded Swiss cheese
   (8 ounces)
¼ cup grated Parmesan cheese

1. In covered 3-quart saucepan over low heat, in hot oil and butter, cook onions 15 minutes or until tender, stirring occasionally.

2. Uncover; stir in sugar. Over medium heat, cook 30 minutes more or until onions are golden, stirring frequently.

3. Add broth and water. Heat to boiling; reduce heat to low. Cover; simmer 25 minutes.

4. Preheat oven to 350°F. Ladle soup into six 12-ounce oven-safe bowls; place bowls on jelly-roll pan. Place French bread in each bowl and top each with Swiss cheese and Parmesan.

5. Bake 20 minutes or until cheese is melted and top is browned. Makes about 6½ cups or 6 servings.

Bavarian Pea Soup

SPLIT PEA AND MEATBALL SOUP

1 cup dry green split peas, rinsed
  and drained
1 can (10½ ounces) Campbell's
  condensed chicken broth
2 cups water
1 cup chopped onions
½ teaspoon rubbed sage
⅛ teaspoon pepper
½ pound bulk pork sausage

¼ cup soft bread crumbs
1 egg
1 tablespoon chopped fresh parsley
1 clove garlic, minced
1 cup chopped carrots
1 cup frozen mixed vegetables
1 can (14½ ounces) stewed
  tomatoes

1. In 4-quart Dutch oven over high heat, combine peas, broth, water, onion, sage and pepper. Heat to boiling; reduce heat to low. Cover; simmer 1 hour.

2. To make meatballs: In medium bowl, combine sausage, bread crumbs, egg, parsley and garlic. Mix lightly, but well. Shape into 36 balls, using 1 rounded teaspoonful for each. Set aside.

3. Add carrots, mixed vegetables and tomatoes to soup mixture. Over high heat, heat to boiling. Add meatballs; reduce heat to low. Cover; simmer 30 minutes or until vegetables are tender. Makes about 8 cups or 6 servings.

PASTA AND BEAN SOUP

2 tablespoons vegetable oil
½ cup diced cooked ham
½ cup chopped onion
½ cup chopped celery
½ cup shredded carrot
1 clove garlic, minced
1 can (10½ ounces) Campbell's
  condensed vegetable soup
1 soup can water

1 can (19 ounces) white kidney
  beans
½ teaspoon dried thyme leaves,
  crushed
1 bay leaf
⅛ teaspoon pepper
½ cup small shell macaroni,
  uncooked

1. In 4-quart Dutch oven over medium heat, in hot oil, cook ham until lightly browned, stirring occasionally. Add onion, celery, carrot and garlic; cook until vegetables are tender, stirring occasionally.

2. Stir in soup, water, beans with their liquid, thyme, bay leaf and pepper. Heat to boiling; reduce heat to low. Cover; simmer 15 minutes.

3. Stir in macaroni; cook about 12 minutes more or until macaroni is tender. Discard bay leaf. Makes about 5 cups or 4 servings.

CHEESE-TOPPED SANDWICH STACKS

4 English muffins, split and toasted
8 slices bacon, halved, cooked and drained
1⅓ cups shredded lettuce
8 ounces thinly sliced cooked ham
2 medium Campbell's Fresh tomatoes, sliced
1 can (10¾ ounces) Campbell's condensed cream of mushroom soup

¼ cup milk
1½ cups shredded Cheddar cheese (6 ounces)
1 tablespoon Worcestershire sauce
½ teaspoon dry mustard

1. Place toasted English muffins on cookie sheet. Top each half with bacon, lettuce, ham and tomato slices. Set aside.

2. In 2-quart saucepan, combine soup and milk. Over medium heat, heat through, stirring occasionally. Add cheese, Worcestershire and dry mustard. Heat until cheese melts, stirring constantly. Pour sauce over each muffin.

3. Broil 4 inches from heat 1 to 2 minutes or until tops start to brown. Makes 4 servings.

Tip: For a light meal, make the cheese sauce as in step 2. Serve over toast or toasted English muffins as you would serve Welsh rarebit.

CHILI BEEF SANDWICHES

1 pound ground beef
½ cup chopped onion
½ cup chopped green pepper
1 clove garlic, minced
1 can (11¼ ounces) Campbell's condensed chili beef soup
1 can (10¾ ounces) Campbell's condensed tomato soup

¼ cup water
2 tablespoons vinegar
1 teaspoon dry mustard
¼ teaspoon pepper
8 hamburger buns, split and toasted

1. In 10-inch skillet over medium heat, cook ground beef, onion, green pepper and garlic until meat is browned and vegetables are tender, stirring often to separate meat. Spoon off fat.

2. Stir in soups, water, vinegar, mustard and pepper. Heat to boiling, stirring occasionally. Reduce heat to low. Simmer 10 minutes or until desired consistency, stirring often. Serve in buns, using about ⅓ cup per serving. Makes 8 servings.

To microwave: In 2-quart microwave-safe casserole, crumble beef. Add onion, green pepper and garlic. Cover; microwave on HIGH 6 to 8 minutes or until meat is browned and vegetables are tender, stirring twice during cooking. Spoon off fat. Stir in soups, water, vinegar, mustard and pepper. Cover; microwave on HIGH 7 to 9 minutes or until boiling, stirring twice during cooking. Serve as in step 2.

SAUSAGE-VEGETABLE ROLLS

½ pound bulk pork sausage
1 cup chopped onions
1 cup frozen chopped broccoli,
   thawed and drained
1 can (10¾ ounces) Campbell's
   condensed golden mushroom
   soup

1 loaf (1 pound) frozen bread dough,
   thawed
½ cup grated Romano cheese,
   divided
1 egg, beaten
1 tablespoon sesame seed

1. Preheat oven to 350°F. Grease large cookie sheet.

2. In 10-inch skillet over medium heat, cook sausage until it begins to
brown, stirring to separate meat. Add onion and broccoli; cook about
5 minutes or until meat is browned and vegetables are tender, stirring
occasionally. Spoon off fat. Stir in soup. Cool to room temperature.

3. Divide thawed dough into 6 equal parts. On floured surface, roll out 1 part
to 6-inch round. Place about ½ cup of the sausage mixture on dough,
spreading to within 1 inch of edges. Sprinkle with 1 generous tablespoon of
cheese. Fold over to form a half circle. Pinch edges to seal. Place on prepared
cookie sheet. Repeat with remaining dough.

4. Brush rolls with egg; sprinkle with sesame seed. Bake 25 minutes or until
golden brown. Let stand 10 minutes. Serve warm. Makes 6 servings.

SAUSAGE AND PEPPER SANDWICHES

1 pound mild Italian sausage, cut
   into 4 pieces
2 tablespoons olive oil
2 packages (8 ounces *each*)
   Campbell's Fresh mushrooms,
   thickly sliced

1 large green pepper, cut into strips
1 large onion, cut into thin wedges
2 cloves garlic, minced
4 long hard rolls, split lengthwise

1. In 10-inch skillet, place sausage. Add water to ½-inch depth. Over high
heat, heat to boiling. Reduce heat to low. Cover; simmer 20 minutes or until
sausage is done. Remove sausage from skillet. Spoon off any liquid.

2. In same skillet over medium heat, in hot oil, cook mushrooms, pepper,
onion and garlic until tender and liquid is evaporated, stirring occasionally.

3. Return sausage to skillet; heat through. Serve on rolls. Makes 4 servings.

Sausage Vegetable Rolls

SCRAMBLED EGGS IN PITA POCKETS

4 pita breads (6-inch diameter
   sandwich pockets)
8 eggs
1 can (10¾ ounces) Campbell's
   condensed cream of mushroom
   soup

1 cup sliced Campbell's Fresh
   mushrooms
6 slices bacon, diced
2 tablespoons butter or margarine
1 cup shredded Cheddar cheese
   (4 ounces)

1. Cut each pita bread in half forming two pockets. Wrap pita bread halves in aluminum foil; bake at 350°F. for 15 minutes or until warm.

2. Meanwhile, in large bowl with whisk or rotary beater, beat eggs until foamy. Stir in soup and mushrooms; set aside.

3. In 10-inch skillet over medium heat, cook bacon until crisp, stirring occasionally. Spoon off fat.

4. Add butter to skillet; heat until foamy. Add egg mixture; cook until set but still slightly moist, stirring and lifting eggs so uncooked portion flows to bottom.

5. Stuff warm pita pockets with egg mixture. Top each with cheese.
Makes 8 servings.

VEGETABLE MELT SANDWICH

2 tablespoons olive oil
1 package (8 ounces) Campbell's
   Fresh mushrooms, sliced
1 medium zucchini, thinly sliced
1 medium onion, thinly sliced
1 clove garlic, minced
1 tablespoon fresh basil leaves or 1
   teaspoon dried basil leaves,
   crushed

1 loaf Italian bread (about 14 inches
   long), cut in half lengthwise
2 large Campbell's Fresh tomatoes,
   thinly sliced
2 cups shredded mozzarella cheese
   (8 ounces)

1. Preheat oven to 350°F. In 10-inch skillet over medium heat, in hot oil, cook mushrooms, zucchini, onion, garlic and basil until vegetables are tender and liquid is evaporated, stirring occasionally.

2. On cookie sheet, place bread halves, cut-side up. Arrange tomatoes on bread; top with mushroom mixture. Sprinkle with cheese. Bake 20 minutes or until cheese is melted. Cut into thick slices. Makes 4 main-dish or 8 appetizer servings.

CHILI DOGS

1 can (11¼ ounces) Campbell's condensed chili beef soup
2 tablespoons water
2 tablespoons ketchup
6 frankfurters

6 Pepperidge Farm frankfurter rolls, split
3 slices American cheese, cut into triangles

1. In small microwave-safe bowl, combine soup, water and ketchup. Cover with vented plastic wrap; microwave on HIGH 3 minutes or until very hot, stirring once during cooking.

2. Arrange frankfurters on 10-inch microwave-safe plate lined with plain white paper towels. Microwave, uncovered, on HIGH 2 minutes or until hot.

3. Place cooked frankfurters in rolls. Spoon a heaping tablespoon of soup mixture over each. Arrange cheese triangles over soup mixture.

4. Arrange rolls on same plate lined with plain white paper towels. Microwave, uncovered, on HIGH 1 minute or until cheese melts. Makes 6 servings.

CALZONES

1 tablespoon olive oil
1 package (8 ounces) Campbell's Fresh mushrooms, sliced
1 small onion, chopped
½ cup chopped green pepper
1 clove garlic, minced
1 loaf (1 pound) frozen white bread dough, thawed

½ cup Prego spaghetti sauce
1½ cups (6 ounces) shredded mozzarella cheese
18 thin slices pepperoni (about 2 ounces)
1 egg, beaten
Grated Parmesan cheese

1. Preheat oven to 425°F. Grease large cookie sheet.

2. In 10-inch skillet over medium heat, in hot oil, cook mushrooms, onion, green pepper and garlic until mushrooms are tender and liquid is evaporated, stirring occasionally. Set aside.

3. To make calzones: Divide thawed dough into 6 equal pieces. On floured surface, roll 1 piece into 7-inch round. Place 1 tablespoon of the spaghetti sauce on dough, spreading to within ½ inch of edges. Sprinkle with ¼ cup of the mozzarella cheese; place 3 slices of the pepperoni on one half of the circle. Spoon about ¼ cup of the mushroom mixture over pepperoni. Fold over to form a half circle. Pinch edges to seal. Place on prepared cookie sheet. Repeat to make 5 more calzones.

4. Brush calzones with egg; sprinkle with Parmesan. Bake 15 minutes or until golden brown. Serve warm or at room temperature. Makes 6 servings.

CHICKEN-STUFFED PITAS

2 cups sliced Campbell's Fresh mushrooms
2 cups chopped cooked chicken or turkey
½ cup mayonnaise
½ cup plain yogurt
1 large carrot, shredded
¼ cup golden raisins
¼ cup chopped toasted almonds
1 teaspoon curry powder
¼ teaspoon salt
4 pita breads (6-inch-diameter sandwich pockets), cut in half crosswise
Campbell's Fresh butterhead lettuce leaves

1. In large bowl, combine all ingredients except pita breads and lettuce; mix until well blended.

2. In each pita bread half, arrange lettuce and about ½ cup of the chicken mixture. Makes 4 servings.

CHICKEN SALAD CROISSANTS

2 cans (5 ounces *each*) Swanson premium chunk chicken
2 tablespoons mayonnaise or plain yogurt
1 tablespoon finely chopped onion
1 teaspoon lemon juice
Dash pepper
4 Pepperidge Farm croissants, split
Campbell's Fresh butterhead lettuce leaves
2 medium nectarines or peaches, thinly sliced

1. In medium bowl, combine chicken, mayonnaise, onion, lemon juice and pepper. Cover; refrigerate until serving time, at least 1 hour.

2. To serve: On bottom half of each croissant, layer lettuce, chicken salad and nectarines. Top with croissant tops. Makes 4 servings.

ENGLISH MUFFIN PIZZAS

2 English muffins, split and toasted
¼ cup Prego spaghetti sauce
¼ cup shredded mozzarella cheese (1 ounce)
Vlasic sliced pitted ripe olives
Sliced Campbell's Fresh mushrooms
Pepperoni or frankfurter slices
Green pepper strips

1. Spread each muffin half with 1 tablespoon of the spaghetti sauce; sprinkle with 1 tablespoon of the cheese. Sprinkle with toppings of your choice.

2. Arrange pizzas in circle on microwave-safe plate lined with plain white paper towels. Microwave, uncovered, on HIGH 1½ minutes or until cheese melts, rotating plate once during cooking. Makes 4 pizzas.

Eggs & Cheese

Greek-Style Puffy Pancake (page 56)

GREEK-STYLE PUFFY PANCAKE

Puffy Pancake (recipe follows)
**2 cups sliced Campbell's Fresh
  mushrooms**
1 large onion, sliced
1 cup shredded carrots
¾ cup V8 vegetable juice
1 teaspoon cornstarch

**½ teaspoon dried basil leaves,
  crushed**
**¾ cup crumbled feta cheese, divided
  (4 ounces)**
**2 tablespoons sliced Vlasic pitted
  ripe olives**
2 tablespoons chopped fresh parsley

1. Prepare Puffy Pancake.

2. Meanwhile, spray 10-inch nonstick skillet with vegetable cooking spray. Over medium-high heat, cook mushrooms, onion and carrots 5 minutes or until vegetables are tender, stirring often.

3. In small bowl, combine V8 juice, cornstarch and basil. Stir V8 mixture into skillet; cook 4 minutes or until slightly thickened, stirring often.

4. Sprinkle ½ of the feta onto pancake. Spoon vegetable mixture over feta. Sprinkle with remaining feta, olives and parsley. Cut into wedges. Makes 4 servings.

PUFFY PANCAKE: Preheat oven to 450°F. Place 10-inch oven-safe skillet on middle rack in oven 5 minutes. Meanwhile, in medium bowl with mixer at medium speed, beat ½ cup all-purpose flour, ½ cup milk, 2 eggs and ⅛ teaspoon salt until well blended. Add 1 tablespoon vegetable oil to skillet, tilting to coat bottom and sides. Pour batter into pan. Bake 10 minutes. Reduce heat to 350°F.; bake 10 minutes more or until puffed and browned.

EGGS GOLDENROD

**1 can (10¾ ounces) Campbell's
  condensed cream of celery soup**
½ cup milk
2 tablespoons chopped fresh parsley

¼ teaspoon dry mustard
4 hard-cooked eggs
4 slices bread, toasted

1. In small saucepan, combine soup, milk, parsley and mustard until smooth.

2. Separate egg yolks and whites. Chop whites coarsely; add to soup mixture. Over medium heat, heat through, stirring occasionally.

3. Meanwhile, force egg yolks through sieve. Serve soup mixture on toast, using about ½ cup per serving; garnish with sieved yolks. Makes about 2 cups or 4 servings.

Tip: To make this dish a little more special, sprinkle with fresh alfalfa sprouts.

To microwave: In 1½-quart microwave-safe casserole, stir together soup, milk, parsley and mustard. Cover; microwave on HIGH 2 to 3 minutes until hot, stirring once during cooking. Meanwhile, separate eggs and chop whites as in step 2. Add whites to soup mixture. Cover; microwave on HIGH 1 to 2 minutes until heated through. Stir. Serve as in step 3.

CHEESY CHICKEN CREPES

3 eggs
1 cup milk
2/3 cup all-purpose flour
1 can (10¾ ounces) Campbell's condensed cream of chicken soup

1/3 cup water
2 tablespoons dry sherry
1½ cups shredded Cheddar cheese, divided (6 ounces)
2 cups diced cooked chicken

1. In medium bowl, combine eggs, milk and flour; beat until smooth.

2. Over medium heat, heat 8-inch crepe pan or skillet. When hot, brush lightly with vegetable oil. Add scant ¼ cup batter to skillet, rotating pan to spread batter evenly. Cook until surface is dry and edges are browned. Turn over; cook other side a few seconds. Remove from pan, stacking crepes as they are made. Repeat to make 10 crepes, brushing pan with oil as needed.

3. In 2-quart saucepan over medium heat, heat soup, water and sherry; stir to mix well. Add 1 cup of the cheese, stirring until cheese melts. Stir 1 cup of the sauce into chicken; reserve remaining sauce. Spoon about 3 tablespoons of the filling mixture down center of each crepe. Roll up. Repeat with remaining crepes.

4. Arrange rolled crepes, seam-side down, in 12- by 8-inch baking dish. Pour remaining sauce over all; sprinkle with remaining ½ cup cheese. Cover; bake at 350°F. for 25 minutes or until heated through. Makes 5 servings.

To microwave: Prepare crepes as in steps 1 and 2. In 1-quart microwave-safe casserole, combine soup, water and sherry; stir well. Add 1 cup of the cheese. Cover; microwave on HIGH 4 to 6 minutes or until cheese is melted, stirring occasionally during cooking. Stir 1 cup of the sauce into chicken; reserve remaining sauce. Fill and roll crepes as directed. Arrange rolled crepes, seam-side down, in 12- by 8-inch microwave-safe dish. Pour remaining sauce over all. Cover; microwave on HIGH 7 to 9 minutes until hot, rotating dish once during cooking. Sprinkle with remaining ½ cup cheese. Microwave on HIGH 2 minutes or until cheese is melted.

CAMPBELLED EGGS

1 can (10¾ ounces) Campbell's condensed cream of chicken soup
8 eggs

Dash pepper
2 tablespoons butter or margarine
Chopped fresh parsley for garnish

1. In medium bowl, stir soup until smooth; beat in eggs and pepper.

2. In 10-inch skillet over low heat, melt butter. Pour in egg mixture. As eggs begin to set, stir lightly so uncooked egg flows to bottom. Cook until set but still very moist. Garnish with parsley. Serve immediately. Makes 4 servings.

To microwave: Omit butter. In 3-quart microwave-safe casserole, stir soup until smooth. Beat in eggs and pepper. Cover with lid; microwave on HIGH 6½ minutes or until eggs are nearly set, stirring 3 times during cooking. Let stand, covered, 2 minutes. Garnish with parsley.

MUSHROOM-CHIVE OMELET

3 tablespoons butter or margarine,
  divided
1 package (8 ounces) Campbell's
  Fresh mushrooms, sliced
1 tablespoon fresh or frozen
  chopped chives

¼ teaspoon salt, divided
3 eggs
3 tablespoons milk
Dash pepper

1. In 8-inch skillet over medium heat, in 2 tablespoons hot butter, cook mushrooms until tender and liquid is evaporated, stirring occasionally. Stir in chives and ⅛ teaspoon of the salt; keep warm.

2. Meanwhile, to prepare omelet: In medium bowl, beat together eggs, milk, remaining salt and the pepper.

3. In 10-inch omelet pan or skillet over medium heat, melt remaining butter. Pour in egg mixture. As eggs set around edge, lift egg, tilting skillet to allow uncooked egg mixture to run underneath.

4. When omelet is set but still moist on surface; increase heat slightly to brown bottom. Remove from heat. Spoon ½ of mushroom mixture in center of omelet. Lift edge of omelet and fold in half. Slide omelet onto warm plate. Top with remaining mushroom mixture. Makes 2 servings.

APPLE-CHEDDAR OMELET

4 slices bacon, chopped
1 can (11 ounces) Campbell's
  condensed Cheddar cheese
  soup, divided
8 eggs

⅓ cup milk
1 small apple, peeled and chopped
1 cup shredded Cheddar cheese
  (4 ounces)
⅛ teaspoon pepper

1. Place bacon in 9-inch microwave-safe pie plate. Cover with plain white paper towel; microwave on HIGH 3 minutes or until crisp, stirring once during cooking. Drain bacon on paper towels; reserve drippings.

2. In medium bowl, stir ½ cup of the soup until smooth. Add eggs; beat until well blended. Set aside.

3. To make sauce: In 1-quart microwave-safe casserole, stir remaining soup until smooth; stir in milk, apple, cheese and pepper. Cover with lid; microwave on HIGH 4 minutes or until hot and bubbling, stirring once during cooking. Let stand, covered, while preparing omelets.

4. Brush 1 teaspoon of the bacon drippings over bottom and side of same pie plate. Pour in ½ of the egg mixture. Cover with waxed paper; microwave on HIGH 2 minutes. With spatula, gently move cooked outer edge of omelet to center, letting uncooked portion flow to edge. Cover; microwave on HIGH 2 minutes or until center is set. Fold omelet in half; slide onto serving plate.

5. Repeat step 4 with 1 teaspoon of the bacon drippings and remaining egg mixture. Spoon sauce over each; sprinkle with bacon. Makes 4 servings.

Mushroom-Chive Omelet

SWISS CHEESE-VEGETABLE OMELET

6 eggs, separated	1 cup sliced Campbell's Fresh
¼ cup milk	mushrooms
¼ cup grated Parmesan cheese	½ cup diced sweet red pepper
⅛ teaspoon pepper	½ teaspoon dried Italian seasoning,
1 cup shredded Swiss cheese,	crushed
divided (4 ounces)	1½ cups V8 vegetable juice
1 cup broccoli flowerets	1 tablespoon cornstarch

1. Preheat oven to 350°F. In large bowl with mixer at high speed, beat egg whites until stiff peaks form. In small bowl with mixer at high speed, beat egg yolks, milk, Parmesan and pepper until foamy. Carefully fold egg yolk mixture and ½ cup of the Swiss cheese into beaten egg whites.

2. Spray oven-safe 10-inch nonstick skillet with vegetable cooking spray. Over medium heat, heat skillet; add egg mixture. Reduce heat to low. Cook 5 minutes or until golden on underside. Place skillet in oven; bake 10 minutes or until top is puffed and golden brown.

3. Meanwhile, to prepare sauce: Spray another 10-inch nonstick skillet with vegetable cooking spray. Over medium heat, cook broccoli, mushrooms, red pepper and Italian seasoning until vegetables are tender-crisp, stirring often.

4. In small bowl, combine V8 juice and cornstarch; stir V8 into skillet. Over medium heat, heat until boiling, stirring often.

5. To serve: Run spatula under omelet; slide onto plate. Top with remaining Swiss cheese. Spoon sauce over; cut into wedges. Makes 6 servings.

HUEVOS RANCHEROS

1 tablespoon vegetable oil	¼ cup water
¼ cup chopped green pepper	4 eggs
¼ cup chopped onion	4 corn tortillas (6-inch)
2 teaspoons chili powder	¼ cup shredded Cheddar cheese
1 can (10¾ ounces) Campbell's	Chopped fresh parsley or cilantro
condensed tomato soup	for garnish

1. In 2-quart casserole, stir together first 4 ingredients. Cover with lid; microwave on HIGH 3 minutes or until vegetables are tender, stirring once.

2. Stir in soup and water. Cover; microwave on HIGH 5 minutes or until edges are hot and bubbling, stirring once during cooking.

3. Gently break each egg, sliding onto soup mixture and arranging around edge of casserole. With toothpick, pierce each yolk. Cover; microwave on MEDIUM (50% power) 4 minutes or until eggs are almost set, rotating dish once during cooking. Let stand, covered, 2 minutes.

4. Meanwhile, wrap stack of tortillas in damp plain white paper towels. Microwave on HIGH 30 seconds or until warm. Spoon 1 egg and some sauce onto each tortilla. Sprinkle 1 tablespoon cheese over each egg. Garnish with parsley. Makes 4 servings.

Swiss Cheese-Vegetable Omelet

ITALIAN MUSHROOM OMELET

3 tablespoons butter or margarine,
divided
1 package (8 ounces) Campbell's
Fresh mushrooms, sliced
2 tablespoons chopped green
pepper
1 jar (14 ounces) Prego spaghetti
sauce (1¾ cups)

2 tablespoons sliced Vlasic pitted
ripe olives
8 eggs
½ cup milk
½ teaspoon salt
½ cup shredded Cheddar cheese
(2 ounces)

1. In 1½-quart microwave-safe casserole, combine 1 tablespoon of the butter,
the mushrooms and green pepper. Cover with lid; microwave on HIGH
3 minutes or until vegetables are tender, stirring once during cooking. Stir in
spaghetti sauce and olives. Cover; microwave on HIGH 3 minutes or until
hot and bubbling. Stir and set aside.

2. Place 1 tablespoon of the butter in 9-inch microwave-safe pie plate. Cover;
microwave on HIGH 20 seconds or until melted. Brush evenly onto pie plate.

3. In medium bowl, beat eggs, milk and salt until well blended. Pour ½ of
the egg mixture into prepared pie plate. Cover with waxed paper; microwave
on HIGH 2 minutes. With spatula, gently move cooked outer edge of omelet
to center, letting uncooked portion flow to edge. Cover; microwave on HIGH
2 minutes or until center is set. Remove omelet to serving plate.

4. Repeat steps 2 and 3 with remaining butter and egg mixture. Spoon about
½ cup of the sauce in center of each omelet; fold omelet in half. Top with
more sauce and the cheese. Serve with remaining sauce. Makes 4 servings.

SHIITAKE STRATA

1 package (3.5 ounces) Campbell's
Fresh shiitake mushrooms
3 slices bread, toasted and buttered
2 tablespoons butter or margarine
½ cup chopped onion
1 clove garlic, minced
1½ cups milk

3 eggs
1 teaspoon dry mustard
1 cup shredded Swiss cheese
(4 ounces)
1 cup fresh bread crumbs
2 tablespoons grated Parmesan
cheese

1. Trim woody portions of mushroom stems and discard. Remove and chop
stems; slice mushroom caps.

2. In 8- by 8-inch baking dish, arrange toasted bread, buttered-side down,
cutting as needed to cover bottom of dish.

3. In 10-inch skillet over medium heat, in hot butter, cook mushrooms, onion
and garlic until tender, stirring occasionally. Spoon over toast.

4. In medium bowl, beat together milk, eggs and mustard. Stir in Swiss
cheese; pour over mushroom mixture. Sprinkle with bread crumbs and
Parmesan. Bake at 325°F. for 35 minutes or until set. Makes 4 servings.

Italian Mushroom Omelet

CHEESE OMELET ROLL

1 can (10¾ ounces) Campbell's condensed cream of celery soup	1 cup shredded Cheddar cheese (4 ounces)
6 eggs, separated	½ pound bacon, cooked and crumbled
¼ teaspoon cream of tartar	1 cup cooked chopped broccoli

1. Preheat oven to 350°F. Oil 15- by 10-inch jelly-roll pan; line with foil, extending 3 inches beyond pan on each end. Oil and flour bottom and sides of foil.

2. In 1-quart saucepan over medium heat, heat soup, stirring occasionally. Remove from heat. In small bowl, beat egg yolks. Stir some of the hot soup into yolks, then return to soup. Over low heat, cook 1 minute, stirring constantly. Remove from heat.

3. In large bowl with mixer at high speed, beat egg whites and cream of tartar until stiff peaks form. Fold soup mixture into whites. Spread in prepared pan. Bake 20 minutes or until puffy and browned.

4. Invert onto waxed paper; gently remove foil (some of the omelet may stick to foil). Sprinkle with cheese, bacon and broccoli. With aid of waxed paper, roll up jelly-roll fashion, starting at narrow side. Roll onto serving plate. Serve at once. Makes 6 servings.

Tip: Omelet is delicious served plain or with stewed tomatoes or a cheese sauce.

SAVORY VEGETABLE TART

1 unbaked piecrust (10-inch)	½ cup toasted slivered almonds
2 tablespoons butter or margarine	1½ cups shredded mild Cheddar cheese (6 ounces)
1 package (8 ounces) Campbell's Fresh mushrooms, sliced	2 eggs
¼ cup finely chopped shallots or onion	½ cup mayonnaise
1½ cups cauliflowerets, blanched 1 minute	½ cup milk
	⅛ teaspoon pepper
	⅛ teaspoon ground nutmeg

1. Preheat oven to 350°F. With a fork, prick bottom and sides of piecrust. Bake 10 minutes.

2. In 10-inch skillet over medium heat, in hot butter, cook mushrooms and shallots until tender and liquid is evaporated, stirring occasionally. Stir in cauliflowerets and almonds; arrange in prebaked piecrust. Sprinkle with cheese.

3. In small bowl, beat eggs until foamy. Add remaining ingredients; beat until smooth. Pour over cheese. Bake 30 minutes or until golden brown and knife inserted in center comes out clean. Let stand 10 minutes before serving. Serve warm or chilled. Makes 6 servings.

Cheese Omelet Roll

EASY CHEESE SOUFFLE

EASY CHEESE SOUFFLE

**1 can (11 ounces) Campbell's
condensed Cheddar cheese
soup**

**1 cup shredded sharp Cheddar
cheese (4 ounces)
Dash ground red pepper
6 eggs, separated**

1. In 1-quart saucepan, combine soup, cheese and red pepper. Over low heat, heat until cheese is melted, stirring occasionally. Remove from heat.

2. In large bowl with mixer at high speed, beat egg whites until stiff peaks form; set aside. In small bowl with mixer at high speed, beat egg yolks until thick and lemon-colored. Gradually stir in soup mixture; fold into beaten egg whites.

3. Pour into ungreased 2-quart casserole or souffle dish. Bake at 300°F. for 1 hour or until souffle is lightly browned. Serve immediately. Makes 6 servings.

Tip: For best results when beating egg whites, bring them to room temperature before you begin beating. Be sure to use a very clean bowl and beaters; even a small amount of fat or yolk will inhibit the beating.

BAKED MANICOTTI

**2 tablespoons vegetable oil
½ cup finely chopped onion
1 clove garlic, minced
½ teaspoon dried basil leaves,
crushed
1 can (10¾ ounces) Campbell's
condensed tomato soup
1 soup can water
1 can (6 ounces) tomato paste
2 tablespoons grated Parmesan
cheese**

**1 bay leaf
1 container (15 ounces) ricotta
cheese
1 cup shredded mozzarella cheese
(4 ounces)
½ cup grated Parmesan cheese,
divided
1 egg
1 tablespoon chopped fresh parsley
10 manicotti shells, cooked and
drained**

1. To make sauce: In 3-quart saucepan over medium heat, in hot oil, cook onion, garlic and basil until onion is tender, stirring frequently. Stir in soup, water, tomato paste, 2 tablespoons Parmesan and bay leaf. Heat to boiling; reduce heat to low. Simmer 30 minutes or until desired consistency, stirring occasionally. Discard bay leaf.

2. To make filling: In medium bowl, combine ricotta, mozzarella, ¼ cup of the Parmesan, the egg and parsley; stir to mix well. Using spoon or pastry bag, fill each manicotti shell with ¼ cup of the cheese filling.

3. Spoon 1 cup of the sauce into 12- by 8-inch baking dish; arrange stuffed manicotti over sauce. Top with remaining sauce and remaining ¼ cup Parmesan. Bake at 350°F. for 30 minutes or until hot. Makes 5 servings.

Easy Cheese Souffle

SOUPER EASY QUICHE

4 eggs
1 can (11 ounces) Campbell's
 condensed Cheddar cheese
 soup
½ cup light cream

1 cup shredded sharp Cheddar
 cheese (4 ounces)
½ cup diced cooked ham
½ cup cooked chopped broccoli
1 unbaked piecrust (9-inch)
 Ground nutmeg

1. In medium bowl, beat eggs until foamy. Gradually add soup and cream, mixing well.

2. Sprinkle cheese, ham and broccoli evenly over piecrust. Pour soup mixture over all. Sprinkle with nutmeg.

3. Bake at 350°F. for 50 minutes or until center is set. Let stand 10 minutes before serving. Makes 6 servings.

NEAPOLITAN PIZZA

1 pouch Campbell's dry onion soup
 and recipe mix
2 cups all-purpose flour, divided
1 tablespoon sugar
1 package active dry yeast
¾ cup very warm water (120° to
 130°F.)

2 tablespoons olive or vegetable oil
2 Campbell's Fresh tomatoes, thinly
 sliced
1 jar (6 ounces) marinated artichoke
 hearts, drained and cut up
2 cups shredded mozzarella cheese
 (8 ounces)

1. In medium bowl, combine soup mix, 1 cup of the flour, the sugar and yeast; mix well. With mixer at low speed, gradually pour warm water and oil into dry ingredients; beat until just mixed. At medium speed, beat 4 minutes, scraping bowl often.

2. With spoon, stir in about ¾ cup of the flour or enough to make a soft dough. On floured surface, knead dough about 5 minutes until smooth and elastic, adding more flour, if necessary.

3. Grease 14-inch pizza pan or cookie sheet. On floured surface, roll dough to 14-inch round. Transfer to prepared pizza pan. Turn edge under to form rim.

4. Let rise in warm place (80° to 85°F.), free from draft, for 20 minutes.

5. Preheat oven to 400°F. Bake crust 5 minutes; remove from oven. Arrange tomato slices and artichoke hearts over crust; sprinkle with cheese. Bake 15 minutes more or until lightly browned. Makes 4 servings.

Souper Easy Quiche

LAYERED VEGETABLE PIE

2 tablespoons vegetable or olive oil
2 packages (8 ounces *each*)
   Campbell's Fresh mushrooms,
   sliced
¼ cup finely chopped shallots or
   onion
1 clove garlic, minced
1 package (10 ounces) frozen
   chopped spinach, cooked and
   well drained
1 tablespoon all-purpose flour
4 eggs, slightly beaten
1 container (15 ounces) ricotta
   cheese

¼ cup grated Parmesan cheese
¾ cup diced fontinella or mozzarella
   cheese
¼ teaspoon ground nutmeg
¼ teaspoon pepper
   Pastry for 2-crust 10-inch pie
1 egg, separated
1 jar (6 ounces) roasted red
   peppers, drained and cut into
   strips
1 tablespoon sour cream or heavy
   cream

1. In 10-inch skillet over medium heat, in hot oil, cook mushrooms, shallots and garlic until tender, stirring occasionally. Add spinach; cook 2 minutes or until liquid is evaporated, stirring constantly. Stir in flour; set aside.

2. Preheat oven to 375°F. In large bowl, beat together 4 eggs, cheeses, nutmeg and pepper. Stir 1 cup of the cheese mixture into mushroom mixture.

3. On lightly floured surface, roll ½ of the pastry into 13-inch round. Line 10-inch deep-dish pie plate with pastry; trim even with rim, saving scraps. Prick with a fork. Brush with beaten egg white. Bake 10 minutes.

4. In prebaked piecrust, layer, in order, 2 cups of the mushroom mixture, 1 cup of the cheese mixture, remaining mushroom mixture, red peppers and remaining cheese mixture.

5. Roll remaining pastry to 12-inch round. Cut slits in top. Place over filling; trim edge to ½ inch beyond rim of pie plate. Fold top crust under, forming a ridge. Flute edge. Reroll any pastry scraps and use to decorate top of pastry. In cup, combine egg yolk and sour cream; brush on pastry.

6. Place pie plate on cookie sheet. Bake 1 hour or until golden brown. Let stand on wire rack 20 minutes. Cut into wedges. Makes 6 main-dish or 12 appetizer servings.

Layered Vegetable Pie

EGGPLANT PARMESAN

1 egg	1 jar (14 ounces) Prego spaghetti
2 tablespoons milk	sauce (1¾ cups)
1 cup Italian-seasoned fine dry	2 cups shredded mozzarella cheese
bread crumbs	(8 ounces)
1 medium eggplant, peeled and cut	2 tablespoons grated Parmesan
into ¼-inch slices (1 pound)	cheese

1. In pie plate, beat together egg and milk. Place bread crumbs in another pie plate. Dip eggplant slices in egg mixture, then in crumbs to coat well.

2. Arrange ½ of the eggplant slices on 10-inch microwave-safe plate lined with plain white paper towels. Microwave, uncovered, on HIGH 4 minutes or until tender, rearranging slices once during cooking. Repeat with remaining eggplant.

3. Spread ¼ cup of the spaghetti sauce in 8- by 8-inch microwave-safe baking dish. Layer ½ of the eggplant, ½ of the mozzarella and ½ of the remaining spaghetti sauce in dish; repeat layers. Sprinkle with Parmesan.

4. Cover with vented plastic wrap; microwave on HIGH 4 minutes or until hot. Rotate dish. Microwave, covered, on MEDIUM (50% power) 10 minutes or until hot and bubbling, rotating dish once during cooking. Let stand, covered, 5 minutes. Makes 4 servings.

MACARONI AND CHEESE

1 can (10¾ ounces) Campbell's	1½ cups elbow macaroni (6 ounces),
condensed cream of mushroom	cooked and drained
soup	2 cups shredded Cheddar cheese,
¾ cup milk	divided (8 ounces)
1 teaspoon prepared mustard	1 can (2.8 ounces) French-fried
⅛ teaspoon pepper	onions

1. In 1½-quart casserole, combine soup, milk, mustard and pepper. Stir in cooked macaroni and 1½ cups of the cheese. Bake at 400°F. for 25 minutes or until hot; stir.

2. Sprinkle with remaining ½ cup cheese and the onions; bake 5 minutes more or until cheese is melted. Makes 6 servings.

To microwave: In 2-quart microwave-safe casserole, combine soup, milk, mustard, pepper, cooked macaroni and 1½ cups of the cheese. Cover; microwave on HIGH 7 to 10 minutes until hot, stirring twice during cooking. Sprinkle with remaining ½ cup cheese and the onions. Microwave, uncovered, on HIGH 30 to 45 seconds or until cheese is melted.

Eggs &
Cheese

SMOKY ZITI AND CHEESE

1 can (10¾ ounces) Campbell's
  condensed cream of celery soup
¾ cup milk
¾ cup shredded mozzarella cheese
  (3 ounces)
½ cup shredded smoked mozzarella
  or smoked gouda cheese
  (2 ounces)

½ cup shredded Cheddar cheese
  (2 ounces)
¼ teaspoon white pepper
8 ounces ziti, cooked and drained
  (6 cups cooked)
2 tablespoons grated Parmesan
  cheese
2 tablespoons buttered bread
  crumbs

Eggs &
Cheese

1. In 3-quart saucepan over medium heat, stir soup until smooth. Add milk, mozzarella, smoked mozzarella, Cheddar cheese and pepper; heat until cheeses are melted, stirring often. Remove from heat. Add cooked ziti; toss to coat.

2. Spoon ziti mixture into 1½-quart casserole. Sprinkle top with Parmesan. Bake at 350°F. for 25 minutes. Sprinkle with bread crumbs. Bake 5 minutes more. Makes 6 cups or 6 main-dish servings.

CHEDDAR BROCCOLI LASAGNA

2 tablespoons olive or vegetable oil
1 large onion, chopped
1 clove garlic, minced
1 teaspoon dried Italian seasoning,
  crushed
2 packages (10 ounces *each*) frozen
  chopped broccoli, thawed and
  drained
1 can (10¾ ounces) Campbell's
  condensed cream of chicken
  soup

2 cups shredded sharp Cheddar
  cheese (8 ounces)
1 egg
1 jar (30 ounces) Prego spaghetti
  sauce (3½ cups)
½ cup Burgundy or other dry red wine
9 lasagna noodles, cooked and
  drained
2 cups shredded mozzarella cheese
  (8 ounces)

1. To make filling: In 10-inch skillet over medium heat, in hot oil, cook onion, garlic and Italian seasoning until onion is tender, stirring occasionally. Stir in broccoli; cook until broccoli is tender and liquid is evaporated, stirring occasionally. Remove from heat; stir in soup, Cheddar cheese and egg. Set aside.

2. In medium bowl, stir together spaghetti sauce and wine; pour ½ of the sauce mixture into 13- by 9-inch baking dish. Set remainder aside.

3. Arrange 3 lasagna noodles over sauce; spread with ½ of the vegetable filling. Sprinkle with ⅓ of the mozzarella. Arrange 3 more noodles over cheese; spread with remaining filling. Sprinkle with another ⅓ of the mozzarella. Top with remaining 3 noodles and remaining sauce.

4. Bake at 350°F. for 40 minutes or until hot. Sprinkle with remaining ⅓ of the mozzarella; bake 5 minutes more. Let stand 15 minutes before serving. Makes 6 servings.

Eggs & Cheese

SPINACH LASAGNA ROLL-UPS

2 tablespoons olive oil
1 package (12 ounces) Campbell's Fresh mushrooms, sliced
1 medium onion, chopped
2 cloves garlic, minced
1 container (15 ounces) ricotta cheese
1½ cups shredded fontina or provolone cheese
1 package (10 ounces) frozen chopped spinach, thawed and well drained

1 egg
½ teaspoon salt
¼ teaspoon pepper
8 lasagna noodles, cooked and drained
1 jar (14 ounces) Prego spaghetti sauce (1¾ cups)
¼ cup grated Parmesan cheese

1. In 10-inch skillet over medium heat, in hot oil, cook mushrooms, onion and garlic until tender and liquid is evaporated, stirring occasionally. Reserve ½ cup of the mixture.

2. In large bowl, combine remaining mushroom mixture, ricotta, fontina, spinach, egg, salt and pepper; mix well. Spoon about ½ cup of the mixture down center of each lasagna noodle; roll up, jelly-roll fashion.

3. In small bowl, combine reserved mushroom mixture and spaghetti sauce. Spoon about ½ cup sauce mixture in 12- by 8-inch baking dish. Arrange roll-ups, seam-side down, in sauce. Spoon remaining sauce over roll-ups.

4. Cover; bake at 350°F. for 35 minutes or until heated through. Uncover; sprinkle with Parmesan. Bake 5 minutes more or until cheese is melted. Makes 8 servings.

TORTELLINI IN CREAM SAUCE

1 teaspoon olive or vegetable oil
2 cloves garlic, minced
½ cup chopped sweet red pepper
¼ cup chopped onion
1 can (10¾ ounces) Campbell's condensed cream of mushroom soup
½ cup half-and-half or milk

¼ cup Chablis or other dry white wine
¼ teaspoon dried tarragon leaves, crushed
8 ounces cheese tortellini, cooked and drained
½ cup crumbled feta or grated Parmesan cheese
¼ cup sliced green onions

1. In 2-quart microwave-safe casserole, combine oil, garlic, red pepper and onion. Cover with lid; microwave on HIGH 2 minutes or until vegetables are tender.

2. Stir in soup until smooth. Stir in half-and-half, wine and tarragon. Cover; microwave on HIGH 5 minutes or until hot and bubbling, stirring once during cooking. Let stand, covered, 5 minutes.

3. Toss with hot tortellini. Sprinkle with cheese and green onions. Makes 4 servings.

Spinach Lasagna Roll-Ups

SPINACH TOFU LASAGNA

1 jar (14 ounces) Prego spaghetti
   sauce (1¾ cups)
1 pound tofu, well drained
2 eggs
½ cup ricotta cheese
½ cup grated Parmesan cheese,
   divided
1 package (10 ounces) frozen
   chopped spinach, thawed and
   well drained
½ teaspoon dried Italian seasoning,
   crushed
⅛ teaspoon pepper
6 lasagna noodles, cooked and
   drained
2 cups shredded mozzarella cheese
   (8 ounces)

1. Heat spaghetti sauce according to label directions.

2. Meanwhile, in large bowl, mash tofu with fork. Stir in eggs, ricotta, ¼ cup
of the Parmesan, spinach, Italian seasoning and pepper until well mixed.

3. Spread 2 tablespoons of the spaghetti sauce in 8- by 8-inch microwave-
safe baking dish. Fit 2 noodles into baking dish, cutting and piecing as
needed. Layer ⅓ of the remaining sauce, ½ of the tofu mixture and ½ of the
mozzarella over noodles. Repeat layers of 2 noodles, ⅓ of the sauce,
remaining tofu mixture and remaining mozzarella. Top with remaining
2 noodles, remaining sauce and remaining ¼ cup Parmesan.

4. Cover with vented plastic wrap; microwave on HIGH 8 minutes or until
hot. Rotate dish. Microwave, covered, on MEDIUM (50% power) 12 minutes
or until hot and bubbling, rotating dish twice during cooking. Let stand,
covered, 5 minutes. Makes 6 servings.

BROCCOLI-CHEESE PIE

1 can (11 ounces) Campbell's
   condensed Cheddar cheese
   soup, divided
1½ cups cooked rice
4 eggs, divided
1 package (10 ounces) frozen
   chopped broccoli, cooked and
   drained
1 cup ricotta cheese or cream-style
   cottage cheese
1 sweet red pepper, cut into
   matchstick-thin strips
¼ teaspoon pepper

1. In medium bowl, stir ⅓ cup of the soup until smooth; stir in rice and 1 of
the eggs. Press mixture onto bottom and side of 9-inch microwave-safe pie
plate, forming a shell. Microwave, uncovered, on HIGH 2 minutes or until
almost set. Let stand while preparing filling.

2. In large bowl, stir remaining soup until smooth; stir in remaining 3 eggs,
the broccoli, ricotta, red pepper and pepper. Spoon into rice shell.

3. Microwave, uncovered, on MEDIUM (50% power) 22 minutes or until
center is set, rotating dish 3 times during cooking. Let stand, uncovered,
10 minutes. Makes 6 servings.

Meats

Flank Steak with Southwest Sauce (page 78)

FLANK STEAK WITH SOUTHWEST SAUCE

½ cup Burgundy or other dry red wine
¼ cup vegetable oil
2 cloves garlic, minced and divided
1½ pounds beef flank steak
⅓ cup chopped onion
1 can (16 ounces) stewed tomatoes, undrained
¾ cup Open Pit original flavor barbecue sauce
1 to 2 tablespoons seeded and chopped Vlasic hot jalapeno peppers

½ teaspoon dried oregano leaves, crushed
½ teaspoon ground cumin
¼ teaspoon ground coriander
Sweet red pepper rings for garnish
Vlasic hot jalapeno peppers for garnish
Fresh cilantro for garnish

1. To make marinade: In large nonmetal dish, combine wine, oil and ½ of the minced garlic. Add steak; turn to coat. Cover; refrigerate at least 4 hours or overnight, turning occasionally. Drain steak; reserve ¼ cup marinade.

2. To make sauce: In 2-quart saucepan over medium-high heat, heat reserved marinade to boiling. Add remaining garlic and onion; cook until tender, stirring often. Stir in tomatoes, barbecue sauce, chopped peppers, oregano, cumin and coriander; heat to boiling. Reduce heat to low. Simmer 15 minutes or until reduced to 2 cups, stirring occasionally.

3. On grill rack, place meat directly above medium-hot coals. Grill, uncovered, until desired doneness (allow 10 minutes for rare and 14 minutes for medium); turn once. Thinly slice meat across grain. Garnish with pepper rings, jalapeno peppers and cilantro. Serve with sauce. Makes 6 servings.

TEXAS BEEF BRISKET

1½ cups Open Pit original flavor barbecue sauce
⅓ cup Worcestershire sauce
⅓ cup molasses or dark corn syrup
½ teaspoon garlic powder
½ teaspoon onion powder

5- to 6-pound beef brisket
Avocado slices for garnish
Campbell's Fresh tomato wedges for garnish
Curly endive for garnish

1. To make sauce: In medium bowl, combine barbecue sauce, Worcestershire, molasses, garlic power and onion powder.

2. In covered grill, arrange preheated coals around drip pan; test for low heat above pan. On grill rack, place meat over pan. Grill, covered, 2½ to 3 hours or until tender (allow 30 minutes per pound). Adjust vents; add more charcoal as needed. Turn; brush often with sauce during last hour.

3. To serve: Thinly slice meat across grain. Garnish with avocado, tomato and endive. Heat remaining sauce; serve with meat. Makes 15 servings.

BEER-BASTED BEEF ROAST

3- to 3½-pound boneless beef top
    loin roast
¼ cup packed brown sugar
2 tablespoons spicy brown mustard
½ teaspoon salt

1 cup beer
½ cup Open Pit original flavor
    barbecue sauce
2 teaspoons molasses

1. Using long-tined fork, pierce meat several times; place in large shallow nonmetal dish. In small bowl, combine sugar, mustard and salt; rub over meat. Pour beer into dish. Cover; refrigerate at least 12 hours or overnight, turning occasionally. In small bowl, combine barbecue sauce and molasses.

2. In covered grill, arrange preheated coals around drip pan; test for medium-low heat above pan. Drain meat, reserving marinade. Insert meat thermometer into thickest part of meat, without touching fat.

3. On grill rack, place roast over pan but not over coals. Grill, covered, 45 minutes, brushing with reserved marinade after 30 minutes. Grill 30 to 60 minutes more or until desired doneness (allow 25 minutes per pound for rare or 140°F. and 30 minutes per pound for medium or 160°F.). Adjust vents and add more charcoal as necessary. Brush with sauce every 20 to 30 minutes during the remaining time. Serve with sauce. Makes 12 to 14 servings.

GARDEN SWISS STEAK

¼ cup all-purpose flour
1 pound round steak, cut ½ inch
    thick
2 tablespoons vegetable oil
1 clove garlic, minced
1 bay leaf
⅛ teaspoon pepper
1 can (10¾ ounces) Campbell's
    condensed cream of mushroom
    soup

½ cup water
1 medium green pepper, cut into
    strips
6 green onions, sliced
½ cup chopped Campbell's Fresh
    tomato
Hot cooked rice

1. On cutting board with meat mallet, pound flour into both sides of steak until all flour is absorbed and meat is slightly flattened. Cut steak into 4 serving-size pieces. In 10-inch skillet over medium-high heat, in hot oil, cook meat until browned on both sides.

2. Add garlic, bay leaf and pepper. Spoon soup over meat; add water. Heat to boiling. Reduce heat to low. Cover; simmer 1 hour, stirring occasionally.

3. Add green pepper, green onions and tomato. Cover; simmer 30 minutes more or until meat is tender. Discard bay leaf. Serve with rice. Makes 4 servings.

SAVORY STEAK

1½ cups V8 vegetable juice
¼ cup Burgundy or other dry red wine
2 cloves garlic, minced

¼ teaspoon coarsely ground pepper
2 pounds round steak

1. To make marinade: In 12- by 8-inch baking dish, combine V8 juice, wine, garlic and pepper. Add steak to marinade, turning to coat. Cover; refrigerate at least 4 hours, turning steak occasionally.

2. Remove steak from marinade, reserving marinade. Place steak on grill or on rack in broiler pan. Grill or broil steak 4 inches from heat 15 minutes on each side or until desired doneness, basting occasionally with marinade.

3. Meanwhile, in small saucepan over medium-high heat, heat remaining marinade to boiling. Serve with steak. Makes 8 servings.

VEGETABLE-STUFFED FLANK STEAK

1 tablespoon olive oil or vegetable oil
1 cup chopped Campbell's Fresh mushrooms
1 package (10 ounces) frozen chopped spinach, thawed and drained
½ cup chopped onion
1 clove garlic, minced
1 cup shredded carrots

½ cup shredded muenster or Swiss cheese (2 ounces)
½ teaspoon dried basil leaves, crushed
⅛ teaspoon pepper
1½ pounds beef flank steak, pounded to ¼-inch thickness
1 can (10¾ ounces) Campbell's condensed cream of onion soup
2 tablespoons dry sherry

1. In 1½-quart microwave-safe casserole, combine oil, mushrooms, spinach, onion and garlic. Cover with lid; microwave on HIGH 5 minutes or until vegetables are tender, stirring once during cooking. Drain. Stir in carrots, cheese, basil and pepper; mix well.

2. Spread vegetable mixture over steak to within 1 inch of edges. Roll up from long end, jelly-roll fashion, tucking ends of steak into roll. Secure with wooden toothpicks or tie with kitchen string. Place, seam-side down, in 12- by 8-inch microwave-safe baking dish.

3. In small bowl, stir soup until smooth. Stir in sherry. Pour over meat. Cover with vented plastic wrap; microwave on HIGH 10 minutes, rotating dish once during cooking.

4. Spoon pan juices over meat. Cover; microwave on MEDIUM (50% power) 20 minutes or until meat is tender, rotating dish twice during cooking. Let stand, covered, 10 minutes. Makes 6 servings.

Savory Steak

BEEF EN CROUTE WITH DUXELLES

4-pound beef tenderloin (filet mignon)
2 tablespoons butter or margarine
2 packages (8 ounces *each*) Campbell's Fresh mushrooms, finely chopped
¼ cup finely chopped onion
2 tablespoons brandy or port wine

1 tablespoon chopped fresh parsley
Dash salt
Dash pepper
1 package (17¼ ounces) Pepperidge Farm frozen puff pastry sheets, thawed
1 egg white, beaten
Chasseur Sauce (see page 262)

1. On rack in roasting pan, place filet. Roast, uncovered, at 450°F. for 30 minutes or until meat thermometer inserted in center reaches 120°F. (very rare). Cool to room temperature.

2. Meanwhile, in 10-inch skillet over medium heat, in hot butter, cook mushrooms and onion until tender and liquid is evaporated, stirring occasionally. Stir in brandy, parsley, salt and pepper; simmer 1 minute. Cool to room temperature.

3. Preheat oven to 425°F. Unfold puff pastry sheets; on floured surface, press long edges together to form one piece of pastry. Roll out pastry to form rectangle large enough to encase filet. Trim pastry; save trimmings for decoration. Brush pastry with egg white. Spread mushroom mixture on pastry to within 2 inches of edges.

4. Place filet in center of pastry. Fold pastry around filet, sealing edges with egg white. On jelly-roll pan, place filet seam-side down. Decorate top of pastry with trimmings; brush with egg white.

5. Bake 20 minutes or until pastry is golden. Let stand 10 minutes before slicing. Serve with Chasseur Sauce. Makes 8 servings.

Tip: For glossy crust, brush pastry with 1 egg yolk beaten with 1 teaspoon milk.

To use Pepperidge Farm patty shells: Substitute 2 packages (10 ounces *each*) Pepperidge Farm frozen patty shells, thawed for puff pastry sheets. Arrange patty shells 3 by 4 with sides touching; roll out into large pastry rectangle to fit around filet.

Beef en Croute with Duxelles

BEEF STEW

2 pounds beef for stew, cut into
   1-inch cubes
¼ cup all-purpose flour
4 tablespoons vegetable oil, divided
2 medium onions, sliced
2 cloves garlic, minced
1 teaspoon dried thyme leaves,
   crushed
1 bay leaf

1 can (10¾ ounces) Campbell's
   condensed beefy mushroom
   soup
½ cup water
3 medium potatoes, peeled and
   cubed
2 medium carrots, cut into 2- by
   ½-inch strips
1 cup fresh or frozen cut green beans

1. Coat beef cubes with flour; reserve remaining flour.

2. In 4-quart Dutch oven over medium-high heat, in 2 tablespoons hot oil, cook beef, a few pieces at a time, until browned on all sides. Remove beef as it browns. Reduce heat to medium.

3. Add remaining 2 tablespoons oil to skillet. In hot oil, cook onions, garlic, thyme and bay leaf until onions are tender, stirring occasionally. Stir in reserved flour. Gradually add soup and water; heat to boiling. Return meat to pan. Reduce heat to low. Cover; simmer 1 hour, stirring occasionally.

4. Add potatoes, carrots and green beans. Cover; simmer 25 minutes or until vegetables are tender. Discard bay leaf. Makes about 6 cups or 8 servings.

CLASSIC POT ROAST

2 tablespoons vegetable oil
3½- to 4-pound beef chuck pot roast
1 pouch Campbell's dry onion soup
   and recipe mix
1 cup water

4 carrots, cut into 2-inch pieces
2 large potatoes, peeled and cubed
2 tablespoons water
1 tablespoon all-purpose flour

1. In 6-quart Dutch oven over medium-high heat, in hot oil, cook roast until browned on all sides. Spoon off fat.

2. Add soup mix and 1 cup water. Heat to boiling. Reduce heat to low. Cover; simmer 2½ hours or until meat is nearly tender, adding more water if needed.

3. Add carrots and potatoes; simmer 30 to 45 minutes until vegetables are tender. Remove meat and vegetables to platter; keep warm.

4. Skim fat from cooking liquid. In small bowl, combine 2 tablespoons water and the flour; stir into cooking liquid. Heat to boiling, stirring constantly; simmer 1 minute. Serve gravy with meat and vegetables. Makes 8 servings.

Beef Stew

STIR-FRIED BEEF AND VEGETABLES

½ pound boneless beef sirloin steak,
   cut ¾ inch thick
1 can (10½ ounces) Campbell's
   condensed beef broth (bouillon)
1 tablespoon cornstarch
1 tablespoon soy sauce
3 tablespoons vegetable oil, divided

1 clove garlic, minced
4 green onions, cut into 1-inch pieces
1 cup broccoli flowerets
1 can (8 ounces) sliced bamboo
   shoots, drained
Shredded lettuce or hot cooked
   rice

1. Freeze steak 1 hour to make slicing easier. Trim and discard excess fat from steak. Slice across grain into very thin strips.

2. In small bowl, combine broth, cornstarch and soy sauce; stir to blend. Set aside.

3. In 10-inch skillet or wok over medium-high heat, in 2 tablespoons hot oil, cook beef strips and garlic stirring quickly and frequently (stir-frying) until meat is browned. Remove from skillet.

4. Add remaining 1 tablespoon oil to skillet. Add green onions and broccoli; stir-fry 1 minute. Add bamboo shoots; stir-fry 30 seconds more.

5. Return beef to skillet. Stir broth mixture; stir into skillet. Heat to boiling; cook 1 minute more. Spoon over shredded lettuce. Makes about 2½ cups or 2 servings.

EASY BEEF STROGANOFF

1 pound boneless beef sirloin steak,
   cut ¾ inch thick
2 tablespoons vegetable oil
1 pouch Campbell's dry onion
   mushroom soup and recipe mix

2 tablespoons all-purpose flour
1½ cups water
½ cup sour cream
Hot cooked noodles

1. Freeze steak 1 hour to make slicing easier. Trim and discard excess fat from steak. Slice across grain into very thin strips.

2. In 10-inch skillet over medium-high heat, in hot oil, cook meat until browned, stirring often.

3. In medium bowl, combine soup mix and flour; whisk in water until smooth. Pour into skillet; heat to boiling, stirring constantly.

4. Reduce heat to low. Cover; simmer 30 minutes or until meat is tender.

5. Stir in sour cream until blended. Heat through, but do not boil. Serve over noodles. Makes 4 servings.

Stir-Fried Beef and Vegetables

BEEF WITH SNOW PEAS

1 pound boneless beef sirloin steak, cut ¾ inch thick
3 tablespoons soy sauce
2 tablespoons dry sherry
1 tablespoon rice wine vinegar
2 tablespoons packed brown sugar
1 clove garlic, minced
2 teaspoons cornstarch
3 tablespoons peanut or vegetable oil, divided
1 package (8 ounces) Campbell's Fresh mushrooms, sliced
1 cup sliced celery
1 cup sweet red pepper cut into ¾-inch squares
1 cup snow peas cut in half lengthwise

1. Freeze meat 1 hour to firm for easier slicing. Trim and discard excess fat from steak. Slice across grain into very thin strips.

2. In cup, combine soy sauce, sherry, vinegar, sugar, garlic and cornstarch; set aside.

3. In 10-inch skillet over medium heat, in 1 tablespoon hot oil, cook mushrooms until tender and liquid is evaporated, stirring occasionally. Remove to bowl; set aside.

4. In same skillet in remaining 2 tablespoons hot oil, stir-fry meat until color just changes, stirring quickly and frequently. Push to one side. Add celery and red pepper; stir-fry until tender-crisp. Add snow peas; stir-fry 1 minute.

5. Stir in soy mixture. Cook until mixture boils and thickens, stirring often. Add mushrooms; heat through. Makes 6 cups or 6 servings.

BEEF AND MUSHROOM SATE

1 pound boneless beef sirloin steak, cut 1 inch thick
¼ cup finely chopped onion
¼ cup soy sauce
3 tablespoons lemon or lime juice
3 tablespoons rice wine or dry sherry
2 tablespoons vegetable oil
2 tablespoons packed brown sugar
3 cloves garlic, minced
½ teaspoon crushed red pepper
1 package (8 ounces) Campbell's Fresh mushrooms
1 large green pepper, cut into squares
Peanut Dipping Sauce (page 262)

1. Freeze meat 1 hour to firm for easier slicing. Trim and discard excess fat from steak. Slice across grain into very thin strips.

2. In large bowl, combine onion, soy sauce, lemon juice, wine, oil, sugar, garlic and red pepper. Add meat and mushrooms; toss to coat well. Cover; refrigerate at least 2 hours, stirring occasionally.

3. On four 12-inch skewers, alternately thread meat, mushrooms and green pepper. Place skewers on grill 6 inches above glowing coals. Grill 8 minutes or until meat is desired doneness and mushrooms are tender, turning often and brushing with remaining marinade. Serve with Peanut Dipping Sauce. Makes 4 servings.

Beef with Snow Peas

TEX-MEX CHILI

1 pound lean ground beef
1 cup chopped onions
2 cloves garlic, minced
3 tablespoons chili powder
2 teaspoons ground cumin
¼ teaspoon pepper
1 tablespoon all-purpose flour

3 cups V8 vegetable juice or no salt
   added V8 vegetable juice
1 can (20 ounces) kidney beans,
   drained
Sweet red and green pepper rings
   for garnish
Celery leaves for garnish

1. In 3-quart saucepan over medium heat, cook beef, onions, garlic, chili powder, cumin and pepper until beef is browned and onion is tender, stirring to separate meat. Spoon off fat.

2. Stir in flour; cook 1 minute, stirring constantly. Gradually stir in V8 juice. Heat to boiling, stirring often. Reduce heat to low. Simmer 30 minutes, stirring occasionally.

3. Add beans. Simmer 15 minutes more, stirring occasionally.

4. To serve: Garnish with pepper rings and celery leaves. Ladle into bowls; serve with shredded Cheddar cheese, chopped green onions, chopped tomatoes and chopped green pepper, if desired. Makes 6½ cups or 6 servings.

CHIMICHANGAS

1 pound ground beef
1 medium onion, chopped
1 clove garlic, minced
1 can (10¾ ounces) Campbell's
   condensed tomato soup
1 can (4 ounces) chopped green
   chilies, drained
1 tablespoon vinegar

1 teaspoon dried oregano leaves,
   crushed
½ teaspoon ground cumin
8 flour tortillas (8-inch)
1 cup shredded Monterey Jack
   cheese (4 ounces)
Vegetable oil
Shredded lettuce for garnish
Taco sauce for garnish

1. In 10-inch skillet over medium heat, cook beef, onion and garlic until browned, stirring occasionally to separate meat. Spoon off fat. Stir in soup, chilies, vinegar, oregano and cumin. Reduce heat to low. Simmer 10 to 15 minutes or until most of liquid evaporates. Remove from heat; cool slightly.

2. Spoon ¼ cup filling down center of one tortilla. Top with 2 tablespoons of the cheese. Fold in sides of tortilla; roll up tortilla around filling. Secure with a wooden toothpick. Assemble 2 or 3 at a time.

3. In 10-inch skillet, heat 1-inch oil to 350°F. Fry chimichangas 2 minutes or until golden, turning once. Remove and drain on paper towels. Garnish with lettuce and taco sauce. Makes 8 servings.

Tex-Mex Chili

CHILI IN TORTILLA CUPS

Tortilla Cups (recipe follows)
¾ pound lean ground beef
½ cup chopped onion
1 tablespoon chili powder
1 teaspoon ground cumin
1½ cups V8 vegetable juice
1 can (16 ounces) kidney beans,
    drained
Dash hot pepper sauce

1 cup shredded Colby or Monterey
    Jack cheese (4 ounces)
½ cup diced green pepper
¾ cup diced Campbell's Fresh tomato
2½ cups shredded iceberg lettuce
Chopped green pepper for garnish
Chopped tomato for garnish
Shredded cheese for garnish

1. Prepare Tortilla Cups.

2. In 10-inch nonstick skillet over medium-high heat, cook beef, onion, chili powder and cumin until beef is browned and onion is tender, stirring to separate meat. Spoon off fat.

3. Stir in V8 juice, kidney beans and hot pepper sauce. Heat to boiling. Reduce heat to low. Simmer 15 minutes, stirring occasionally.

4. In large bowl, toss cheese, green pepper and tomato with meat mixture.

5. To serve: Divide lettuce among Tortilla Cups. Fill each with about ¾ cup meat mixture. Garnish with green pepper, tomato and cheese. Makes 6 servings.

TORTILLA CUPS: Preheat oven to 400°F. On cookie sheet, place 6 balls of foil (4-inch diameter). Spray 10-inch nonstick skillet with vegetable cooking spray. Over high heat, heat one 8-inch flour tortilla 5 seconds on each side until tortilla is softened. Drain on paper towels. Immediately drape tortilla over foil ball on baking sheet. Repeat with 5 additional tortillas. Bake 5 minutes or until golden. Remove from oven; cool on foil balls.

TACOS

1 pound ground beef
½ cup chopped onion
2 cloves garlic, minced
1 tablespoon chili powder
1 can (10¾ ounces) Campbell's
    condensed tomato soup

8 taco shells
1 cup shredded Cheddar cheese
    (4 ounces)
Shredded lettuce
1 cup chopped Campbell's Fresh
    tomatoes

1. Preheat oven to 350°F. In 10-inch skillet over medium heat, cook beef, onion, garlic and chili powder until meat is well browned, stirring to separate meat. Spoon off fat. Stir in soup. Heat through, stirring occasionally.

2. Place about ¼ cup meat mixture in each taco shell. Place on cookie sheet. Bake 5 minutes. Top with cheese, lettuce and tomatoes. Makes 8 tacos or 4 servings.

Chili in Tortilla Cups

FAST CHILI

1 pound ground beef
1 cup chopped onions
2 cloves garlic, minced
1 tablespoon chili powder
1 can (8 ounces) tomatoes,
   undrained, cut up
¼ cup Open Pit original flavor
   barbecue sauce

1 can (28 ounces) Campbell's pork
   & beans in tomato sauce or
2 cans (15½ ounces *each*)
   Campbell's Ranchero beans
2 tablespoons seeded and chopped
   Vlasic mild cherry peppers
Corn bread or hot cooked rice

1. In 10-inch skillet over medium-high heat, cook beef, onions, garlic and chili powder until beef is browned and onions are tender, stirring to separate meat. Spoon off fat.

2. Stir in tomatoes and barbecue sauce; cook 1 minute. Stir in beans; heat to boiling. Reduce heat to low. Simmer 10 minutes, stirring occasionally. Stir in peppers.

3. To serve: Spoon over corn bread or rice. Makes 6 cups or 6 servings.

To microwave: In 2-quart microwave-safe casserole, combine beef, onions, garlic and chili powder. Cover; microwave on HIGH 5 minutes or until no pink remains in meat, stirring once during cooking. Spoon off fat. Stir in tomatoes, barbecue sauce and beans. Cover; microwave on HIGH 7 minutes or until heated through, stirring twice during cooking. Stir in peppers. Serve as in step 3.

CINCINNATI-STYLE CHILI

2 pounds ground beef
1 cup coarsely chopped onions
3 cloves garlic, minced
5 cups Campbell's tomato juice
1 can (6 ounces) tomato paste
2 tablespoons cider vinegar
2 bay leaves
1 tablespoon ground cumin
1½ teaspoons dried oregano leaves,
   crushed

1 teaspoon salt
1 teaspoon ground cinnamon
½ teaspoon ground red pepper
1 can (20¾ ounces) Campbell's
   pork & beans in tomato sauce
Hot cooked vermicelli (thin
   spaghetti)
Shredded Cheddar cheese for
   garnish
Chopped onion for garnish

1. In 4-quart Dutch oven over medium-high heat, cook beef, onions and garlic until beef is browned and onions are tender, stirring occasionally to separate meat. Spoon off fat.

2. Stir in tomato juice, tomato paste, vinegar, bay leaves, cumin, oregano, salt, cinnamon and red pepper. Heat to boiling. Reduce heat to low. Simmer 30 minutes, stirring occasionally. Stir in beans; heat through. Remove bay leaves.

3. Spoon over vermicelli. Sprinkle with cheese and additional chopped onion. Makes 10 cups or 10 servings.

Fast Chili

HEARTLAND BURGERS

1 pound ground beef
1 cup thinly sliced Campbell's Fresh
  mushrooms
¼ cup finely chopped onion
½ teaspoon Worcestershire sauce
¼ teaspoon salt
  Generous dash pepper
⅓ cup Open Pit original flavor
  barbecue sauce

4 whole wheat hamburger buns,
  split, toasted and buttered
Campbell's Fresh butterhead
  lettuce leaves
Sliced Campbell's Fresh tomato
Vlasic hamburger relish
Sliced onion

1. In large bowl, combine beef, mushrooms, chopped onion, Worcestershire, salt and pepper. Shape into four 1-inch-thick patties.

2. On grill rack, place patties directly above medium coals. Grill, uncovered, until desired doneness (allow 10 minutes for medium and 12 minutes for well-done), turning and brushing often with barbecue sauce.

3. To serve: Place patties on buns with lettuce, tomato, relish and sliced onion. Makes 4 servings.

To broil: Arrange patties on rack in broiler pan. Broil 4 inches from heat until desired doneness (allow 15 minutes for medium and 18 minutes for well-done), turning and brushing often with barbecue sauce. Serve as in step 2.

BURGERS U.S.A.

1½ pounds ground beef
⅓ cup Open Pit original flavor
  barbecue sauce, divided
2 tablespoons finely chopped onion
½ teaspoon dried basil leaves,
  crushed

½ teaspoon dried oregano leaves,
  crushed
6 hamburger buns, split and toasted
  Vlasic original hamburger dill
  chips or hamburger relish

1. In large bowl, combine beef, 2 tablespoons of the barbecue sauce, the onion, basil and oregano. Shape into six 1-inch-thick patties.

2. On grill rack, place patties directly above medium coals. Grill, uncovered, until desired doneness (allow 10 minutes for medium and 12 minutes for well-done), turning and brushing often with remaining barbecue sauce.

3. To serve: Place patties on buns with dill chips. Makes 6 servings.

To broil: Arrange patties on rack in broiler pan. Broil 4 inches from heat until desired doneness (allow 15 minutes for medium and 18 minutes for well-done), turning and brushing often with remaining barbecue sauce. Serve as in step 3.

Heartland Burgers

MEATBALL STEW

1 pound ground beef
½ cup soft bread crumbs
½ teaspoon dried savory leaves,
    crushed
1 egg
1 clove garlic, minced
2 tablespoons vegetable oil
1 can (10½ ounces) Campbell's
    condensed French onion soup

¼ cup water
3 medium potatoes, peeled and
    quartered
3 medium carrots, cut into 1-inch
    chunks
1 medium onion, cut into thin
    wedges
Chopped fresh parsley for garnish

1. In medium bowl, combine beef, bread crumbs, savory, egg and garlic; mix thoroughly. Shape into 20 meatballs.

2. In 10-inch skillet over medium heat, in hot oil, cook meatballs until browned on all sides. Spoon off fat.

3. Stir soup and water into skillet; stir in potatoes, carrots and onion. Heat to boiling. Reduce heat to low. Cover; simmer 30 minutes or until vegetables are tender, adding more water if needed. Garnish with parsley.
Makes 4 servings.

KOREAN BEEF IN LETTUCE

10 romaine lettuce leaves
2 tablespoons water
1 pound ground beef
1 pouch Campbell's dry onion soup
    and recipe mix

1 package (8 ounces) Campbell's
    Fresh mushrooms, chopped
¼ cup hoisin sauce
1 tablespoon dry sherry or rice wine
2 teaspoons cornstarch
1½ cups hot cooked rice

1. Arrange romaine leaves in 12- by 8-inch microwave-safe baking dish; add water. Cover with vented plastic wrap; microwave on HIGH 3 minutes or until wilted. Drain and set aside.

2. Crumble beef into 2-quart microwave-safe casserole. Cover with lid; microwave on HIGH 5 minutes or until beef is no longer pink, stirring once during cooking to separate meat. Spoon off fat.

3. Stir in soup mix, mushrooms and hoisin sauce. In cup, combine sherry and cornstarch; stir into meat mixture. Cover; microwave on HIGH 5 minutes or until very hot, stirring once during cooking.

4. Lay drained lettuce leaves on counter. Mound 2 heaping tablespoons of rice in center of each; top with about ¼ cup of the meat mixture. Fold in sides and roll up to form bundles. Makes 10 bundles or 5 servings.

Meatball Stew

VEGETABLE-STUFFED MEAT CUPS

1 package (10 ounces) frozen mixed vegetables	1 pouch Campbell's dry onion soup and recipe mix
1 cup shredded Swiss cheese, divided (4 ounces)	1 egg
1½ pounds ground beef	½ cup fresh bread crumbs
	2 tablespoons ketchup

1. Place vegetables in small microwave-safe bowl. Cover with vented plastic wrap; microwave on HIGH 3½ minutes or until tender-crisp. Drain. Add ½ cup of the cheese; toss to mix well. Set aside.

2. In large bowl, combine beef, soup mix, egg, bread crumbs and ketchup; mix well. Divide meat mixture into 8 equal parts. Press into bottoms and up sides of eight 6-ounce custard cups or individual casseroles. Divide vegetable mixture among meat cups.

3. Arrange 4 meat cups in a circle in the microwave oven. Microwave, uncovered, on HIGH 4 minutes or until meat is no longer pink, rearranging cups once during cooking. Sprinkle each with 1 tablespoon of the remaining cheese. Repeat with remaining meat cups. Makes 8 servings.

BEST-EVER MEAT LOAF

1 can (10¾ ounces) Campbell's condensed golden mushroom soup, divided	1 egg, beaten
	⅓ cup finely chopped onion
2 pounds ground beef	1 tablespoon Worcestershire sauce
½ cup fine dry bread crumbs	⅓ cup water

1. In large bowl, thoroughly mix ½ cup of the soup, the beef, bread crumbs, egg, onion and Worcestershire. In 12- by 8-inch baking pan, firmly shape meat into 8- by 4-inch loaf.

2. Bake at 350°F. for 1¼ hours or until done. Remove meat loaf to platter; keep warm.

3. Spoon off all but 3 tablespoons drippings from pan. Stir remaining soup and the water into drippings in pan, scraping up brown bits from bottom. Over medium heat, heat soup mixture until hot, stirring constantly. Serve gravy with meat loaf. Makes 8 servings.

Vegetable-Stuffed Meat Cups

MARINATED KABOBS

1 pouch Campbell's dry onion
  mushroom soup and recipe mix
1½ cups water, divided
¼ cup Burgundy or other dry red wine
2 tablespoons vegetable oil
1 clove garlic, minced
1 teaspoon dried basil leaves,
  crushed
2 bay leaves
¼ teaspoon black pepper

1 pound boneless lamb, cut into
  1-inch pieces
1 green pepper, cut into
  1-inch squares
1 sweet red pepper, cut into
  1-inch squares
1 sweet yellow pepper, cut into
  1-inch squares
2 tablespoons chutney
Hot cooked rice

1. To make marinade: In 2-cup measure, combine soup mix, ½ cup of the water, the wine, oil, garlic, basil, bay leaves and black pepper; mix well with a fork.

2. Place lamb in shallow dish or bowl; pour marinade over all. Cover; refrigerate several hours or overnight.

3. Drain lamb, reserving marinade. On each of four 8-inch skewers, alternate lamb and pepper squares. Arrange skewers in broiler pan. Broil 6 inches from heat 10 minutes or until lamb is desired doneness, turning occasionally and brushing with reserved marinade.

4. To make sauce: Pour remaining marinade into 1-quart saucepan. Add remaining 1 cup water and the chutney. Over medium-high heat, heat to boiling, stirring often. Reduce heat to low. Simmer 5 minutes. Remove bay leaves.

5. Serve kabobs on rice with sauce. Makes 4 servings.

MINI MEAT LOAVES

1 pouch Campbell's dry onion soup
  and recipe mix
1½ pounds ground beef
½ pound bulk pork sausage
½ cup fine dry bread crumbs
1 egg

½ cup Open Pit original flavor
  barbecue sauce, divided
3 small Vlasic sweet pickles, cut in
  half lengthwise
2 slices (1 ounce *each*) process
  Cheddar cheese, each cut into
  3 thin strips

1. Preheat oven to 350°F. In large bowl, combine soup mix, beef, sausage, bread crumbs, egg and ¼ cup of the barbecue sauce; mix well.

2. Divide meat mixture into 6 equal portions. Flatten each into 4-inch patty. Place pickle half on each; fold meat over to enclose pickle. Shape each into small loaf. Place loaves in large shallow baking pan.

3. Bake 30 minutes. Remove from oven; spoon fat from pan. Spread remaining ¼ cup barbecue sauce over loaves; top with cheese strips. Bake 2 minutes more or until cheese melts. Makes 6 servings.

Marinated Kabobs

LAMB CURRY

1 tablespoon butter or margarine
1 cup chopped onions
2 tablespoons curry powder
1½ pounds boneless lamb, cut into
    ½-inch pieces
¼ cup all-purpose flour
1 cup Swanson clear ready to serve
    chicken broth

2 apples, peeled and chopped
1 can (8 ounces) tomatoes, drained,
    cut up
¼ cup chutney
½ cup sour cream or plain yogurt
Hot cooked rice
Chopped peanuts for garnish

1. In 3-quart microwave-safe casserole, combine butter, onions and curry powder. Cover with lid; microwave on HIGH 4 minutes or until onion is tender, stirring once during cooking.

2. In large bowl, toss lamb with flour; stir into casserole. Cover; microwave on HIGH 6 minutes or until meat is no longer pink, stirring once during cooking.

3. Stir in broth, apples, tomatoes and chutney. Cover; microwave on HIGH 7 minutes or until boiling, stirring once during cooking. Stir again.

4. Microwave on MEDIUM (50% power) 30 minutes or until meat is tender, stirring 3 times during cooking. Let stand, covered, 5 minutes.

5. Stir in sour cream. Serve over rice; garnish with peanuts. Makes about 5 cups or 6 servings.

LAMB STEW

1½ pounds boneless lamb, cut into
    1-inch pieces
1 can (10½ ounces) Franco-
    American mushroom gravy
4 small potatoes, cut into quarters

1 tablespoon chopped fresh mint
    leaves or ½ teaspoon dried
    mint leaves, crushed
1 cup frozen peas
1 cup quartered Campbell's Fresh
    mushrooms

1. Place lamb in 3-quart microwave-safe casserole. Cover with lid; microwave on HIGH 6 minutes or until lamb is no longer pink, stirring once during cooking. Drain off excess liquid.

2. Stir in gravy, potatoes and mint. Cover; microwave on HIGH 5 minutes or until bubbling. Stir again.

3. Cover; microwave on MEDIUM (50% power) 25 minutes or until meat is nearly tender, stirring twice during cooking.

4. Stir in peas and mushrooms. Cover; microwave on MEDIUM 5 minutes or until vegetables and meat are tender, stirring once during cooking. Let stand, covered, 5 minutes. Makes about 5½ cups or 6 servings.

ROSEMARY LAMB RIBLETS

1 tablespoon vegetable oil
¼ cup finely chopped onion
2 cloves garlic, minced
1 teaspoon dried rosemary leaves,
   crushed

1 cup Open Pit original flavor
   barbecue sauce
2 pounds lamb breast riblets
   (about 12), cut into serving-size
   pieces

1. To make sauce: In 1-quart saucepan over medium heat, in hot oil, cook onion, garlic and rosemary until onion is tender, stirring often. Stir in barbecue sauce; heat through, stirring occasionally.

2. In covered grill, arrange preheated coals around drip pan; test for medium heat above pan.

3. On grill rack, place ribs, fat-side up, over pan but not over coals. Grill, covered, 1¼ hours or until tender. Adjust vents and add more charcoal as necessary. Turn and brush often with sauce during the last 45 minutes. Makes 2 to 3 servings.

KENTUCKY BARBECUED LAMB

Hickory chips
5- pound lamb leg roast
Black Dip (recipe follows)

Kentucky Barbecue Sauce
   (recipe follows)

1. At least 1 hour before grilling, soak wood chips in enough water to cover. Drain wood chips.

2. In covered grill, arrange preheated coals around drip pan; test for low heat above pan. Sprinkle 4 cups wood chips over coals. Sprinkle lamb with salt; insert meat thermometer into thickest part without touching fat or bone.

3. On grill rack, place meat, fat-side up, over pan but not over coals. Grill, covered, 3 hours or until medium doneness or 160°F. (allow 30 to 35 minutes per pound). Adjust vents and add more charcoal and wood chips as necessary. Prepare Black Dip and Kentucky Barbecue Sauce. Brush meat with Black Dip every 30 minutes.

4. To serve: Let meat stand 15 minutes; thinly slice across the grain. Serve with Kentucky Barbecue Sauce. Makes 12 servings.

To roast: Place meat, fat-side up, on rack in roasting pan. Roast, uncovered, at 325°F. for 2 to 2½ hours or until medium doneness or 160°F. Brush with Black Dip every 30 minutes. Serve as in step 4.

BLACK DIP: In 1-quart saucepan, combine 1 cup vinegar, ½ cup water, ¼ cup Worcestershire sauce, 1½ teaspoons lemon juice and ¼ teaspoon pepper. Over high heat, heat to boiling. Makes 1¾ cups.

KENTUCKY BARBECUE SAUCE: In 1-quart saucepan, combine 1 cup Open Pit original flavor barbecue sauce, 1 cup tomato puree and 1 tablespoon butter or margarine. Over medium heat, heat through, stirring until butter is melted. Serve warm. Makes 2 cups.

VEAL CUTLETS WITH OYSTER MUSHROOMS

1 package (3.8 ounces) Campbell's
   Fresh oyster mushrooms
1 pound thinly sliced veal cutlets,
   ¼ inch thick
¼ cup all-purpose flour
½ teaspoon salt
¼ teaspoon pepper

¼ cup butter or margarine
¼ cup sliced green onions
½ cup Swanson clear ready to serve
   chicken broth
½ cup Chablis or other dry white wine
1 cup light cream

1. Cut any large mushrooms in half. With meat mallet, pound cutlets to ⅛-inch thickness. On waxed paper, mix flour, salt and pepper; coat cutlets with mixture.

2. In 10-inch skillet over medium heat, in hot butter, cook cutlets, a few at a time, until lightly browned on both sides, removing pieces as they brown.

3. Reduce heat to low; add mushrooms to hot drippings. Cook until mushrooms are tender, stirring occasionally. Add green onions; cook 1 minute.

4. Stir in chicken broth and wine, scraping to loosen brown bits. Simmer until liquid is reduced to ½ cup, about 10 minutes. Stir in cream; add veal. Heat through, but do not boil. Makes 6 servings.

VEAL WITH VEGETABLES DIJON

1 tablespoon vegetable oil
1 pound veal cutlets
1½ cups sliced Campbell's Fresh
   mushrooms
½ cup carrots cut into 2-inch strips
½ cup chopped parsnip

½ cup chopped onion
1 cup V8 vegetable juice
1 teaspoon Dijon-style mustard
½ teaspoon grated lemon peel
   Chopped fresh parsley for garnish.

1. In 10-inch nonstick skillet over medium heat, in hot oil, cook veal, a few pieces at a time, until browned on both sides. Remove to warm platter. Cover; keep warm.

2. In same skillet over medium heat, cook mushrooms, carrots, parsnip and onion until tender, stirring occasionally.

3. Stir V8 juice, mustard and lemon peel into skillet. Reduce heat to low. Simmer 10 minutes or until desired consistency, stirring occasionally. Spoon sauce over veal. Garnish with parsley. Makes 4 servings.

MUSHROOM VEAL PICCATA

1 pound veal cutlets, ¼ inch thick
2 tablespoons all-purpose flour
¼ teaspoon salt
⅛ teaspoon pepper
¼ cup butter or margarine, divided
1 package (8 ounces) Campbell's
Fresh mushrooms, sliced

½ cup Swanson clear ready to serve
chicken broth
¼ cup Chablis or other dry white wine
2 tablespoons lemon juice
Lemon slices
Chopped fresh parsley for garnish

1. With meat mallet, pound cutlets to ⅛-inch thickness. On waxed paper, mix flour, salt and pepper; coat cutlets with mixture. Reserve 1 teaspoon flour mixture.

2. In 10-inch skillet over medium heat, in 2 tablespoons hot butter, cook cutlets, a few at a time, until lightly browned on both sides, removing pieces as they brown. Keep warm.

3. In same skillet over medium heat, in remaining hot butter, cook mushrooms until tender and liquid is evaporated, stirring occasionally. Stir in reserved flour mixture; cook 1 minute. Gradually stir in broth, wine and lemon juice; cook until mixture boils and thickens, stirring often.

4. Arrange lemon slices on veal; pour sauce over all. Garnish with parsley. Makes 4 servings.

VEAL STEW

1 pound veal for stew, cut into
½-inch pieces
2 tablespoons all-purpose flour
1 can (10¾ ounces) Campbell's
condensed cream of mushroom
soup
½ cup milk
1 cup frozen baby carrots or fresh
carrots cut into sticks

½ cup fresh or frozen pearl onions
¼ teaspoon dried thyme leaves,
crushed
⅛ teaspoon pepper
2 tablespoons chopped fresh parsley
1 teaspoon lemon juice

1. In 3-quart microwave-safe casserole, combine veal and flour. Cover with lid; microwave on HIGH 5 minutes or until veal is no longer pink, stirring once during cooking.

2. In small bowl, combine soup and milk; blend well. Stir soup mixture into meat. Stir in carrots, onions, thyme and pepper. Cover; microwave on MEDIUM (50% power) 25 minutes or until veal is tender, stirring 3 times during cooking. Stir in parsley and lemon juice. Let stand, covered, 5 minutes. Makes about 3½ cups or 4 servings.

Meats

CROWN ROAST OF PORK

6- pound pork crown roast
(12 to 16 small ribs)
¼ cup butter or margarine
1 package (12 ounces) Campbell's
Fresh mushrooms, sliced
½ cup thinly sliced celery

½ cup water
1 package (8 ounces) Pepperidge
Farm corn bread stuffing
1 cup coarsely chopped apple
⅛ teaspoon ground allspice
⅓ cup apricot preserves, melted

1. In roasting pan, place roast, bones pointing up. Cover bone tips with small pieces of foil. Insert meat thermometer into thickest part of meat, not touching bone. Roast at 325°F. for 1½ hours.

2. Meanwhile, to prepare stuffing: In 10-inch skillet over medium heat, in hot butter, cook mushrooms and celery until tender; stirring occasionally. Stir in water; heat to boiling.

3. In large bowl, combine corn bread stuffing, apple and allspice. Pour mushroom mixture over stuffing mixture; toss to mix well. Spoon stuffing mixture into center of roast, mounding high. Cover stuffing with foil. Roast 1 hour more. Remove foil from stuffing.

4. Brush melted preserves over roast. Roast 30 minutes more or until internal temperature reaches 170°F., brushing often with preserves.

5. Let roast stand 15 minutes for easier carving. Remove foil from bones before serving. Makes 8 servings.

HONEY-GLAZED COUNTRY-STYLE RIBS

1 tablespoon vegetable oil
½ cup finely chopped onion
2 cloves garlic, minced

1 cup Open Pit original flavor
barbecue sauce
⅓ cup honey
5 pounds pork country-style ribs

1. To make sauce: In 2-quart saucepan over medium heat, in hot oil, cook onion and garlic until onion is tender, stirring often. Stir in barbecue sauce and honey. Heat to boiling. Reduce heat to low. Simmer 10 minutes, stirring occasionally.

2. In covered grill, arrange preheated coals around drip pan; test for medium heat above pan.

3. On grill rack, place ribs, fat-side up, over pan but not over coals. Grill, covered, 1½ to 2 hours or until well-done. Adjust vents and add more charcoal as necessary. Turn and brush with sauce every 30 minutes. Makes 10 servings.

To roast: Place ribs, fat-side up, on rack in roasting pan. Roast, uncovered, at 350°F. for 1½ to 2 hours or until well-done. Turn and brush often with sauce during last 30 minutes.

Crown Roast of Pork

MAPLE-GLAZED PORK ROAST

½ cup Open Pit original flavor
   barbecue sauce
¼ cup maple syrup
2 teaspoons slivered orange peel
1 teaspoon ground ginger

½ teaspoon salt
3- pound boneless pork loin roast
   Red and green grapes for garnish
   Italian parsley for garnish

1. To make sauce: In small bowl, combine barbecue sauce, syrup and peel. In another small bowl, combine ginger and salt; rub over meat.

2. In covered grill, arrange preheated coals around drip pan; test for medium heat above pan. Insert meat thermometer into thickest part of meat, without touching fat.

3. On grill rack, place meat, fat-side up, over pan but not over coals. Grill, covered, 2 to 2½ hours or until well-done or 170°F. (allow 40 to 50 minutes per pound). Adjust vents and add more charcoal as necessary. Brush often with sauce during the last hour. Thinly slice meat across the grain. Garnish with grapes and parsley. Makes 12 servings.

To roast: Place meat, fat-side up, on rack in roasting pan. Roast, uncovered, at 325°F. for 1¾ to 2 hours or until well-done or 170°F. (allow 35 to 40 minutes per pound). Brush often with sauce during the last hour. Garnish as in step 3.

PORK CHOPS AND SAUERKRAUT

2 slices bacon, chopped
½ cup chopped onion
1 jar (32 ounces) Vlasic Polish
   sauerkraut, rinsed and drained

2 apples, peeled and chopped
¼ teaspoon pepper
4 pork chops (about 1½ pounds)

1. In 3-quart microwave-safe casserole, combine bacon and onion. Cover with lid; microwave on HIGH 3½ minutes or until bacon is crisp and onion is tender, stirring once during cooking.

2. Stir in sauerkraut, apples and pepper. Arrange pork chops over sauerkraut, placing thicker portions toward edge of dish. Cover; microwave on HIGH 8 minutes or until very hot. Rearrange pork chops.

3. Cover; microwave on MEDIUM (50% power) 20 minutes or until pork is no longer pink in center, rearranging chops once during cooking. Let stand, covered, 5 minutes. Makes 4 servings.

Maple-Glazed Pork Roast

MUSHROOM-STUFFED IOWA CHOPS

1 tablespoon butter or margarine
2 cups thinly sliced Campbell's
  Fresh mushrooms
½ cup shredded carrot
⅓ cup sliced green onions
2 tablespoons chopped fresh parsley
1 tablespoon lemon juice
¼ teaspoon rubbed sage
  Dash pepper

4 pork rib chops, each cut
  1½ inches thick with
  pocket for stuffing
1 tablespoon vegetable oil
½ teaspoon dried thyme leaves,
  crushed
½ cup Open Pit original flavor
  barbecue sauce

1. To make filling: In 10-inch skillet over medium heat, in hot butter, cook mushrooms until tender, stirring occasionally. Remove from heat. Stir in carrot, onions, parsley, lemon juice, sage and pepper.

2. Stuff each chop with ¼ cup of the filling, pressing firmly into opening. Secure with wooden toothpicks. Brush chops with oil. Rub thyme over chops.

3. On grill rack, place chops directly above medium coals. Grill, uncovered, 35 to 40 minutes or until well-done, turning and brushing often with barbecue sauce during the last 20 minutes. Makes 4 servings.

To broil: Arrange chops on rack in broiler pan. Broil 4 inches from heat 25 to 30 minutes or until well-done, turning and brushing often with barbecue sauce during the last 10 minutes.

GRILLED STUFFED PORK CHOPS

½ cup olive oil
2 tablespoons tarragon vinegar
2 teaspoons Dijon-style mustard
2 teaspoons dried tarragon leaves,
  crushed
1 clove garlic, minced
6 pork chops, each cut 1½ inches
  thick with pocket for stuffing

3 tablespoons butter or margarine
1 cup sliced Campbell's Fresh
  mushrooms
1 medium onion, chopped
2 cups Pepperidge Farm corn bread
  stuffing
1 tablespoon water
1 egg

1. In 12- by 8-inch baking dish, combine oil, vinegar, mustard, tarragon and garlic. Add pork chops, turning to coat well. Cover; refrigerate 4 hours or overnight.

2. In 10-inch skillet over medium heat, in hot butter, cook mushrooms and onion until tender and liquid is evaporated, stirring occasionally.

3. To prepare stuffing: In bowl, combine corn bread stuffing, water, egg and mushroom mixture; toss to mix well.

4. Remove chops from marinade, reserving marinade. Stuff each chop with ½ cup of the stuffing mixture, securing with wooden toothpicks, if necessary.

5. Place pork chops on grill 6 inches above glowing coals. Grill 30 minutes or until meat is no longer pink, turning often and brushing with remaining marinade. Makes 6 servings.

APPLE-GLAZED PORK CHOPS

1 can (10¼ ounces) Franco-
   American beef gravy
¼ cup apple jelly
1 tablespoon cider vinegar
¼ teaspoon ground cloves

⅛ teaspoon pepper
6 pork chops, each cut ¾ inch thick
Grapes for garnish
Apple slices for garnish
Fresh oregano for garnish

1. To make glaze: In 1½-quart saucepan, combine gravy, jelly, vinegar, cloves and pepper. Over medium-high heat, heat to boiling, stirring constantly.

2. On grill rack, place chops directly above medium coals. Grill, uncovered, 20 minutes or until well-done, turning and brushing often with glaze during the last 15 minutes.

3. To serve: Heat any remaining glaze; serve with chops. Garnish with grapes, apple slices and oregano. Makes 6 servings.

To broil: Arrange chops on rack in broiler pan. Broil 4 inches from heat 20 to 30 minutes or until well-done, turning and brushing often with glaze during the last 10 minutes. Serve as in step 3.

SWEET JALAPENO RIBS

1½ cups Open Pit original flavor
   barbecue sauce
½ cup jalapeno jelly
¼ cup cider vinegar

2 tablespoons seeded and chopped
   Vlasic hot jalapeno peppers
2 teaspoons garlic powder
6 pounds pork spareribs (2 slabs)

1. To make sauce: In 1-quart saucepan, combine barbecue sauce, jelly, vinegar, peppers and garlic powder. Over medium heat, heat until jelly melts, stirring often.

2. In covered grill, arrange coals around drip pan; test for medium heat above pan. On grill rack, place ribs, fat-side up, over pan but not over coals. Grill, covered, 1½ to 2 hours or until well-done. Adjust vents and add more charcoal as necessary. Turn and brush often with sauce during the last 30 minutes. Makes 6 servings.

To roast: Place ribs, fat-side up, on rack in roasting pan. Roast, uncovered, at 350°F. for 1½ to 2 hours or until well-done. Turn and brush often with sauce during the last 30 minutes.

Meats

BARBECUED PORK SPARERIBS

1 can (10¼ ounces) Franco-American beef gravy	3 pounds pork spareribs (1 slab)
¾ cup Open Pit original flavor barbecue sauce	Arugula for garnish
2 tablespoons packed brown sugar	Campbell's Fresh mushrooms for garnish

1. To make sauce: In small bowl, combine gravy, barbecue sauce and sugar.

2. In covered grill, arrange preheated coals around drip pan; test for medium heat above pan.

3. On grill rack, place ribs, fat-side up, over pan but not over coals. Grill, covered, 1½ to 2 hours or until well-done. Adjust vents and add more charcoal as necessary. Turn and brush with sauce every 30 minutes. Garnish with arugula and mushrooms. Makes 4 servings.

To roast: Place ribs, fat-side up, on rack in roasting pan. Roast, uncovered, at 350°F. for 1½ to 2 hours or until well-done. Turn and brush with sauce every 30 minutes. Garnish as in step 3.

BARBECUED ONION SPARERIBS

1 pouch Campbell's dry onion soup and recipe mix	2 tablespoons vinegar
½ cup water	1 teaspoon chili powder
½ cup ketchup	¼ teaspoon hot pepper sauce
¼ cup packed brown sugar	2½ pounds pork spareribs, cut into individual ribs

1. To prepare sauce: In small bowl, combine soup mix, water, ketchup, sugar, vinegar, chili powder and hot pepper sauce.

2. In 12- by 8-inch microwave-safe dish, arrange ribs, placing thicker portions toward edges of dish. Pour sauce over ribs. Cover with vented plastic wrap; microwave on HIGH 5 minutes. Rearrange ribs.

3. Cover; microwave on MEDIUM (50% power) 40 minutes or until ribs are tender, rearranging ribs and spooning off fat twice during cooking. Let stand, covered, 5 minutes. Spoon off fat. Makes 4 servings.

Barbecued Pork Spareribs

CURRIED PORK

1 pound boneless pork, cut into
   ¾-inch cubes
2 tablespoons all-purpose flour
2 tablespoons butter or margarine,
   divided
1 large onion, chopped

1 medium apple, chopped
2 cloves garlic, minced
2 teaspoons curry powder
1½ cups V8 vegetable juice
2 tablespoons raisins
Hot cooked rice

1. In medium bowl, toss pork with flour to coat.

2. In 10-inch nonstick skillet over medium heat, in 1 tablespoon hot butter, cook ½ of the pork until browned on all sides; remove with slotted spoon. Repeat with remaining butter and pork; remove from skillet.

3. In same skillet over medium heat, cook onion, apple, garlic and curry powder until onion is nearly tender, stirring often. Stir in V8 juice, raisins and pork. Heat to boiling, stirring occasionally. Reduce heat to low. Cover; simmer until pork is no longer pink, about 10 minutes. Serve over rice. Makes 4 cups or 4 servings.

ORIENTAL PORK

1 teaspoon sesame oil
1 teaspoon vegetable oil
1 teaspoon grated fresh ginger
1 tablespoon soy sauce
1 tablespoon dry sherry
1 clove garlic, minced
1 pound boneless pork, cut into
   2- by ¼-inch strips

1 can (10½ ounces) Campbell's
   condensed beef broth (bouillon)
2 tablespoons cornstarch
1 cup fresh snow peas
1 sweet red pepper, cut into thin
   strips
1 cup sliced Campbell's Fresh
   mushrooms
Hot cooked rice

1. In 3-quart microwave-safe casserole, combine oils, ginger, soy sauce, sherry and garlic. Stir in pork to coat. Cover with lid; refrigerate 1 hour.

2. Microwave, covered, on HIGH 5 minutes or until pork is no longer pink, stirring once during cooking.

3. In small bowl, combine broth and cornstarch; add to pork mixture along with peas, pepper and mushrooms. Cover; microwave on HIGH 7 minutes or until hot and bubbling, stirring 3 times during cooking. Serve over rice. Makes about 5 cups or 5 servings.

Curried Pork

STUFFED CABBAGE LEAVES

1 pound ground pork	¼ cup chopped fresh parsley
½ cup chopped onion	½ teaspoon dried mint leaves,
1 can (10½ ounces) Campbell's	crushed (optional)
condensed beef broth (bouillon)	1 medium head cabbage
½ cup bulgur wheat, uncooked	1 can (10½ ounces) Campbell's
½ teaspoon grated lemon peel	condensed tomato soup
½ cup chopped apple	1 tablespoon lemon juice
¼ cup chopped walnuts	¼ teaspoon ground cinnamon

1. In 10-inch skillet over medium heat, cook pork and onion until meat is well browned, stirring occasionally to separate meat. Spoon off fat. Add beef broth, bulgur and lemon peel. Heat to boiling. Reduce heat to low. Cover; simmer 20 to 25 minutes or until bulgur is done, adding a little water if mixture becomes dry. Remove from heat. Stir in apple, walnuts, parsley and mint.

2. Meanwhile, in 4-quart saucepan over high heat, heat about 6 cups water to boiling. Add whole head of cabbage to boiling water. Reduce heat to low. Cover; simmer 1 to 2 minutes or until outer leaves are softened. Remove cabbage from water. Carefully remove 6 outer leaves. Reserve remaining cabbage for another use.

3. Drain cabbage leaves on paper towels. Lay leaves flat on cutting board and cut out any tough stems. Spoon about ¾ cup of the meat filling into center of one leaf. Fold in sides, then roll up from stem end to form a bundle. Repeat with remaining leaves and filling.

4. In medium bowl, combine soup, lemon juice and cinnamon. Pour ½ of the soup mixture into 12- by 8-inch baking dish. Place cabbage rolls, seam-side down, in prepared dish. Pour remaining soup mixture over all. Cover with foil. Bake at 350°F. for 35 minutes or until heated through. Makes 6 servings.

SWEET GEORGIA BARBECUED RIBS

1 bottle (18 ounces) Open Pit	¼ cup Worcestershire sauce
original flavor barbecue sauce	3 tablespoons butter or margarine
¾ cup packed brown sugar	2 tablespoons dry mustard
⅓ cup cider vinegar	6 pounds pork spareribs (2 slabs)

1. To make sauce: In 2-quart saucepan, combine barbecue sauce, sugar, vinegar, Worcestershire, butter and mustard. Over high heat, heat to boiling. Reduce heat to low. Simmer 5 minutes, stirring often. Let stand 1 hour.

2. In covered grill, arrange preheated coals around drip pan; test for medium heat above pan. On grill rack, place ribs, fat-side up, over pan but not over coals. Grill, covered, for 1½ to 2 hours or until well-done. Adjust vents and add more charcoal as necessary. Turn and brush with sauce every 30 minutes. Makes 6 servings.

Stuffed Cabbage Leaves

TOSTADAS

1 can (11¼ ounces) Campbell's condensed chili beef soup
1 cup finely chopped cooked pork
1 package (3 ounces) cream cheese, cubed
½ teaspoon dried oregano leaves, crushed
¼ cup water
Vegetable oil

6 corn tortillas (6-inch)
Shredded lettuce
Chopped Campbell's Fresh tomato
1 cup shredded Cheddar cheese (4 ounces)
⅓ cup guacamole
Taco sauce
Vlasic sliced pitted ripe olives

1. In 2-quart saucepan over low heat, heat soup, pork, cream cheese, oregano and water until hot, stirring occasionally.

2. To make tostada shells: In small skillet over medium heat, heat ½ inch oil to 350°F. Fry tortillas, one at a time, until golden brown (about 1 minute), turning once. Remove and drain on paper towels.

3. Top each tostada shell with ¼ cup of the soup mixture. Top with lettuce, tomato, cheese, guacamole and taco sauce. Sprinkle with olives. Makes 6 servings.

To microwave: Prepare tostada shells as in step 2. While shells are draining, in 1½-quart microwave-safe casserole, combine soup, pork, cream cheese, oregano and water. Cover; microwave on HIGH 5 to 8 minutes until hot, stirring occasionally during cooking. Proceed as in step 3.

SPICED MIXED MEAT KABOBS

½ cup Open Pit original flavor barbecue sauce
½ teaspoon grated orange peel
2 tablespoons orange juice
2 tablespoons vegetable oil
1 tablespoon packed brown sugar
¼ teaspoon ground cinnamon

1 whole chicken breast, skinned, boned and cut into strips
½ pound boneless pork tenderloin, cut into 1-inch pieces
½ pound boneless beef sirloin, cut into ¾-inch pieces

1. To marinate: In large shallow nonmetal dish, combine barbecue sauce, orange peel, orange juice, oil, sugar and cinnamon. Add chicken, pork and beef pieces; stir to coat. Cover; refrigerate 4 hours, stirring occasionally.

2. Drain meats, reserving marinade. On 6 metal skewers, alternately thread meats. On grill rack, place kabobs directly above hot coals. Grill, uncovered, 10 minutes or until chicken and pork are well-done, turning and brushing often with marinade. Makes 6 servings.

To broil: Arrange kabobs on rack in broiler pan. Broil 4 inches from heat 10 minutes or until well-done, turning and brushing often with marinade.

Tostadas

PINEAPPLE-GLAZED HAM AND SWEETS

1 can (8 ounces) pineapple slices in juice, undrained
1 package (12 ounces) Mrs. Paul's frozen candied sweet potatoes
1 tablespoon Dijon-style mustard
¾ pound cooked ham, cut into 3 slices

1. Drain pineapple, reserving 2 tablespoons juice. To make sauce: In small bowl, combine reserved pineapple juice, candied sauce mix and mustard.

2. Arrange ham slices in center of 10-inch microwave-safe pie plate. Cut pineapple slices in half; arrange pineapple and sweet potatoes around edge of dish. Spoon sauce over all.

3. Cover with vented plastic wrap; microwave on HIGH 10 minutes or until potatoes are tender, rotating dish once during cooking. Spoon sauce over ham and sweet potatoes before serving. Makes 3 servings.

HOLIDAY STUFFED HAM

6 tablespoons butter or margarine
4 packages (8 ounces *each*) Campbell's Fresh mushrooms, finely chopped
½ cup finely chopped onion
2 tablespoons chopped fresh parsley
1 teaspoon grated orange peel
¼ teaspoon ground nutmeg
⅛ teaspoon salt
Dash pepper
2 cups soft bread crumbs
7- to 8-pound fully cooked smoked shank half ham
½ cup orange marmalade
1 tablespoon frozen orange juice concentrate

1. To make stuffing: In 10-inch skillet over medium heat, in hot butter, cook mushrooms and onion until tender and liquid is evaporated, stirring occasionally. Stir in parsley, orange peel, nutmeg, salt and pepper; add bread crumbs.

2. Remove rind from ham; trim excess fat. Slice ham to bone at 1-inch intervals. Spoon stuffing between slices. Place ham on rack in roasting pan; cover with foil. Bake at 325°F. for about 2 hours (15 minutes per pound).

3. Meanwhile, in small saucepan, heat marmalade and orange juice concentrate until melted. Uncover ham during last 30 minutes of baking and brush often with marmalade mixture. Makes 12 servings.

HAM-SAUCED SWEET POTATOES

3 sweet potatoes (about 8 ounces *each*)
1 can (10¾ ounces) Campbell's condensed golden mushroom soup

1 cup cooked ham cut into thin strips
½ teaspoon grated orange peel
⅓ cup orange juice
¼ cup raisins

1. Pierce potatoes with fork in several places; arrange in circular pattern on microwave-safe plate. Microwave, uncovered, on HIGH 8 minutes or until tender, rearranging potatoes once during cooking. Let stand, uncovered, while making sauce.

2. In medium microwave-safe bowl, combine remaining ingredients. Cover with vented plastic wrap; microwave on HIGH 4 minutes or until hot, stirring once during cooking. Split potatoes; spoon sauce over each. Makes 3 servings.

SAUSAGE AND PEPPERS

1 pound Italian sausage, cut into 2-inch pieces
2 tablespoons water
2 large green peppers, cut into ½-inch strips
1 medium onion, sliced and separated into rings

2 cloves garlic, minced
1 can (11 ounces) Campbell's condensed tomato bisque soup
½ cup water
½ teaspoon dried basil leaves, crushed
Polenta (recipe follows)

1. In 10-inch covered skillet over medium heat, cook sausage in 2 tablespoons water 5 minutes. Uncover; cook until sausage is browned on all sides.

2. Add green peppers, onion and garlic; cook until vegetables are tender, stirring frequently.

3. Stir in soup, ½ cup water and basil. Reduce heat to low. Cover; simmer 10 minutes. Serve with polenta. Makes 4 servings.

POLENTA: In heavy 4-quart saucepan, heat 4 cups water to boiling. With wire whisk, gradually stir in 1 cup cornmeal. Reduce heat to low. Simmer 20 to 25 minutes, stirring often. Pour into buttered 9-inch pie plate. Let stand 10 minutes; cut into wedges.

GLAZED SMOKED SAUSAGE

⅓ cup Open Pit original flavor
   barbecue sauce
¼ cup packed brown sugar

3 tablespoons cider vinegar
1 pound cooked smoked sausage
   (kielbasa)

1. To make glaze: In small bowl, combine barbecue sauce, sugar and vinegar.

2. Score sausage diagonally. On grill rack, place sausage directly above medium coals. Grill, uncovered, 20 minutes or until hot, turning and brushing often with glaze. Makes 4 servings.

To broil: Place sausage on rack in broiler pan. Broil 4 inches from heat 15 minutes or until hot, turning and brushing often with glaze.

EASY FRANKS 'N' BEANS

2 cans (16 ounces *each*) Campbell's
   pork & beans in tomato sauce
4 frankfurters, thickly sliced
3 green onions, sliced

1 tablespoon prepared mustard
¼ teaspoon pepper
½ cup shredded sharp Cheddar
   cheese (2 ounces)

In 10-inch skillet, combine beans, frankfurters, onions, mustard and pepper. Over medium heat, heat to boiling. Reduce heat to low. Simmer 10 minutes, stirring occasionally. Top with cheese; heat until cheese is melted. Makes 4 cups or 4 servings.

To microwave: In 1½-quart microwave-safe casserole, combine beans, frankfurters, onions, mustard and pepper. Cover; microwave on HIGH 7 minutes or until heated through, stirring twice during cooking. Top with cheese; microwave, uncovered, on HIGH 1 minute or until cheese is melted.

Poultry

Blackened Chicken (page 126)

BLACKENED CHICKEN

½ teaspoon salt
½ teaspoon garlic powder
½ teaspoon paprika
¼ teaspoon onion powder
¼ teaspoon black pepper
¼ teaspoon ground cumin
3 whole chicken breasts, split,
    skinned and boned (1½ pounds
    boneless)

2 tablespoons seeded and chopped
    Vlasic hot chili or jalapeno
    peppers
¼ cup butter or margarine
    Plum tomato slices for garnish
    Snipped fresh parsley for garnish

1. In small bowl, combine salt, garlic powder, paprika, onion powder, black pepper and cumin. With meat mallet or rolling pin, pound chicken breasts to ¼-inch thickness. Rub hot chili peppers evenly over one side of each breast half. In 8-inch skillet over low heat, melt butter. Dip chicken into butter. Rub seasoning mixture evenly over both sides of chicken. Reserve remaining butter.

2. On grill rack, place chicken directly above hot coals. Carefully drizzle 1 teaspoon reserved butter over each piece. Grill, uncovered, 3 minutes. Turn chicken. Drizzle with remaining butter. Grill 2 minutes more or until tender and juices run clear. Garnish with tomato and parsley. Makes 6 servings.

SAUTEED CHICKEN CUTLETS

¼ cup all-purpose flour
¼ teaspoon salt
⅛ teaspoon pepper
2 whole chicken breasts, split,
    skinned and boned (1 pound
    boneless)
3 tablespoons butter or margarine

1 package (8 ounces) Campbell's
    Fresh mushrooms, sliced
1 small onion, chopped
¾ cup Swanson clear ready to serve
    chicken broth
½ cup vermouth or other dry white
    wine
    Chopped fresh parsley for garnish

1. In plastic bag, combine flour, salt and pepper. Shake chicken in flour mixture to coat.

2. In 10-inch skillet over medium heat, in hot butter, cook chicken until tender and browned on both sides, about 10 minutes. Remove to platter; keep warm.

3. In same skillet over medium heat, in hot drippings, cook mushrooms and onion until tender and liquid is evaporated, stirring occasionally. Stir in broth and vermouth; heat to boiling. Reduce heat to low. Simmer until sauce is slightly thickened, about 5 minutes, stirring occasionally. Serve over chicken; garnish with parsley. Makes 4 servings.

STUFFED CHICKEN BREASTS TARRAGON

3 tablespoons butter or margarine,
    divided
1 package (8 ounces) Campbell's
    Fresh mushrooms, finely
    chopped
3 green onions, chopped
½ teaspoon dried tarragon leaves,
    crushed

2 tablespoons dry sherry
¼ cup soft bread crumbs
¼ teaspoon salt
2 whole chicken breasts, split (about
    1½ pounds)
Paprika

1. To make stuffing: In 10-inch skillet over medium heat, in 1 tablespoon hot butter, cook mushrooms, onions and tarragon until mushrooms are tender, stirring occasionally. Add sherry; cook until liquid is evaporated, stirring occasionally. Stir in bread crumbs and salt.

2. To make pockets for stuffing: Cut lengthwise slit in thickest part of each breast. Stuff each with ¼ of the stuffing.

3. In 12- by 8-inch baking dish, arrange chicken skin-side up. Melt remaining 2 tablespoons butter; brush chicken with butter. Sprinkle with paprika. Bake at 400°F. for 30 minutes or until chicken is tender and juices run clear.. Makes 4 servings.

SPIRITED CHICKEN AND VEGETABLES

4 slices bacon, chopped
1 cup carrots cut into matchstick-
    thin strips
1 pouch Campbell's dry onion
    mushroom soup and recipe mix
1 cup water

½ cup Chablis or other dry white wine
⅛ teaspoon pepper
2 whole chicken breasts, split,
    skinned and boned (1 pound
    boneless)

1. Place bacon in 3-quart microwave-safe casserole. Cover with plain white paper towel; microwave on HIGH 3 minutes or until crisp, stirring once during cooking. Drain bacon on paper towels, reserving drippings in casserole.

2. Add carrots to drippings. Cover with lid; microwave on HIGH 3 minutes or until carrots are tender. Stir in soup mix, water, wine and pepper until well blended.

3. Add chicken breasts, placing thicker portions toward edge of dish. Cover; microwave on HIGH 10 minutes or until chicken is tender and juices run clear, rearranging chicken once during cooking. Let stand, covered, 5 minutes. Sprinkle with reserved bacon. Makes 4 servings.

CHICKEN 'N' STEAK FAJITAS

½ cup Chablis or other dry white wine
½ cup prepared oil-and-vinegar
  salad dressing
¼ cup soy sauce
1 pound flank steak
1 whole chicken breast, split,
  skinned and boned (½ pound
  boneless)

1 cup Marie's refrigerated avocado
  goddess salad dressing
1 Campbell's Fresh tomato, chopped
½ cup coarsely chopped onion
6 to 8 (8-inch) flour tortillas, heated
  Sliced Vlasic pitted ripe olives
  Shredded Cheddar cheese
  Sour cream (optional)

1. To marinate: In large shallow nonmetal dish, combine wine, oil-and-vinegar salad dressing and soy sauce. Add steak and chicken; turn to coat. Cover; refrigerate at least 4 hours or overnight, turning occasionally.

2. In medium bowl, combine avocado salad dressing, tomato and onion. Cover; refrigerate until serving time.

3. Drain steak and chicken. On grill rack, place steak and chicken directly above medium-hot coals. Grill, uncovered, until steak is desired doneness and chicken is tender and juices run clear (allow 10 minutes for rare steak, 14 minutes for medium steak and 15 minutes for chicken). Turn once during cooking.

4. To serve: Thinly slice steak and chicken into strips. Arrange strips down center of each tortilla. Top with avocado mixture, olives, cheese and sour cream, if desired. Wrap up. Makes 6 to 8 servings.

TEQUILA-ORANGE CHICKEN

½ cup orange juice
¼ cup tequila
2 tablespoons seeded and finely
  chopped Vlasic hot jalapeno
  peppers

½ teaspoon grated orange peel
1 can (10½ ounces) Franco-
  American chicken gravy
3 whole chicken breasts, split (about
  2¼ pounds)

1. To make sauce: In 1-quart saucepan, combine orange juice, tequila, peppers and orange peel. Over high heat, heat to boiling. Reduce heat to low. Simmer 10 minutes or until mixture is reduced by half. Add gravy; heat through, stirring constantly.

2. On grill rack, place chicken, skin-side up, directly above medium coals. Grill, uncovered, 1 hour or until tender and juices run clear, turning and brushing often with sauce during the last 30 minutes. Makes 6 servings.

To broil: Arrange chicken, skin-side up, on rack in broiler pan. Broil 6 inches from heat 40 minutes or until tender and juices run clear, turning and brushing often with sauce during the last 20 minutes.

Chicken 'n' Steak Fajitas

ROLLED CHICKEN BREASTS FLORENTINE

2 whole chicken breasts, split, skinned and boned (1 pound boneless)
4 thin slices (1 ounce *each*) cooked ham
4 thin slices (1 ounce *each*) Swiss cheese
1 package (10 ounces) frozen chopped spinach, thawed and well drained

1 can (10¾ ounces) Campbell's condensed golden mushroom soup
⅓ cup water
¼ cup sliced green onions
⅛ teaspoon dried thyme leaves, crushed

1. With meat mallet or rolling pin, pound chicken to ¼-inch thickness. Place a ham slice, cheese slice and ¼ of the spinach on each chicken piece. Roll up chicken from short end, jelly-roll fashion. Secure with wooden toothpicks, if needed.

2. Place chicken, seam-side down, in 12- by 8-inch microwave-safe dish. Cover with vented plastic wrap; microwave on HIGH 5 minutes.

3. In small bowl, stir soup until smooth; stir in water, onions and thyme. Pour over chicken. Cover; microwave on HIGH 10 minutes or until chicken is tender and juices run clear, rotating dish once during cooking. Let stand, covered, 5 minutes. Makes 4 servings.

Tip: To thaw 1 package (10 ounces) frozen spinach, place frozen spinach in 1½-quart microwave-safe casserole. Cover with lid; microwave on HIGH 5 minutes, stirring once during heating. Drain thoroughly.

CHICKEN AND MUSHROOM KABOBS

¼ cup soy sauce
¼ cup packed brown sugar
2 tablespoons dry sherry
1 tablespoon grated fresh ginger
1 tablespoon vegetable oil

2 whole chicken breasts, split, skinned, boned and cut into 1-inch pieces (1 pound boneless)
1 package (12 ounces) Campbell's Fresh mushrooms
1 green pepper, cut into 1-inch pieces

1. In large bowl, combine soy sauce, sugar, sherry, ginger and oil. Stir in chicken and mushrooms. Cover; marinate in refrigerator 1 hour.

2. On eight 10-inch wooden skewers, alternately thread chicken, mushrooms and green pepper, leaving small spaces between pieces. Arrange skewers across 12- by 8-inch microwave-safe dish. Microwave, uncovered, on HIGH 12 minutes or until chicken is tender and juices run clear, rearranging kabobs and basting with marinade twice during cooking. Makes 4 servings.

Rolled Chicken Breasts Florentine

CASHEW CHICKEN

2 tablespoons cornstarch
1 tablespoon dry sherry
1 tablespoon soy sauce
1 teaspoon grated fresh ginger
1½ whole chicken breasts, split,
    skinned, boned and cut into
    ⅛-inch strips (¾ pounds)
3 tablespoons peanut or vegetable
    oil, divided

3 cups broccoli flowerets
1 cup snow peas, cut in half
1½ cups water
1 pouch Campbell's dry noodle soup
    and recipe mix
1 cup sliced radishes
½ cup toasted cashews

1. In medium bowl, combine cornstarch, sherry, soy sauce and ginger; mix well. Add chicken strips; stir to coat well.

2. In 10-inch skillet over high heat, in 1 tablespoon hot oil, cook broccoli, stirring quickly and frequently (stir-frying) 1 minute. Add snow peas; stir-fry 3 minutes or until vegetables are tender-crisp. Remove vegetables to plate.

3. In same skillet, in remaining 2 tablespoons oil, stir-fry chicken along with its marinade until chicken is no longer pink.

4. Stir in water and soup mix. Heat to boiling, stirring constantly. Reduce heat to low. Cover; simmer 5 minutes or until noodles are tender, stirring occasionally.

5. Return cooked vegetables to skillet; add radishes and cashews. Cook until heated through. Makes 4 servings.

STIR-FRIED CHICKEN AND ZUCCHINI

2 tablespoons olive oil
2 whole chicken breasts, split,
    skinned, boned and cut into
    1-inch pieces (1 pound boneless)
2 cups sliced zucchini
1 sweet red pepper, cut into strips
½ cup tiny white onions cut into
    halves

¼ cup chopped green onions
1 clove garlic, minced
1½ cups V8 vegetable juice
1 tablespoon cornstarch
1 tablespoon soy sauce
1 teaspoon packed brown sugar
½ teaspoon grated fresh ginger
    Hot cooked rice

1. In 10-inch skillet over medium heat, in hot oil, cook chicken pieces, a few at a time, until lightly browned. Remove with slotted spoon; set aside. In same skillet over high heat, cook zucchini, red pepper, white and green onions and garlic, stirring quickly and frequently (stir-frying), until tender-crisp. Add 1 tablespoon oil, if necessary.

2. In small bowl, combine V8 juice, cornstarch, soy sauce, sugar and ginger. Gradually stir into vegetables. Cook until mixture boils and thickens, stirring occasionally. Stir in chicken; heat through. Serve over rice. Makes 3½ cups or 4 servings.

Cashew Chicken

FRENCH-STYLE COUNTRY STEW

2 tablespoons olive oil
1 whole chicken breast, split, skinned, boned and cut into 1-inch pieces (½ pound boneless)
½ pound boneless pork shoulder, cut into 1-inch pieces
1 tablespoon chopped fresh thyme leaves or 1 teaspoon dried thyme leaves, crushed
1 package (12 ounces) Campbell's Fresh mushrooms, sliced
1 large onion, chopped
2 stalks celery, chopped
½ pound kielbasa (Polish sausage), sliced
1½ cups Campbell's tomato juice
1 cup Chablis or other dry white wine
1 bay leaf
2 cans (20 ounces *each*) cannellini (white kidney beans) or great northern beans
½ cup chopped fresh parsley

1. In 4-quart Dutch oven over medium-high heat, in hot oil, cook chicken, pork and thyme, a few pieces at a time, until browned on all sides. Remove meat as it browns.

2. Add mushrooms, onion and celery to hot drippings; cook until vegetables are tender and liquid is evaporated, stirring occasionally.

3. Add browned meat, kielbasa, tomato juice, wine and bay leaf; heat to boiling. Reduce heat to low. Cover; simmer 45 minutes or until meat is fork-tender, stirring occasionally.

4. Stir in beans and parsley; simmer, uncovered, 15 minutes more to blend flavors. Discard bay leaf. Serve in shallow bowls with crusty French bread, if desired. Makes 10 cups or 8 servings.

DOWN-HOME CHICKEN GRILL

6 chicken legs (about 2 pounds)
¾ cup Open Pit original flavor barbecue sauce, divided
2 cans (16 ounces *each*) Campbell's pork & beans in tomato sauce
1 can (8 ounces) whole kernel golden corn, drained

1. On grill rack, place chicken, skin-side down, directly above medium coals. Grill, uncovered, 1 hour or until tender and juices run clear. Turn and brush often with ½ cup of the barbecue sauce during the last 30 minutes.

2. Meanwhile, in 10-inch cast-iron skillet combine beans, corn and remaining ¼ cup barbecue sauce. Place skillet on grill for the last 15 minutes or until mixture is heated through, stirring occasionally. Add chicken to skillet; spoon bean mixture over. Makes 6 servings.

ORANGE-HONEY CHICKEN

1½ cups V8 vegetable juice
2 tablespoons lemon juice
4 teaspoons honey
½ teaspoon grated orange peel
¼ teaspoon garlic powder
⅛ teaspoon pepper
2½- to 3-pound broiler-fryer chicken, cut up

1. To make marinade: In 12- by 8-inch baking dish, combine V8 juice, lemon juice, honey, orange peel, garlic powder and pepper. Add chicken to marinade, turning to coat. Cover; refrigerate at least 2 hours, turning chicken occasionally.

2. Remove chicken from marinade, reserving marinade. Arrange chicken on rack in broiler pan; broil 6 inches from heat 35 minutes or until chicken is tender and juices run clear, basting chicken with marinade and turning occasionally. Makes 6 servings.

ARROZ CON POLLO

1 tablespoon olive or vegetable oil
1 clove garlic, minced
1 can (10½ ounces) Campbell's condensed chicken broth
1 can (8 ounces) tomatoes, undrained, cut up
¾ cup regular long-grain rice, uncooked
⅛ teaspoon ground turmeric
2 pounds chicken thighs, skinned
1 cup frozen peas

1. In 12- by 8-inch microwave-safe dish, combine oil and garlic. Cover with vented plastic wrap; microwave on HIGH 1 minute.

2. Stir in broth and tomatoes. Cover; microwave on HIGH 5 minutes or until bubbling.

3. Stir in rice and turmeric. Arrange chicken thighs over rice, with thicker portions toward edges of dish. Cover; microwave on HIGH 8 minutes.

4. Remove chicken. Stir peas into rice; rearrange chicken over rice. Cover; microwave on HIGH 15 minutes or until chicken is no longer pink, rotating dish once during cooking. Let stand, covered, 10 minutes before serving. Makes 6 servings.

Poultry

BARBECUED CHICKEN

2 cloves garlic, minced	½ cup Open Pit original flavor
¼ teaspoon salt	barbecue sauce
2 broiler-fryer chickens, quartered	Celery leaves for garnish
(2½ to 3 pounds *each*)	

1. In small bowl, combine garlic and salt. With finger, loosen skin from chicken; rub garlic mixture under skin of each piece.

2. On grill rack, place chicken, skin-side down, directly above medium coals. Grill, uncovered, 1 hour or until tender and juices run clear, turning and brushing with barbecue sauce every 10 minutes. Garnish with celery leaves. Makes 8 servings.

To broil: Arrange chicken, skin-side down, on rack in broiler pan. Broil 6 inches from heat 40 minutes or until tender and juices run clear, turning and brushing with barbecue sauce after 30 minutes. Garnish as in step 2.

CHICKEN JAMBALAYA

½ pound bulk pork sausage	1 can (about 15 ounces) tomatoes,
2 pounds chicken parts	undrained, cut up
1 green pepper, chopped	1 cup water
1 cup sliced celery	1 pouch Campbell's dry onion soup
2 cloves garlic, minced	and recipe mix
½ teaspoon dried thyme leaves,	½ teaspoon hot pepper sauce
crushed	¾ cup regular long-grain rice,
	uncooked

1. In 10-inch skillet over medium-high heat, cook sausage until browned, stirring often to separate meat. Remove sausage, reserving drippings in pan.

2. In same skillet over medium-high heat, in hot drippings, cook chicken 10 minutes or until browned on all sides, turning occasionally. Remove chicken from pan.

3. Add green pepper, celery, garlic and thyme to skillet; cook until vegetables are tender, stirring often.

4. Stir in tomatoes, water, soup mix and hot pepper sauce. Heat to boiling. Stir in rice. Return chicken and sausage to skillet.

5. Reduce heat to low. Cover; simmer 35 minutes or until chicken is tender and juices run clear. Makes 6 servings.

CHICKEN PAPRIKA

2 tablespoons vegetable oil
2 pounds chicken parts
1 can (10¾ ounces) Campbell's
    condensed cream of chicken
    soup
1 cup quartered Campbell's Fresh
    mushrooms

1 medium onion, sliced and
    separated into rings
1 clove garlic, minced
2 teaspoons paprika
½ cup sour cream
Hot cooked noodles

1. In 10-inch skillet over medium heat, in hot oil, cook chicken until browned on all sides. Spoon off fat. Stir in soup, mushrooms, onion, garlic and paprika. Heat to boiling. Reduce heat to low. Cover; simmer 30 to 40 minutes or until chicken is tender and juices run clear.

2. Remove chicken to platter; keep warm. Stir sour cream into sauce; over low heat, heat through, stirring constantly. Spoon some of sauce over chicken. Serve chicken with noodles; serve with remaining sauce. Makes 4 servings.

CHICKEN AND BROWN RICE

2 tablespoons vegetable oil
2 pounds chicken thighs and
    drumsticks
½ cup chopped green pepper
1 medium onion, sliced
1 clove garlic, minced
1 cup brown rice, uncooked

1 can (10½ ounces) Campbell's
    condensed chicken broth
1 can (14½ ounces) stewed
    tomatoes
½ cup water
1 teaspoon dried basil leaves,
    crushed

1. In 6-quart Dutch oven over medium heat, in hot oil, cook chicken until browned on all sides. Remove from pan.

2. In hot drippings, cook green pepper, onion and garlic until tender, stirring frequently. Add rice; cook 1 minute, stirring constantly. Stir in broth, tomatoes, water and basil.

3. Arrange chicken over rice. Heat to boiling. Reduce heat to low. Cover; simmer 1 hour or until rice is tender, stirring occasionally. Add more water during cooking if mixture appears dry. Uncover; let stand 5 minutes before serving. Makes 4 servings.

Tip: Use white rice instead of brown rice to reduce cooking time. Prepare as in steps 1 through 3, but substitute 1 cup regular rice for brown rice. In step 3, simmer 30 to 40 minutes or until chicken is tender and juices run clear.

Poultry

BRUNSWICK STEW

5 pounds stewing chicken, cut up	1 can (16 ounces) whole tomatoes,
6 cups water	undrained, cut up
2 bay leaves	1 can (8 ounces) whole kernel
2 teaspoons salt	golden corn, drained
½ teaspoon pepper	1 cup frozen lima beans
4 slices bacon, cut into ½-inch	1 tablespoon Worcestershire sauce
pieces	1 can (20 ounces) Campbell's pork
2 medium onions, sliced and	& beans in tomato sauce
separated into rings	2 tablespoons chopped fresh parsley
2 medium potatoes, peeled and	
cubed	

1. In 6-quart Dutch oven, combine chicken, water, bay leaves, salt and pepper. Heat to boiling. Reduce heat to low. Cover; simmer 2½ hours or until chicken is tender.

2. Skim fat; strain broth. Reserve 4 cups broth (adding water, if necessary, to equal 4 cups). Discard bay leaves. When cool, remove chicken from bones; cut up.

3. In same Dutch oven, cook bacon until crisp. Drain on paper towels, reserving 2 tablespoons drippings in pan. Add onions; cook until tender, stirring often. Stir in potatoes, tomatoes, corn, lima beans, Worcestershire, reserved broth and chicken. Heat to boiling. Reduce heat to low. Simmer 30 minutes.

4. Stir in beans. Simmer 30 minutes more. Stir in bacon. Add parsley. Makes 12 cups or 12 servings.

CHICKEN STROGANOFF

2 tablespoons vegetable oil	1 cup water
2 pounds chicken parts	½ cup sour cream
1 pouch Campbell's dry onion	
mushroom soup and recipe mix	

1. In 10-inch skillet over medium-high heat, in hot oil, cook chicken until browned on all sides, turning occasionally. Spoon off fat.

2. Stir soup mix and water into skillet. Heat to boiling; reduce heat to low. Cover; simmer 30 minutes or until chicken is tender and juices run clear. Remove chicken to platter.

3. Skim fat from cooking liquid. Stir sour cream into skillet. Heat through, but do not boil. Spoon sauce over chicken. Makes 4 servings.

Brunswick Stew

CLASSIC GLORIFIED CHICKEN

2½- to 3-pound broiler-fryer chicken,
  cut up
1 tablespoon butter or margarine,
  melted

1 can (10¾ ounces) Campbell's
  condensed cream of chicken
  soup

1. In 12- by 8-inch baking dish, arrange chicken skin-side up. Drizzle with butter. Bake at 375°F. for 40 minutes.

2. Spoon soup over chicken. Bake 20 minutes more or until chicken is tender and juices run clear. Stir sauce before serving. Makes 4 servings.

Variation: This recipe can be cooked in a skillet instead of the oven. Omit butter and use 2 tablespoons vegetable oil. In 10-inch skillet over medium heat, in 2 tablespoons hot oil, cook chicken about 10 minutes or until browned on all sides. Spoon off fat. Stir in soup. Reduce heat to low. Cover; simmer 35 minutes or until chicken is tender and juices run clear, stirring occasionally. Makes 4 servings.

LEMON-TARRAGON CHICKEN

2 tablespoons vegetable oil
2 pounds chicken parts
1 can (10¾ ounces) Campbell's
  condensed cream of chicken
  soup
2 tablespoons lemon juice

½ teaspoon paprika
¼ teaspoon dried tarragon leaves,
  crushed
⅛ teaspoon pepper
Lemon slices for garnish
Hot cooked rice

1. In 10-inch skillet over medium heat, in hot oil, cook chicken about 10 minutes until browned on all sides. Spoon off fat.

2. Stir in soup, lemon juice, paprika, tarragon and pepper. Heat to boiling; reduce to low. Cover; simmer 30 to 40 minutes or until chicken is tender and juices run clear, stirring occasionally. Garnish with lemon slices. Serve with rice. Makes 4 servings.

To microwave: Omit oil. In 12- by 8-inch microwave-safe dish, arrange chicken with thicker pieces toward edge of dish. Cover; microwave on HIGH 8 to 10 minutes, rotating dish once during cooking. Spoon off fat and rearrange pieces. In small bowl, combine soup, lemon juice, paprika, tarragon and pepper. Spoon evenly over chicken. Cover; microwave on HIGH 8 to 10 minutes or until chicken is tender and juices run clear, rotating dish once during cooking. Let stand, covered, 5 minutes. Remove chicken to serving platter. Stir soup mixture until smooth. Pour over chicken. Garnish with lemon slices; serve with rice.

CRISPY BAKED CHICKEN

1 can (11 ounces) Campbell's
    condensed Cheddar cheese
    soup
½ teaspoon dried oregano leaves,
    crushed

½ cup water
2 cups finely crushed corn flakes
¼ cup sesame seed
⅓ cup all-purpose flour
2 pounds chicken parts

1. In deep pie plate, combine soup, oregano and water until smooth. On waxed paper, combine corn flake crumbs and sesame seed. On second sheet of waxed paper, place flour. Coat chicken with flour, then soup mixture, then crumb mixture. Place on wire rack in jelly-roll pan.

2. Bake at 375°F. for 50 minutes or until chicken is tender and juices run clear. Makes 4 servings.

CHICKEN AND HAM SUPREME

1 package (9 ounces) frozen
    artichoke hearts
1 can (10¾ ounces) Campbell's
    condensed cream of mushroom
    soup
½ cup plain yogurt
½ cup shredded Swiss cheese
    (2 ounces)

1 teaspoon dried basil leaves,
    crushed
⅛ teaspoon ground red pepper
2 cups cooked rice
1½ cups cubed cooked chicken
1 cup cubed cooked ham
Chopped fresh parsley for garnish

1. Place artichoke hearts in small microwave-safe bowl. Cover with vented plastic wrap; microwave on HIGH 4 minutes or until heated through, stirring once during cooking. Drain; set aside.

2. In small bowl, stir soup until smooth; stir in yogurt, cheese, basil and pepper.

3. In 8- by 8-inch microwave-safe dish, combine rice and ½ cup of the soup mixture; spread evenly in dish. Top with chicken, ham and artichoke hearts. Spoon remaining soup mixture over all.

4. Cover with vented plastic wrap; microwave on HIGH 8 minutes or until heated through, rotating dish once during cooking. Let stand, covered, 2 minutes. Garnish with parsley. Makes 4 servings.

Poultry

SUPPER A LA KING

2 tablespoons butter or margarine	¾ cup milk
½ cup diced green pepper	2 cups cubed cooked chicken
⅓ cup chopped onion	¾ cup shredded American cheese
1 can (10¾ ounces) Campbell's	(3 ounces)
condensed cream of chicken	¼ cup diced pimento
soup	⅛ teaspoon pepper

1. In 2-quart microwave-safe casserole, combine butter, green pepper and onion. Cover with lid; microwave on HIGH 2 minutes or until vegetables are tender.

2. Stir in soup and milk; blend well. Stir in chicken, cheese, pimento and pepper. Cover with lid; microwave on HIGH 7 minutes or until heated through, stirring occasionally. Serve over steamed shredded zucchini, cooked noodles, split baked potatoes or biscuits. Makes 3½ cups or 6 servings.

CHICKEN TETRAZZINI

1 can (10½ ounces) Franco-	6 ounces spaghetti, cooked and
American chicken gravy	drained
½ cup light cream	¼ cup chopped roasted red pepper
2 tablespoons dry sherry	or pimento
1 tablespoon lemon juice	½ cup grated Parmesan cheese,
1 package (8 ounces) Campbell's	divided
Fresh mushrooms, sliced	1½ cups cubed cooked chicken

1. In 3-quart microwave-safe casserole, combine gravy, cream, sherry and lemon juice. Cover with lid; microwave on HIGH 2 minutes or until hot.

2. Stir in mushrooms, spaghetti, red pepper, ¼ cup of the Parmesan and the chicken. Cover; microwave on HIGH 7 minutes or until heated through, stirring once during cooking.

3. Top with remaining ¼ cup Parmesan. Microwave, uncovered, on HIGH 2 minutes. Let stand, uncovered, 2 minutes. Makes 4 servings.

Supper a la King

SOUPER ENCHILADAS

½ cup vegetable oil
8 corn tortillas (6-inch)
1 cup chopped onions
1 clove garlic, minced
1 can (11 ounces) Campbell's
    condensed bean with bacon
    soup
2 cups shredded cooked chicken

½ cup water
1 teaspoon ground cumin
1 can (4 ounces) chopped green
    chilies, drained
1 jar (8 ounces) taco sauce
1 cup shredded Cheddar cheese
    (4 ounces)

1. In 8-inch skillet over medium heat, in hot oil, fry tortillas, one at a time, 2 to 3 seconds on each side. Drain tortillas on paper towels.

2. Spoon about 2 tablespoons of the hot oil into 10-inch skillet. Over medium heat, in the 2 tablespoons oil, cook onions and garlic until tender, stirring occasionally. Stir in soup, chicken, water, cumin and chilies. Heat through.

3. Spoon about ⅓ cup of the soup mixture onto each tortilla; roll up. Arrange filled tortillas in 12- by 8-inch baking dish. Pour taco sauce evenly over enchiladas. Sprinkle with cheese. Cover with foil.

4. Bake at 350°F. for 25 minutes. Uncover; bake 5 minutes more. Makes 4 servings.

To microwave: Reduce vegetable oil to 1 tablespoon. In 2-quart microwave-safe casserole, combine 1 tablespoon oil, the onions and garlic. Cover; microwave on HIGH 2 to 3 minutes until vegetables are tender. Stir in soup, chicken, water, cumin and chilies. Cover; microwave on HIGH 4 to 6 minutes or until heated through, stirring once during cooking. Let stand, covered. Meanwhile, wrap tortillas in paper towel and place in microwave oven. Microwave on HIGH 2 minutes or until tortillas are pliable. Assemble as in step 3, placing filled tortillas in 12- by 8-inch microwave-safe dish. Pour taco sauce evenly over enchiladas. Cover; microwave on HIGH 8 to 10 minutes or until hot, rotating dish once during cooking. Sprinkle with cheese. Microwave on HIGH 2 to 3 minutes until cheese is melted.

GRILLED CHICKEN TACO SALAD

2 cups cubed grilled chicken
1 cup mild chunky salsa
4 cups shredded lettuce
1 can (28 ounces) Campbell's
    & beans in tomato sauce or
    2 cans (15½ ounces *each*)
    Campbell's Ranchero beans

1 cup crushed tortilla chips
1 cup shredded Monterey Jack
    cheese (4 ounces)

In small bowl, combine chicken and salsa. In 2-quart glass bowl, layer ½ of the lettuce, beans, chicken mixture, chips and cheese. Repeat layers. Cover; refrigerate until serving time, at least 4 hours. Makes 10 cups or 8 servings.

Souper Enchiladas

MEXICALI CHICKEN CASSEROLE

1 tablespoon butter or margarine
2 cups sliced Campbell's Fresh
  mushrooms
½ cup chopped onion
1 can (11 ounces) Campbell's
  condensed nacho cheese
  soup/dip

2 cups chopped cooked chicken
1 Campbell's Fresh tomato, chopped
½ cup sour cream
1 cup shredded Cheddar cheese,
  divided (4 ounces)
2 cups crushed tortilla chips, divided

1. In 2-quart microwave-safe casserole, combine butter, mushrooms and onion. Cover with lid; microwave on HIGH 4 minutes or until vegetables are tender, stirring once during cooking.

2. Stir in soup until smooth. Stir in chicken, tomato and sour cream. Cover; microwave on HIGH 4 minutes or until heated through, stirring once during cooking.

3. Spread ½ of the soup mixture into 10- by 6-inch microwave-safe baking dish. Sprinkle with ½ of the cheese and ½ of the chips. Spread remaining soup mixture over chips and sprinkle with remaining cheese. Cover with waxed paper; microwave on HIGH 4 minutes or until cheese is melted. Let stand, covered, 2 minutes. Sprinkle with remaining chips. Makes 6 servings.

SWEET AND SOUR CHICKEN

1 teaspoon vegetable oil
2 green onions, cut into 1-inch pieces
¼ cup sweet red pepper cut into
  ½-inch pieces
¼ cup green pepper cut into ½-inch
  pieces
1 can (8 ounces) pineapple chunks
  in juice, undrained

1 tablespoon packed brown sugar
1 tablespoon rice wine vinegar
2 teaspoons cornstarch
1 can (5 ounces) Swanson premium
  chunk white chicken, drained
Hot cooked rice
Soy sauce

1. In 2-quart microwave-safe casserole, combine oil, onions and peppers. Cover with lid; microwave on HIGH 2 minutes or until peppers are nearly tender, stirring once during cooking.

2. Drain pineapple, reserving 3 tablespoons juice. In small bowl, combine reserved pineapple juice, sugar, vinegar and cornstarch. Stir into vegetable mixture. Stir in pineapple chunks. Cover; microwave on HIGH 3 minutes or until boiling, stirring twice during cooking.

3. Stir in chicken. Cover; microwave on HIGH 2 minutes or until heated through. Serve with rice and soy sauce. Makes 2 servings.

CREAMED CHICKEN IN PATTY SHELLS

½ cup chopped onion
1 can (11 ounces) Campbell's
  condensed Cheddar cheese
  soup or nacho cheese soup/dip
1 cup shredded Swiss cheese
  (4 ounces)
½ cup milk

3 tablespoons chopped pimento
1 tablespoon dry sherry
2 cans (5 ounces *each*) Swanson
  premium chunk white chicken,
  drained
4 Pepperidge Farm frozen patty
  shells, baked

1. Place onion in 2-quart microwave-safe casserole. Cover with lid; microwave on HIGH 1½ minutes or until tender.

2. Stir in soup until smooth. Stir in cheese, milk, pimento and sherry. Gently fold in chicken. Cover; microwave on HIGH 5 minutes or until hot and bubbling, stirring once during cooking.

3. Serve over patty shells. Makes about 3 cups or 4 servings.

Tip: This sauce is also delicious served over baked potatoes, toast or biscuits.

CHICKEN POTATO TOPPER

1 cup chopped carrots
½ cup thinly sliced celery
¼ cup chopped onion
1 tablespoon water
1 can (10¾ ounces) Campbell's
  condensed golden mushroom
  soup
⅓ cup milk

⅛ teaspoon pepper
⅛ teaspoon rubbed sage
1 can (5 ounces) Swanson premium
  chunk white chicken, drained
3 hot baked potatoes, split
½ cup shredded Cheddar cheese
  (2 ounces)

1. In 1½-quart microwave-safe casserole, combine carrots, celery, onion and water. Cover; microwave on HIGH 5 minutes or until vegetables are tender, stirring once during cooking.

2. Stir in soup, milk, pepper and sage. Cover; microwave on HIGH 3 minutes or until hot. Gently stir in chicken. Cover; microwave on HIGH 2 minutes or until hot and bubbling. Spoon chicken mixture over potatoes. Top with cheese. Makes 3 servings.

To microwave potatoes: Pierce 3 baking potatoes (8 ounces *each*) with fork in several places; arrange in circular pattern on microwave-safe plate. Microwave, uncovered, on HIGH 8 minutes or until tender, rearranging potatoes once during cooking. Let stand while preparing topper.

GARDEN CHICKEN SALAD

½ cup olive or vegetable oil
¼ cup red wine vinegar
1 tablespoon Dijon-style mustard
1 tablespoon finely chopped onion
1 tablespoon chopped fresh parsley
¼ teaspoon salt
¼ teaspoon pepper
½ pound small new potatoes
¼ pound green beans, trimmed
¼ cup water

2 cans (5 ounces *each*) Swanson premium chunk white chicken, drained
Campbell's Fresh butterhead lettuce leaves
2 hard-cooked eggs, sliced
1 medium Campbell's Fresh tomato, cut into wedges
Vlasic pitted ripe olives for garnish

1. To make dressing: In small bowl or shaker jar, combine oil, vinegar, mustard, onion, parsley, salt and pepper until well blended; set aside.

2. Pierce potatoes with fork in several places. Arrange potatoes in corners of 8- by 8-inch microwave-safe dish; arrange green beans in center. Add water. Cover with vented plastic wrap; microwave on HIGH 6 minutes or until vegetables are nearly tender, rearranging vegetables once during cooking. Let stand, covered, 5 minutes. Drain.

3. Cut potatoes into slices. In medium bowl, toss potatoes and beans with ¼ cup of the dressing. In another small bowl, toss chicken with 2 tablespoons of the dressing. Cover; chill if desired.

4. Arrange lettuce on platter. Mound chicken in center and arrange potatoes, beans, eggs and tomato wedges around chicken. Garnish with olives. Serve with remaining dressing. Makes 4 servings.

ORIENTAL CHICKEN SALAD

2 tablespoons soy sauce
2 tablespoons orange juice
1 tablespoon rice wine vinegar
1 teaspoon sesame oil
1 cup carrots cut into matchstick-thin strips
¼ cup sweet red pepper cut into matchstick-thin strips

1 cup snow peas
3 cups shredded Chinese cabbage or lettuce
1 can (5 ounces) Swanson premium chunk white chicken, drained
2 teaspoons toasted sesame seed

1. In 1½-quart microwave-safe casserole, combine soy sauce, orange juice, vinegar and oil. Add carrots and pepper. Cover with lid; microwave on HIGH 2 minutes or until vegetables are tender. Stir in snow peas. Cover; microwave on HIGH 1 minute or until just heated through.

2. Divide cabbage between 2 salad plates; top with chicken. Spoon hot vegetable mixture over chicken. Sprinkle with sesame seed. Makes 2 servings.

Garden Chicken Salad

DUCK WITH CRANBERRY-WILD RICE STUFFING

1 can (14½ ounces) Swanson clear ready to serve chicken broth
½ cup regular rice, uncooked
¼ cup wild rice, uncooked
2 tablespoons butter or margarine
1 package (12 ounces) Campbell's Fresh mushrooms, coarsely chopped
¼ cup finely chopped green onions
1 cup whole berry cranberry sauce
¼ teaspoon salt
⅛ teaspoon pepper
4- to 5-pound duckling
¼ cup orange marmalade
1 tablespoon lemon juice
Lemon leaves for garnish
Campbell's Fresh mushrooms, fluted, for garnish
Lemon peel twist for garnish

1. To make stuffing: In 1½-quart saucepan, combine broth, rice and wild rice. Over high heat, heat to boiling; reduce heat to low. Cover; simmer 30 minutes or until rice is tender and all liquid is absorbed, stirring occasionally.

2. In 10-inch skillet over medium heat, in hot butter, cook chopped mushrooms and onions until mushrooms are tender and liquid is evaporated, stirring occasionally. Remove from heat. Stir in rice, cranberry sauce, salt and pepper.

3. Remove neck and giblets from inside bird. Remove excess fat. Rinse duck with cold running water; drain well. Spoon stuffing loosely into body cavity. Fold skin over stuffing; secure with skewer. With breast-side up, lift wings toward neck, then fold tips under back of bird to balance. Tie legs. With fork, prick skin in several places.

4. To make glaze: In small saucepan, combine marmalade and lemon juice. Over low heat, heat until marmalade is melted, stirring constantly.

5. In covered grill, arrange preheated coals around drip pan; test for medium heat above pan. Insert a meat thermometer into thickest part of duck between breast and thigh, without touching fat or bone. On grill rack, place duck, breast-side up, over pan but not over coals. Grill, covered, 1¼ to 1½ hours or until well-done or 180°F. Adjust vents and add more charcoal as necessary. Brush often with glaze during the last 30 minutes. Garnish with lemon leaves, fluted mushrooms and lemon peel twist. Makes 4 servings.

To roast: Place stuffed bird, breast-side up, on rack in roasting pan. Roast, uncovered, at 350°F. for 2 hours or until well-done or 180°F. Brush often with glaze during the last 30 minutes. Garnish as in step 5.

Tip: To make a starburst mushroom as pictured opposite, mark the center of the cap with a toothpick. Using a can opener or the flat side of a paring knife tip, cut a small star pattern in the center. Hollow out the star, leaving a circle in the center. Press two concentric circles of inverted V-shaped indentations around the star, working from the center to the edge.

Duck with Cranberry-Wild Rice Stuffing

CORNISH HENS WITH BARLEY STUFFING

3 tablespoons butter or margarine, divided
1 package (8 ounces) Campbell's Fresh mushrooms, sliced
1 clove garlic, minced
1 teaspoon dried basil leaves, crushed

1½ cups cooked barley
¼ cup sliced green onions
⅛ teaspoon pepper
⅓ cup coarsely chopped pecans
4 Cornish hens (about 1½ pounds each)

1. To make stuffing: In 10-inch skillet over medium heat, in 1 tablespoon hot butter, cook mushrooms, garlic and basil until mushrooms are tender and liquid is evaporated, stirring occasionally.

2. Add barley, green onions, pepper and pecans; mix well.

3. Remove giblets and neck from inside hens. Rinse hens with cold running water; drain well. Spoon stuffing lightly into body cavities. Fold skin over stuffing; skewer closed.

4. On rack in roasting pan, place hens breast-side up. Melt remaining 2 tablespoons butter; brush hens with butter. Roast, uncovered, at 350°F. for 1½ hours or until tender and juices run clear. Baste occasionally with pan drippings. Makes 4 servings.

TARRAGON CORNISH HENS

2 tablespoons vegetable oil
2 tablespoons butter or margarine
2 Cornish hens, split lengthwise (about 1½ pounds each)
1 cup sliced Campbell's Fresh mushrooms
4 green onions, sliced

2 cloves garlic, minced
½ teaspoon dried tarragon leaves, crushed
1 can (10½ ounces) Campbell's condensed chicken broth
1 tablespoon cornstarch
2 tablespoons cold water

1. In 10-inch skillet over medium-high heat, in hot oil and butter, cook hens until browned on both sides, 2 halves at a time. Remove to 12- by 8-inch baking dish. Reserve drippings in skillet.

2. Reduce heat to medium. Add mushrooms, onions, garlic and tarragon. Cook 2 minutes, stirring constantly. Add broth; heat to boiling. Pour hot mixture over hens. Cover with foil.

3. Bake at 350°F. for 25 minutes. Uncover; baste hens with pan juices. Bake, uncovered, 10 minutes more or until hens are tender and juices run clear.

4. Remove hens to warm platter and keep warm. Pour pan juices into skillet; over high heat, heat to boiling. In cup, combine cornstarch and water; stir into boiling liquid. Boil 1 minute. Spoon some sauce over hens; serve with remaining sauce. Makes 4 servings.

Cornish Hens with Barley Stuffing

Poultry

GLAZED STUFFED CORNISH HENS

2 Cornish hens (1½ pounds *each*)
¼ cup butter or margarine
½ cup chopped onion
½ cup sweet red pepper cut into matchstick-thin strips
½ cup green pepper cut into matchstick-thin strips

1 package (8 ounces) Pepperidge Farm herb seasoned stuffing mix
1 cup Swanson clear ready to serve chicken broth
½ cup apricot preserves

1. Remove giblets and neck from inside hens. Rinse hens; pat dry. Split hens along backbone and breastbone; set aside.

2. In 3-quart microwave-safe bowl, combine butter, onion and peppers. Cover with vented plastic wrap; microwave on HIGH 3 minutes or until tender, stirring once during cooking. Add stuffing and broth; toss to mix well.

3. Pat stuffing mixture into bottom of 12- by 8-inch microwave-safe dish. Arrange hens, skin-side up, over stuffing; set aside.

4. Place preserves in small microwave-safe bowl. Microwave, uncovered, on HIGH 45 seconds or until melted. Brush preserves over hens. Cover with waxed paper; microwave on HIGH 17 minutes or until hens are tender and juices run clear, rotating dish twice and rearranging hens once during cooking. Let stand, covered, 5 minutes. Makes 4 servings.

CURRANT-GLAZED CORNISH HENS

1 can (10½ ounces) Franco-American chicken gravy
½ cup red currant jelly

1 tablespoon Dijon-style mustard
1 teaspoon grated orange peel
3 Cornish hens (1½ pounds *each*)

1. To make glaze: In 1-quart saucepan, combine gravy, jelly, mustard and orange peel. Over medium heat, heat to boiling, stirring often. Reduce heat to low. Simmer 5 minutes, stirring constantly.

2. Remove neck and giblets from inside hens. Cut each hen in half lengthwise. Rinse halves with cold running water; pat dry. Sprinkle with salt and pepper.

3. On grill rack, place hens, skin-side up, directly above medium coals. Grill, uncovered, 30 to 40 minutes or until tender and juices run clear, turning and brushing often with glaze. Makes 6 servings.

To broil: Arrange hens, skin-side down, on rack in broiler pan. Broil 6 inches from heat 30 minutes or until tender and juices run clear, turning and brushing often with glaze.

Glazed Stuffed Cornish Hens

TURKEY WITH MUSHROOM STUFFING

¼ cup butter or margarine
1 package (8 ounces) Campbell's Fresh mushrooms, coarsely chopped
1 package (8 ounces) Pepperidge Farm herb seasoned stuffing mix

1 cup Swanson clear ready to serve chicken broth
½ cup chopped fresh parsley
1 teaspoon grated lemon peel
⅛ teaspoon pepper
10- to 12-pound ready-to-stuff turkey
Mushroom Gravy (see page 259)

1. To prepare stuffing: In 10-inch skillet over medium heat, in hot butter, cook mushrooms until tender, stirring occasionally.

2. In large bowl, toss together stuffing mix, mushrooms, broth, parsley, lemon peel and pepper.

3. Remove neck and giblets from inside turkey. Rinse turkey with cold running water; drain well. Spoon stuffing mixture lightly into neck and body cavities. Fold skin over stuffing; skewer closed. Tie legs.

4. On rack in roasting pan, place turkey breast-side up. Insert meat thermometer into thickest part of turkey between breast and thigh, not touching bone.

5. Roast, uncovered, at 325°F. for 3½ hours or until internal temperature reaches 180°F. and drumstick moves easily. Baste occasionally with pan drippings. When skin turns golden, cover loosely with foil tent. Serve with Mushroom Gravy. Makes 10 to 12 servings.

Note: When you're short on time, just stir a can of Franco-American mushroom gravy into the pan drippings. It has all the flavor of homemade gravy but is a snap to prepare.

TURKEY DIVAN

1 pound broccoli, cut into flowerets
¼ cup water
1 can (10¾ ounces) Campbell's condensed cream of mushroom soup
¼ cup milk

1 tablespoon dry sherry
Generous dash ground nutmeg
2 cups cubed cooked turkey or chicken
¼ cup shredded Cheddar cheese (1 ounce)

1. In 10- by 6-inch microwave-safe dish, combine broccoli and water. Cover with vented plastic wrap; microwave on HIGH 6 minutes or until broccoli is almost tender, rotating dish once during cooking. Let stand, covered, 3 minutes. Drain.

2. In medium bowl, stir soup until smooth. Stir in milk, sherry and nutmeg; stir in turkey. Pour over broccoli. Sprinkle with cheese. Cover with waxed paper; microwave on HIGH 6 minutes or until heated through, rotating dish once during cooking. Let stand, covered, 5 minutes. Makes 4 servings.

Turkey with Mushroom Stuffing

ORIENTAL TURKEY SKILLET

1 pound turkey breast cutlets
3 tablespoons butter or margarine, divided
½ cup green onions cut into ½-inch pieces
2 cloves garlic, minced
1 can (10½ ounces) Campbell's condensed chicken broth
¼ teaspoon ground ginger
1½ cups sliced broccoli
½ cup sliced water chestnuts
2 tablespoons cornstarch
3 tablespoons water
1 carrot, cut into matchstick-thin strips and cooked until tender-crisp

1. With meat mallet, pound cutlets to ¼-inch thickness, if necessary. In 10-inch skillet over medium heat, in 2 tablespoons hot butter, cook ½ of the cutlets until browned on both sides. Remove from skillet. Add remaining 1 tablespoon butter; repeat with remaining cutlets and remove from skillet.

2. Add green onions and garlic to skillet; cook 2 minutes, stirring constantly. Add broth and ginger; heat to boiling. Add cutlets. Stir in broccoli and water chestnuts. Reduce heat to low. Cover; simmer 5 minutes or until cutlets are nearly tender and broccoli is tender-crisp, stirring occasionally.

3. Remove cutlets and vegetables to platter; keep warm. In cup, combine cornstarch and water. Stir into juices in skillet. Over medium heat, heat to boiling, stirring constantly. Cook 1 minute more. Pour over cutlets and vegetables; top with carrot strips. Makes 4 servings.

HICKORY-SMOKED TURKEY BREAST

Hickory chips
½ teaspoon salt
½ teaspoon rubbed sage
7- pound whole turkey breast
½ cup Open Pit original flavor barbecue sauce

1. At least 1 hour before grilling, soak wood chips in enough water to cover. Drain wood chips.

2. In small bowl, combine salt and sage. With finger, loosen skin from turkey; rub sage mixture on meat under skin.

3. In covered grill, arrange preheated coals around drip pan; test for medium heat above pan. Sprinkle 4 cups of the wood chips over coals. Insert a meat thermometer into thickest part of breast, without touching fat or bone.

4. On grill rack, place turkey, skin-side up, over pan but not over coals. Grill, covered, 1½ to 2 hours or until well-done or 170°F. Adjust vents and add more charcoal and wood chips as necessary. Brush often with barbecue sauce during the last 30 minutes. Let stand 10 minutes before serving. Makes 14 servings.

Oriental Turkey Skillet

TURKEY LASAGNA SWIRLS

1 tablespoon vegetable oil
1 pound ground raw turkey
2 cloves garlic, minced
1 tablespoon dried basil leaves,
   crushed
4 cups V8 vegetable juice
3 tablespoons cornstarch
1 container (15 ounces) ricotta
   cheese

2 cups shredded provolone cheese,
   divided (8 ounces)
1½ cups finely chopped cooked
   broccoli
½ cup grated Parmesan cheese
   (2 ounces)
½ teaspoon ground nutmeg
8 lasagna noodles, cooked and
   drained
Fresh basil leaves for garnish

1. In 10-inch skillet over medium heat, in hot oil, cook turkey, garlic and dried basil until turkey is browned, stirring to separate meat. Spoon off fat.

2. In small bowl, combine V8 juice and cornstarch until smooth; gradually stir into turkey. Cook over medium heat until mixture boils and thickens, stirring often. Boil 1 minute; set aside.

3. In medium bowl, combine ricotta cheese, 1 cup of the provolone cheese, the broccoli, Parmesan and nutmeg. Spoon a generous ⅓ cup of the cheese mixture down the center of each lasagna noodle; roll up. Cut each roll-up in half crosswise.

4. On bottom of 13- by 9-inch baking dish, spread 2 cups of the turkey sauce. Arrange roll-up halves, cut-side down, in sauce. Spoon remaining sauce over roll-ups. Cover.

5. Bake at 350°F. for 30 minutes. Uncover; sprinkle with remaining 1 cup provolone cheese. Bake 10 minutes more or until cheese is melted. Garnish with fresh basil. Makes 8 servings.

TURKEY MEATBALLS

1 pound ground raw turkey
1 egg
¾ cup fine dry bread crumbs
⅓ cup finely chopped onion

1 can (10½ ounces) Franco-
   American turkey gravy, divided
3 tablespoons apple jelly
3 tablespoons ketchup
Hot cooked rice

1. In large bowl, thoroughly blend turkey, egg, bread crumbs, onion and ¼ cup of the gravy. Shape into 1-inch meatballs; set aside.

2. In 3-quart microwave-safe casserole, combine remaining gravy, jelly and ketchup. Cover with waxed paper; microwave on HIGH 5 minutes or until jelly is melted, stirring once during cooking.

3. Add meatballs to gravy mixture. Cover; microwave on HIGH 8 minutes or until meatballs are no longer pink, stirring once during cooking. Let stand, covered, 5 minutes. Serve over rice. Makes 5 servings.

Turkey Lasagna Swirls

TURKEY-TOPPED BISCUITS

1 tablespoon butter or margarine	⅛ teaspoon pepper
½ pound ground raw turkey	½ cup chopped onion
1 tablespoon grated Parmesan cheese	1 medium apple, chopped
½ teaspoon rubbed sage	¾ cup V8 vegetable juice
½ teaspoon fennel seed	¼ cup raisins
¼ teaspoon garlic powder	¼ teaspoon ground cinnamon
⅛ teaspoon salt	4 biscuits, split

1. In 10-inch skillet over medium heat, in hot butter, cook turkey, Parmesan, sage, fennel, garlic powder, salt and pepper until turkey is browned, stirring to separate turkey.

2. Add onion and apple; cook until tender, stirring often. Stir in V8 juice, raisins and cinnamon. Cook 5 minutes or until slightly thickened.

3. To serve: Spoon turkey mixture onto bottom halves of biscuits; cover with biscuit tops. Makes 4 servings.

TURKEY-STUFFED SQUASH

2 medium acorn squash	¾ cup V8 vegetable juice
½ pound ground raw turkey	1 can (4 ounces) chopped green chilies
1 cup fresh or frozen whole kernel corn	⅛ teaspoon pepper
1 cup chopped onions	¾ cup cooked brown or white rice
½ cup shredded carrot	¾ cup shredded Cheddar cheese (3 ounces)
½ teaspoon ground cumin	

1. Cut acorn squash in half; spoon out seeds. In 5-quart Dutch oven in 1-inch boiling water, place squash cut-side down. Reduce heat to low. Cover; simmer 10 minutes or until squash is tender. Drain; remove to platter. Keep warm.

2. Meanwhile, spray 10-inch nonstick skillet with vegetable cooking spray. Over medium heat, cook turkey, corn, onions, carrot and cumin until turkey is browned and vegetables are tender, stirring to separate turkey. Spoon off fat; discard.

3. Stir in V8 juice, chilies and pepper. Heat to boiling. Reduce heat to low. Simmer, uncovered, 5 minutes. Stir in rice; heat through. Spoon mixture into squash halves. Top with cheese. Makes 4 servings.

Turkey-Topped Biscuits

TURKEY TERIYAKI

2 tablespoons vegetable oil, divided
1 cup sliced carrots
1 cup sliced Campbell's Fresh
    mushrooms
½ cup sliced celery
¼ cup finely chopped shallots
¾ pound turkey breast cutlets, cut
    into 2-inch strips

1 cup V8 vegetable juice
2 tablespoons teriyaki sauce
1 teaspoon cornstarch
¼ teaspoon pepper
1 small zucchini, cut into
    matchstick-thin strips
Hot cooked rice

1. In 10-inch skillet over medium heat, in 1 tablespoon hot oil, cook carrots, mushrooms, celery and shallots until mushrooms are tender. Remove from skillet. In same skillet over medium heat, in remaining 1 tablespoon hot oil, cook turkey until lightly browned. Add reserved cooked vegetables to skillet with turkey.

2. In bowl, mix V8 juice, teriyaki sauce, cornstarch and pepper. Stir into skillet along with zucchini. Cook until mixture boils and thickens, stirring often. Reduce heat to low. Cover; simmer 5 minutes or until zucchini is tender. Serve over rice. Makes 4 cups or 4 servings.

TURKEY PAPRIKA

1½ cups V8 vegetable juice
1 tablespoon all-purpose flour
2 tablespoons olive oil, divided
2 medium onions, sliced
1 clove garlic, minced

1 pound turkey breast cutlets, cut
    into 2-inch strips
1 tablespoon paprika
¼ cup sour cream
Hot cooked noodles

1. In small bowl, combine V8 juice and flour. Set aside.

2. In 10-inch skillet over medium-high heat, in 1 tablespoon hot oil, cook onions and garlic until onions are browned and tender. Set aside.

3. In same skillet over medium heat, in remaining 1 tablespoon oil, cook turkey until lightly browned.

4. Add onion mixture, V8 juice mixture and paprika. Cook until mixture boils and thickens, stirring often. Reduce heat to low. Cover; simmer 15 minutes. Remove from heat. Stir in sour cream. Serve over noodles. Makes 3½ cups or 4 servings.

Fish & Shellfish

Fish Rolls with Asparagus (page 166)

FISH ROLLS WITH ASPARAGUS

18 asparagus spears (about 4 inches long)
6 flounder fillets (about 1½ pounds)
2 cups sliced Campbell's Fresh mushrooms
1 cup V8 vegetable juice
1 tablespoon fresh dill or ½ teaspoon dried dill weed, crushed
1 tablespoon cornstarch

1. Place 3 asparagus spears on each fish fillet. Roll fillets up jelly-roll fashion; secure with wooden toothpicks, if necessary. Set aside.

2. Spray 10-inch nonstick skillet with vegetable cooking spray. Over medium heat, cook mushrooms until lightly browned.

3. In small bowl, combine V8 juice, dill and cornstarch until smooth. Gradually stir into skillet. Cook over medium heat until mixture boils and thickens.

4. Place fish rolls in sauce. Reduce heat to low. Cover; simmer 15 minutes or until fish flakes easily when tested with fork. Before serving, remove toothpicks. Makes 6 servings.

LEMONY STUFFED FLOUNDER

5 tablespoons butter or margarine, divided
½ cup water
2 cups Pepperidge Farm herb seasoned stuffing mix
½ teaspoon grated lemon peel
½ cup chopped onion
½ cup shredded carrot
4 flounder fillets (about 1 pound)
Paprika
Lemon slices for garnish

1. In 4-cup glass measure, combine 4 tablespoons of the butter and the water. Microwave, uncovered, on HIGH 1½ minutes or until butter is melted. Stir in stuffing mix and lemon peel; set aside.

2. In 10-inch microwave-safe pie plate, combine remaining 1 tablespoon butter, the onion and carrot. Cover with waxed paper; microwave on HIGH 3 minutes or until vegetables are tender, stirring once during cooking. Stir into stuffing mixture.

3. Make 4 mounds of stuffing in same pie plate. Divide fish into 4 parts and arrange over stuffing. Sprinkle with paprika. Cover with waxed paper; microwave on HIGH 8 minutes or until fish is nearly done, rotating dish once during cooking. Let stand, covered, 5 minutes or until fish flakes easily when tested with fork. Garnish with lemon slices. Makes 4 servings.

STUFFED FISH ROLL-UPS

2 tablespoons butter or margarine
1 package (8 ounces) Campbell's
   Fresh mushrooms, chopped
4 green onions, sliced
2 tablespoons Chablis or other dry
   white wine

4 flounder or sole fillets
   (about 1 pound)
2 tablespoons lemon juice
Paprika
Fresh parsley for garnish
Lemon slices for garnish

1. To make stuffing: In 10-inch skillet over medium heat, in hot butter, cook mushrooms and green onions until mushrooms are tender and liquid is evaporated, stirring occasionally. Add wine. Heat to boiling; simmer 1 minute.

2. Sprinkle fillets with lemon juice. Spoon about ¼ cup of the stuffing onto each fillet. Roll fillets up jelly-roll fashion; secure with wooden toothpicks. In 10- by 6-inch baking dish, arrange roll-ups seam-side down; sprinkle with paprika.

3. Bake at 350°F. for 20 minutes or until fish flakes easily when tested with fork. Garnish with parsley and lemon slices. Makes 4 servings.

MICROWAVED FISH PROVENCALE

1 tablespoon olive oil
2 tablespoons chopped onion
1 clove garlic, minced
1 pound firm white fish fillets
1 cup sliced Campbell's Fresh
   mushrooms
1 cup seeded and coarsely chopped
   Campbell's Fresh tomatoes

1 tablespoon Chablis or other dry
   white wine
1 tablespoon cornstarch
¼ teaspoon dried thyme leaves,
   crushed
¼ teaspoon salt
Generous dash pepper
Lemon wedges for garnish

1. In 12- by 8-inch microwave-safe dish, combine oil, onion and garlic. Microwave, uncovered, on HIGH 2 minutes or until onion is tender. Arrange fish over onion mixture with thicker parts toward edges of dish; top with mushrooms and tomatoes.

2. In cup, combine wine, cornstarch, thyme, salt and pepper; mix well. Pour over fish. Cover with waxed paper; microwave on HIGH 8 minutes or until fish flakes easily when tested with fork, rotating dish once during cooking.

3. Transfer fish to serving platter. Stir sauce; pour over fish. Garnish with lemon wedges. Makes 4 servings.

VEGETABLE-STUFFED FISH ROLLS

½ cup chopped Campbell's Fresh
    tomato
½ cup chopped Campbell's Fresh
    mushrooms
¼ cup chopped green onions
1 can (11 ounces) Campbell's
    condensed Cheddar cheese
    soup, divided

6 flounder fillets (about 1½ pounds)
¼ cup dry sherry, milk or water
1 cup shredded Swiss cheese
    (4 ounces)

1. In medium bowl, combine tomato, mushrooms, green onions and ¼ cup of the soup. Place about 3 tablespoons of the mixture on each fish fillet and roll up jelly-roll fashion. Secure with wooden toothpicks, if necessary. Place fish rolls seam-side down in 10- by 6-inch baking dish. Bake at 350°F. for 25 minutes or until fish flakes easily when tested with fork. Discard any liquid in baking dish.

2. Meanwhile, in 2-quart saucepan, combine remaining soup and sherry. Over medium heat, heat through. Pour sauce over fish rolls; sprinkle with cheese.

3. Bake 2 minutes more or until cheese is melted. Makes 6 servings.

FISH FLORENTINE

1 package (10 ounces) frozen
    chopped spinach, thawed and
    well drained
4 haddock steaks, cut ¾ inch thick
    (1½ pounds)
1 small onion, thinly sliced and
    separated into rings
1 can (11 ounces) Campbell's
    condensed Cheddar cheese
    soup

1 tablespoon lemon juice
¼ teaspoon dried oregano leaves,
    crushed
⅛ teaspoon pepper
1 medium Campbell's Fresh tomato,
    sliced

1. In 9- by 9-inch baking dish, arrange spinach. Top with haddock steaks and onion.

2. In small bowl, combine soup, lemon juice, oregano and pepper. Spoon over onion.

3. Bake at 350°F. for 25 to 30 minutes or until fish flakes easily when tested with fork. Top with tomato slices. Bake 5 minutes more. Makes 4 servings.

Vegetable-Stuffed Fish Rolls

SALMON STEAKS IN DILL SAUCE

1 tablespoon butter or margarine
½ cup chopped green onions
1 can (10¾ ounces) Campbell's
    condensed cream of celery soup
½ cup half-and-half
¼ cup Chablis or other dry white wine

2 tablespoons chopped fresh dill or
    1 teaspoon dried dill weed,
    crushed
4 salmon steaks, cut ¾ inch thick
    (about 1½ pounds)
Fresh dill sprig for garnish

1. In 12- by 8-inch microwave-safe dish, combine butter and onions. Cover with vented plastic wrap; microwave on HIGH 2 minutes or until onions are tender, stirring once during cooking.

2. Stir in soup until smooth. Stir in half-and-half, wine and dill; blend well.

3. Arrange salmon steaks in sauce with thicker portions toward edges of dish. Cover; microwave on HIGH 9 minutes or until fish is nearly done, rotating dish twice during cooking. Let stand, covered, 5 minutes or until fish flakes easily when tested with fork. Garnish with dill sprig. Makes 4 servings.

FISH STEAKS IN FOIL

Herbed Butter (recipe follows)
4 fish steaks, cut ¾ inch thick
    (about 1½ pounds)
4 teaspoons lemon juice

1 cup sliced Campbell's Fresh
    mushrooms
½ cup thinly sliced leeks
Lemon wedges

1. Prepare Herbed Butter; set aside.

2. On 12-inch piece heavy-duty or double-thickness foil, place 1 fish steak. Sprinkle with 1 teaspoon lemon juice; season with salt and pepper to taste. Top with ¼ of the mushrooms, leeks and Herbed Butter. Bring edges of foil together; seal tightly. Repeat, making 3 more bundles.

3. Place bundles on grill 6 inches above glowing coals. Grill 5 minutes. Open bundles; continue grilling 5 minutes more or until fish flakes easily when tested with fork. Serve with lemon wedges. Makes 4 servings.

HERBED BUTTER: In small bowl, combine ⅓ cup softened butter, 2 tablespoons fresh or frozen chopped chives, 1 tablespoon chopped fresh tarragon leaves or dill weed and ½ teaspoon dry mustard; mix well. Place on waxed paper and form into 4-inch log. Freeze until firm. To use: Cut into 1-inch pieces.

Salmon Steaks in Dill Sauce

SALMON AND SPINACH PIE

1 can (about 15½ ounces) salmon,
  drained and flaked
⅓ cup fine dry bread crumbs
1 tablespoon lemon juice
⅛ teaspoon pepper
1 can (10¾ ounces) Campbell's
  condensed cream of celery
  soup, divided

3 eggs, divided
1 package (10 ounces) frozen
  chopped spinach, thawed and
  well drained
¼ teaspoon ground nutmeg

1. In medium bowl, thoroughly mix salmon, bread crumbs, lemon juice, pepper, ⅓ cup of the soup and 1 of the eggs. Spread evenly in 9-inch microwave-safe pie plate. Cover with waxed paper; microwave on HIGH 3 minutes or until hot, rotating dish once during cooking.

2. Meanwhile, in same bowl, stir remaining soup until smooth; stir in remaining 2 eggs, the spinach and nutmeg. Spread evenly over salmon mixture.

3. Microwave, uncovered, on MEDIUM (50% power) 20 minutes or until center is set, rotating dish twice during cooking. Let stand, uncovered, 5 minutes. Makes 6 servings.

CHEESY SALMON RICE BAKE

1 can (10¾ ounces) Campbell's
  condensed cream of mushroom
  soup
⅓ cup milk
1 tablespoon chopped fresh parsley
2 cups cooked rice

1 can (about 15½ ounces) salmon,
  drained and flaked
1 cup cooked peas
1 cup shredded sharp Cheddar
  cheese (4 ounces)

1. In large bowl, combine soup, milk and parsley; stir to blend. Stir in rice, salmon and peas. Pour mixture into 10- by 6-inch baking dish.

2. Sprinkle with cheese. Bake at 350°F. for 30 minutes or until heated through. Makes about 7 cups or 6 servings.

To microwave: Prepare as in step 1, but pour rice mixture into 10- by 6-inch microwave-safe dish. Cover; microwave on HIGH 7 to 10 minutes until heated through, stirring once during cooking. Sprinkle with cheese. Microwave on HIGH 2 minutes more or until cheese is melted.

CREAMED LOX IN PATTY SHELLS

2 tablespoons butter or margarine
1 package (8 ounces) Campbell's
    Fresh mushrooms, sliced
2 tablespoons finely chopped
    shallots or onion
2 tablespoons all-purpose flour
1 cup milk
4 ounces thinly sliced lox (smoked
    salmon) or smoked turkey, cut
    into strips

2 tablespoons Chablis or other dry
    white wine
⅛ teaspoon pepper
4 Pepperidge Farm patty shells,
    baked
    Fresh dill sprig or parsley for
    garnish

1. In 3-quart saucepan over medium heat, in hot butter, cook mushrooms and shallots until tender and liquid is evaporated, stirring occasionally. Stir in flour until blended; cook 1 minute, stirring constantly. Gradually stir in milk; cook until mixture boils and thickens, stirring often.

2. Add lox, wine and pepper; heat through. To serve: Spoon ¾ cup lox mixture over each patty shell. Garnish with dill or parsley. Makes 2 cups or 3 servings.

SALMON AND NOODLE SKILLET

1 can (about 15½ ounces) salmon,
    drained and flaked
1 can (10¾ ounces) Campbell's
    condensed cream of celery
    soup, divided
1 cup soft bread crumbs
2 tablespoons finely chopped onion
2 tablespoons chopped fresh parsley
1 tablespoon lemon juice

1 egg, beaten
2 cups fresh or frozen cut asparagus
2 tablespoons butter or margarine
½ cup sour cream
½ cup milk
3 cups medium noodles, cooked and
    drained (4 ounces)
½ teaspoon dried dill weed, crushed

1. In medium bowl, combine salmon, ¼ cup of the soup, the bread crumbs, onion, parsley, lemon juice and egg; mix well. Shape into 4 patties, each about 1 inch thick.

2. In 10-inch skillet over medium heat, in ½ inch boiling water, cook asparagus until tender-crisp; drain in colander.

3. In same skillet over medium heat, in hot butter, cook salmon patties until browned on both sides. Remove from skillet.

4. In same skillet, combine remaining soup, the sour cream and milk, stirring until smooth. Stir in noodles, dill weed and cooked asparagus. Arrange salmon patties over noodle mixture. Cover; cook over low heat 10 minutes or until heated through. Makes 4 servings.

Fish & Shellfish

BAKED STUFFED FISH

6 whole salmon or brook trout
   (about 8 ounces *each*), pan
   dressed
2 tablespoons butter or margarine
1 package (8 ounces) Campbell's
   Fresh mushrooms, sliced
1½ cups flaked crabmeat (about
   6 ounces)
½ cup soft small bread cubes

1 tablespoon chopped fresh or
   frozen chives
1 tablespoon chopped fresh dill
   or 1 teaspoon dried dill
   weed, crushed
1 teaspoon grated lemon peel
⅛ teaspoon pepper
1 tablespoon lemon juice
1 tablespoon olive or vegetable oil
¼ cup Chablis or other dry white wine

1. Oil 15- by 10-inch jelly-roll pan. Arrange fish in pan.

2. To make stuffing: In 10-inch skillet over medium heat, in hot butter, cook mushrooms until tender and liquid is evaporated, stirring occasionally. Remove from heat. Add crabmeat, bread cubes, chives, dill, lemon peel and pepper.

3. For each fish: Season cavity with lemon juice; spoon some stuffing lightly into cavity. Skewer cavity closed; brush fish with oil. Pour wine into pan.

4. Bake at 375°F. for 10 minutes (about 10 minutes for each inch, measuring fish at thickest point) or until fish flakes easily when tested with fork. Makes 6 servings.

WINE-SAUCED FISH FILLETS

¼ cup butter or margarine
1 cup soft bread crumbs
1 cup sliced Campbell's Fresh
   mushrooms
1 green pepper, chopped
½ teaspoon paprika
1 pound firm fish fillets, cut into
   1-inch pieces

2 cups cooked rice
1 can (10¾ ounces) Campbell's
   condensed cream of mushroom
   soup
½ cup milk
¼ cup Chablis or other dry white wine
1 tablespoon chopped pimento
   (optional)

1. Preheat oven to 400°F.

2. In 10-inch skillet over medium heat, melt butter. In small bowl, toss 1 tablespoon of the melted butter with bread crumbs; set aside.

3. In remaining butter, cook mushrooms, green pepper and paprika until mushrooms are tender, stirring often. Add fish; cook 2 minutes more, stirring often. Remove from heat. Divide rice among four 12-ounce casseroles. Divide fish mixture into casseroles.

4. In same skillet, combine soup, milk and wine until smooth. Over medium heat, heat to boiling, stirring constantly. Stir in pimento; pour over fish mixture. Sprinkle with buttered bread crumbs. Bake 20 minutes or until lightly browned. Makes 4 servings.

Baked Stuffed Fish

ORIENTAL PASTA TOSS

⅓ cup vegetable or peanut oil
2 cloves garlic, minced
2 teaspoons grated fresh ginger
½ teaspoon crushed red pepper
1 package (3.5 ounces) Campbell's
  Fresh shiitake mushrooms
1 cup snow peas cut into thin strips
1 package (8 ounces) very thin
  spaghetti

1 pound medium shrimp, cooked,
  shelled and deveined
1½ cups carrots cut into matchstick-
  thin strips
¼ cup diagonally sliced green onions
2 tablespoons soy sauce
2 tablespoons rice wine vinegar

1. In small saucepan over medium heat, combine oil, garlic, ginger and red pepper. Heat 2 minutes; remove from heat. Let stand at least 30 minutes to blend flavors.

2. Trim woody portions of mushroom stems and discard. Remove and chop stems; slice mushroom caps. In 10-inch skillet over medium heat, heat 2 tablespoons of the oil mixture. Add mushrooms; cook until tender, stirring occasionally. Add snow peas; cook 1 minute or until tender-crisp, stirring constantly.

3. Meanwhile, cook spaghetti according to package directions; drain well. In large bowl, combine hot spaghetti, mushroom mixture, shrimp, carrots and onions.

4. In cup, combine remaining oil mixture, the soy sauce and vinegar. Pour over spaghetti mixture; toss to coat well. Serve immediately. Makes 8 cups or 8 servings.

Tip: Can also be served as a chilled main-dish salad. Refrigerate at least 2 hours before serving.

SPAGHETTI WITH CLAMS

½ cup butter or margarine
½ cup vegetable or olive oil
4 cloves garlic, minced
1 can (10½ ounces) Campbell's
  condensed chicken broth
¼ cup chopped parsley

1 can (6½ ounces) chopped clams,
  undrained
12 ounces spaghetti, cooked and
  drained
Grated Parmesan cheese

1. In 3-quart saucepan over medium heat, in hot butter and oil, cook garlic until golden, stirring occasionally. Stir in broth and parsley. Heat to boiling; reduce heat to low. Simmer 10 minutes.

2. Add clams. Simmer 2 minutes more, stirring occasionally. Pour sauce over hot spaghetti, tossing to coat. Serve with Parmesan. Makes 6 servings.

Oriental Pasta Toss

LINGUINE WITH SHRIMP SAUCE

¼ cup vegetable oil
2 cups sliced Campbell's Fresh mushrooms
¾ cup chopped onion
2 cloves garlic, minced
½ pound medium shrimp, shelled and deveined
½ pound bay scallops

1 can (11 ounces) Campbell's condensed Cheddar cheese soup
1 cup half-and-half
¼ cup chopped fresh parsley
8 ounces linguine, cooked and drained
Grated Parmesan cheese

1. In 10-inch skillet over medium heat, in hot oil, cook mushrooms, onion and garlic until tender, stirring occasionally. Add shrimp and scallops; cook 2 minutes more or until shrimp are pink and scallops are opaque, stirring constantly.

2. In medium bowl, combine soup and half-and-half; mix well. Stir into skillet; add parsley. Heat through but do not boil. Serve sauce over linguine. Serve with Parmesan. Makes 4 servings.

LINGUINE WITH CLAM SAUCE

1 can (10¾ ounces) Campbell's condensed cream of mushroom or cream of celery soup
1 can (6½ ounces) minced clams, undrained
¼ cup milk
¼ cup Chablis or other dry white wine

2 tablespoons chopped fresh parsley
2 tablespoons grated Parmesan cheese
1 clove garlic, minced
8 ounces linguine, cooked and drained

1. In 1½-quart microwave-safe casserole, stir soup until smooth; stir in clams, milk, wine, parsley, Parmesan and garlic. Cover with lid; microwave on HIGH 8 minutes or until hot and bubbling, stirring once during cooking.

2. Toss with linguine; serve with additional Parmesan. Makes 4 servings.

Linguine with Shrimp Sauce

SHRIMP AND SCALLOP RAMEKINS

½ cup water
½ cup Chablis or other dry white wine
2 tablespoons chopped green onion
⅛ teaspoon dried thyme leaves,
  crushed
Generous dash pepper
½ pound sea scallops, cut in half or
  ½ pound bay scallops
½ pound medium shrimp, shelled
  and deveined

¼ cup butter or margarine, divided
1 package (8 ounces) Campbell's
  Fresh mushrooms, sliced
2 tablespoons all-purpose flour
1 cup half-and-half
1 tablespoon chopped fresh parsley
⅓ cup soft bread cubes
2 tablespoons grated Parmesan
  cheese

1. In 2-quart saucepan, combine water, wine, onion, thyme and pepper. Over high heat, heat to boiling. Add scallops and shrimp; reduce heat to low. Simmer 5 minutes or until shrimp are pink and scallops are opaque. With slotted spoon, remove scallops and shrimp to bowl; set aside.

2. Over high heat, boil remaining liquid in saucepan until reduced to about ⅔ cup.

3. Meanwhile, in 10-inch skillet over medium heat, in 2 tablespoons hot butter, cook mushrooms until tender and liquid is evaporated, stirring occasionally. Stir in flour until blended; cook 1 minute, stirring constantly.

4. Gradually stir in reduced liquid and the half-and-half. Cook until mixture boils and thickens, stirring often. Stir in scallops, shrimp and parsley. Spoon mixture into 4 broiler-safe scallop shells or ramekins.

5. In same skillet, melt remaining butter. Stir in bread cubes and cheese; sprinkle over mixture.

6. Broil 4 inches from heat until bread cubes are golden brown. Makes 3½ cups or 4 servings.

Shrimp and Scallop Ramekins

GREEK-STYLE SHRIMP

2 tablespoons olive oil
1 cup sliced green onions
4 cloves garlic, minced
1 pound large shrimp, shelled and deveined
¾ cup V8 vegetable juice or no salt added V8 vegetable juice
⅓ cup crumbled feta cheese (about 2 ounces)
2 tablespoons chopped fresh parsley
Dash pepper
8 slices French bread

1. In 10-inch skillet over medium heat, in hot oil, cook onions and garlic until onions are tender.

2. Add shrimp; cook until shrimp are pink and opaque, stirring constantly.

3. Stir in V8 juice. Heat to boiling. Reduce heat to low. Simmer 2 minutes.

4. Sprinkle with cheese, parsley and pepper. Serve with bread. Makes 4 servings.

Note: If desired, use oven-safe skillet. After sprinkling with cheese, broil 3 minutes or until cheese is lightly browned.

CAJUN-STYLE SHRIMP

2 slices bacon
2 tablespoons all-purpose flour
1 medium onion, chopped
½ cup chopped celery
½ cup chopped green pepper
1 clove garlic, minced
½ teaspoon dried thyme leaves, crushed
1½ cups V8 vegetable juice
1 tablespoon Louisiana-style hot sauce
1 pound large shrimp, shelled and deveined
4 cups hot cooked rice

1. In 10-inch skillet over medium heat, cook bacon until crisp. Drain bacon on paper towels, reserving 2 tablespoons drippings in pan. Crumble bacon; set aside.

2. In hot drippings, cook flour 1 minute, stirring constantly. Add onion, celery, green pepper, garlic and thyme. Cook until vegetables are tender, stirring occasionally.

3. Stir in V8 juice, hot sauce and shrimp. Cook until shrimp are pink and opaque. Serve over rice. Makes 4 cups sauce or 4 servings.

Greek-Style Shrimp

CASHEW-SHRIMP SALAD

¾ cup V8 vegetable juice
1 tablespoon soy sauce
1 teaspoon vegetable oil
½ teaspoon grated lemon peel
½ teaspoon grated fresh ginger
¾ pound medium shrimp, cooked,
  shelled and deveined
1½ cups cucumber slices cut in half

1 large carrot, cut into matchstick-
  thin strips (about 1¼ cups)
3 green onions, sliced (about ½ cup)
¼ cup coarsely chopped dry roasted
  unsalted cashews (1 ounce)
Campbell's Fresh butterhead
  lettuce leaves

1. In medium bowl, combine V8 juice, soy sauce, oil, lemon peel and ginger. Add shrimp, cucumbers, carrot and onions; toss to coat well. Cover; refrigerate until serving time, at least 2 hours.

2. Before serving, add cashews; toss to coat well. To serve: On 4 lettuce-lined salad plates, arrange shrimp mixture. Makes 4 cups or 3 servings.

LEMON GARLIC SHRIMP

2 tablespoons cornstarch
1 can (14½ ounces) Swanson clear
  ready to serve chicken broth
2 tablespoons olive oil
4 cloves garlic, minced
¼ teaspoon grated lemon peel
⅛ teaspoon ground red pepper

1½ pounds medium shrimp, shelled
  and deveined
¼ cup chopped fresh parsley
2 tablespoons lemon juice
6 cups hot cooked spaghetti
  (12 ounces uncooked)
Freshly ground pepper

1. In 2-cup glass measure, combine cornstarch and broth until smooth; set aside.

2. In 10-inch skillet over medium heat, in hot oil, cook garlic, lemon peel and red pepper 1 minute, stirring constantly. Add shrimp, parsley and lemon juice. Cook until shrimp are pink and opaque, stirring often.

3. Gradually stir in broth mixture. Over medium heat, cook until mixture boils and thickens, stirring constantly. Toss with spaghetti. Serve with freshly ground pepper. Makes 8 cups or 6 servings.

To microwave: Reduce garlic to 3 cloves. In 2-cup glass measure, combine cornstarch and broth until smooth. Microwave, uncovered, on HIGH 4 minutes or until mixture boils and thickens, stirring after each minute. Cover; set aside.

In 2-quart microwave-safe casserole, combine oil, 3 cloves garlic, lemon peel and red pepper. Cover with lid; microwave on HIGH 1 minute. Stir in shrimp, parsley and lemon juice. Cover; microwave on HIGH 3 minutes or until most shrimp are pink and opaque, stirring once during cooking. Stir in broth mixture. Cover; microwave on HIGH 2 minutes more or until mixture boils, stirring after each minute. Toss with spaghetti. Serve with freshly ground pepper.

Cashew-Shrimp Salad

SWEET 'N' SOUR SKEWERED SHRIMP

⅓ cup Open Pit original flavor
   barbecue sauce
3 tablespoons pineapple preserves
3 tablespoons lime juice
1 tablespoon soy sauce
¼ teaspoon grated fresh ginger

1 pound large shrimp,
   shelled and deveined
1 medium papaya, peeled and cut
   into 1-inch pieces
1 large green pepper, cut into 1-inch
   pieces

1. To make sauce: In 1-quart saucepan, combine barbecue sauce, preserves, lime juice, soy sauce and ginger. Over medium heat, heat to boiling, stirring often.

2. On 6 long or 12 short metal skewers, alternately thread shrimp, papaya and pepper pieces. On grill rack, place kabobs directly above hot coals. Grill, uncovered, 6 minutes or until shrimp are pink and opaque, turning and brushing often with sauce. Makes 6 servings.

To broil: Arrange kabobs on rack in broiler pan. Broil 4 inches from heat 6 minutes or until shrimp are pink and opaque, turning and brushing often with sauce.

BROILED SHRIMP DIJON

1 can (10¾ ounces) Campbell's
   condensed tomato soup
1 clove garlic, minced
2 tablespoons vegetable oil
1 tablespoon brown sugar

1 tablespoon Dijon-style mustard
1 teaspoon lemon juice
½ teaspoon hot pepper sauce
1 pound extra-large shrimp

1. To make marinade: In 2-quart saucepan, combine soup, garlic, oil, sugar, mustard, lemon juice and hot pepper sauce. Over medium heat, cook until mixture boils and sugar is dissolved, stirring occasionally. Remove from heat.

2. Shell and devein shrimp, leaving tails intact. Place in large bowl; add soup mixture. Cover; refrigerate 2 hours.

3. Remove shrimp from bowl, reserving marinade. Arrange shrimp on rack in broiler pan. Broil 4 inches from heat for 8 minutes or until shrimp are pink and opaque, turning once and brushing often with marinade.

4. Meanwhile, in 1-quart saucepan over medium heat, heat reserved marinade to boiling, stirring often. Serve with shrimp. Makes about 4 main-dish servings or 24 appetizers.

Note: To reheat the marinade in the microwave, pour the reserved marinade into 1-cup glass measure. Microwave, uncovered, on HIGH 1 minute or until hot, stirring once during heating.

Sweet 'n' Sour Skewered Shrimp

SHIITAKE AND SHRIMP KABOBS

1 package (3.5 ounces) Campbell's
  Fresh shiitake mushrooms
½ cup olive oil
2 cloves garlic, minced
2 tablespoons lemon juice
2 tablespoons chopped fresh parsley

Dash pepper
16 large shrimp, shelled and
  deveined (about 12 ounces)
1 medium sweet red pepper, cut into
  ¾-inch squares

1. Trim woody portions of mushroom stems and discard. Cut any large mushrooms into quarters.

2. In medium bowl, combine oil, garlic, lemon juice, parsley and pepper. Add mushrooms, shrimp and red pepper; toss to coat well.

3. On four 12-inch skewers, alternately thread mushrooms, shrimp and red pepper.

4. Place skewers on grill 6 inches above glowing coals. Grill 8 minutes or until shrimp are pink and opaque and mushrooms are tender, turning often and brushing with remaining marinade. Makes 4 servings.

To broil: Prepare kabobs as in steps 1 through 3. On rack in broiler pan, arrange kabobs. Broil 6 inches from heat 8 minutes or until shrimp are pink and opaque and mushrooms are tender, turning often and brushing with remaining marinade.

SKEWERED SCALLOPS AND VEGETABLES

1½ cups V8 vegetable juice, divided
2 tablespoons vegetable oil
2 tablespoons lime juice
1 tablespoon teriyaki sauce
½ teaspoon ground ginger
⅛ teaspoon pepper

1 pound sea scallops or swordfish,
  cut into 1½-inch pieces
2 medium zucchini, cut into ½-inch
  slices (about 2 cups)
2 large sweet red peppers, cut into
  1-inch squares
1 tablespoon cornstarch

1. In 12- by 8-inch baking dish, mix ¾ cup of the V8 juice, the oil, lime juice, teriyaki sauce, ginger and pepper. Place scallops and vegetables in marinade. Cover; refrigerate 1 hour, stirring occasionally.

2. Remove scallops and vegetables; reserve marinade. On 6 metal skewers, thread scallops and vegetables. Place on rack in broiler pan.

3. In 1-quart saucepan, mix reserved marinade, remaining ¾ cup V8 juice and the cornstarch until smooth. Over medium heat, heat until mixture boils and thickens, stirring constantly. Broil kabobs 4 inches from heat 10 minutes or until scallops are opaque, basting with V8 sauce and turning frequently. Serve with sauce. Makes 6 servings.

Shiitake and Shrimp Kabobs

LEMON-DILL LOBSTER TAILS

¾ cup Marie's refrigerated sour
   cream and dill salad dressing
1 teaspoon grated lemon peel

1 clove garlic, minced
⅛ teaspoon pepper
4 lobster tails (6 ounces *each*)

1. To make sauce: In small bowl, combine salad dressing, lemon peel, garlic and pepper.

2. With kitchen shears, cut membrane from underside of lobster tails; discard. With sharp knife, loosen meat from shell, leaving meat and shell intact. To prevent tail from curling, bend backwards, breaking at joints.

3. Brush grill rack with oil. On grill rack, place lobster tails, shell-side down, directly above medium coals. Grill, uncovered, 18 minutes or until opaque, turning twice and brushing tops with sauce.

4. To serve: With fork, loosen meat from shell, starting at end and pulling forward. Serve with any remaining sauce. Makes 4 servings.

BOUNTIFUL BOUILLABAISSE

1 can (6½ ounces) chopped clams,
   undrained
1 tablespoon olive oil
4 cloves garlic, minced
1 can (14½ ounces) Swanson clear
   ready to serve chicken broth
1 can (about 16 ounces) tomatoes,
   undrained, cut up
⅓ cup chopped fresh parsley

¼ teaspoon pepper
1 package (10 ounces) Mrs. Paul's
   frozen buttered fish fillets, cut
   into quarters
12 ounces medium shrimp, shelled
   and deveined
1 teaspoon orange peel cut into thin
   strips
   Pepperidge Farm garlic croutons
   (optional)

1. Drain clams, reserving liquid; set aside.

2. In 3-quart saucepan over medium heat, in hot oil, cook garlic until lightly browned, stirring constantly. Add broth, tomatoes with their liquid, reserved clam liquid, parsley and pepper; heat to boiling. Add fillets; heat to boiling. Reduce heat to low. Simmer 5 minutes.

3. Add clams, shrimp and orange peel. Cook until shrimp are pink and opaque and fish flakes easily when tested with fork. Serve with garlic croutons. Makes 6½ cups or 4 servings.

Side Dishes

Mushroom-Snow Pea Stir-Fry (page 192)

MUSHROOM-SNOW PEA STIR-FRY

1 package (3.5 ounces) Campbell's
    Fresh oyster mushrooms or
    1 package (8 ounces)
    Campbell's Fresh mushrooms
2 tablespoons soy sauce
1 tablespoon dry sherry
1 tablespoon rice wine vinegar
1 tablespoon packed brown sugar

1 teaspoon cornstarch
3 tablespoons peanut or vegetable
    oil, divided
1 cup diagonally sliced celery
1 cup diagonally sliced zucchini
1 cup snow peas
1 cup sweet yellow or red pepper
    strips

1. Cut mushrooms in half. In small bowl, combine soy sauce, sherry, vinegar, sugar and cornstarch; stir until smooth.

2. In 10-inch skillet or wok over high heat, in 1 tablespoon hot oil, cook mushrooms, stirring quickly and frequently (stir-frying) until tender. Remove from skillet; set aside. Add remaining 2 tablespoons oil to skillet. Add celery, zucchini, snow peas and pepper. Stir-fry until tender-crisp. Add cooked mushrooms.

3. Stir cornstarch mixture; gradually stir into skillet. Cook over medium heat until mixture boils and thickens, stirring often. Cook 1 minute more. Makes 3½ cups or 4 servings.

VEGETABLE KABOBS

¼ cup olive oil
¼ cup vegetable oil
2 tablespoons lemon juice
3 cloves garlic, minced
1 teaspoon dried oregano leaves,
    crushed

¼ teaspoon pepper
1 package (8 ounces) Campbell's
    Fresh mushrooms
1 medium zucchini, cut into ½-inch
    slices and blanched 1 minute
12 large cherry tomatoes

1. In large bowl, combine oils, lemon juice, garlic, oregano and pepper. Add vegetables; toss to coat well. Let stand 30 minutes at room temperature.

2. On four 12-inch skewers, alternately thread vegetables.

3. Place skewers on grill 6 inches above glowing coals. Grill 8 minutes or until vegetables are tender-crisp, turning often and brushing with remaining marinade. Makes 4 servings.

To broil: Prepare kabobs as in steps 1 and 2. On rack in broiler pan, place skewers. Broil 6 inches from heat 10 minutes or until vegetables are tender-crisp, turning often and brushing with remaining marinade.

VEGETABLE TIMBALES

4 eggs
1 can (10¾ ounces) Campbell's
    condensed cream of asparagus
    soup
1 cup milk
½ teaspoon dried tarragon leaves,
    crushed
1 cup shredded mozzarella cheese
    (4 ounces)

¼ cup butter or margarine
3 cups shredded carrots
1 package (8 ounces) Campbell's
    Fresh mushrooms, chopped
1 package (10 ounces) frozen
    chopped broccoli, thawed and
    drained

1. Generously grease eight 5-ounce custard cups or individual molds.

2. In large bowl, beat eggs until foamy. Stir in soup, milk and tarragon; stir in cheese. Set aside.

3. In 10-inch skillet over medium heat, in hot butter, cook carrots, mushrooms and broccoli until tender and liquid is evaporated, stirring occasionally. Add to soup mixture; stir to mix well.

4. Pour into prepared cups. Place cups in large baking pan on oven rack. Pour boiling water around cups to reach halfway up sides of cups.

5. Bake at 400°F. for 30 minutes or until knife inserted in center comes out clean. Let stand 10 minutes; unmold onto serving platter. Makes 8 servings.

Tip: To make a vegetable casserole, prepare as in steps 2 and 3. Pour into greased 2-quart casserole. Bake at 400°F. for 45 to 50 minutes or until knife inserted in center comes out clean. Let stand 10 minutes before serving.

GREEN BEAN BAKE

1 can (10¾ ounces) Campbell's
    condensed cream of mushroom
    soup
½ cup milk
1 teaspoon soy sauce
    Dash pepper

2 packages (9 ounces *each*) frozen
    cut green beans, cooked and
    drained
1 can (2.8 ounces) French-fried
    onions, divided
¼ cup sliced Vlasic pitted ripe olives
    (optional)

1. In 1½-quart casserole, stir soup, milk, soy sauce and pepper until smooth. Stir in green beans, ½ of the onions and the olives.

2. Bake at 350°F. for 25 minutes or until hot; stir. Top with remaining onions. Bake 5 minutes more. Garnish with additional sliced olives, if desired. Makes about 4 cups or 6 servings.

Side Dishes

HONEY-GLAZED SQUASH

1 can (10½ ounces) Campbell's
    condensed chicken broth
¼ cup honey
1 tablespoon cornstarch
1 teaspoon grated orange peel

⅛ teaspoon ground ginger
2 large acorn squash, cooked,
    drained and cut into 2-inch thick
    slices
Slivered orange peel for garnish

1. In 10-inch skillet, combine broth, honey, cornstarch, grated orange peel and ginger. Over medium heat, cook until thickened, stirring constantly.

2. Add squash. Over low heat, cook 10 minutes or until squash is glazed, basting frequently. Pour into serving bowl; garnish with slivered orange peel. Makes 6 servings.

Tip: Sliver orange peel for garnish an hour or two before you need it, then leave it out to dry; it will become curly.

STUFFED ACORN SQUASH

2 medium acorn squash
2 tablespoons butter or margarine
1 package (8 ounces) Campbell's
    Fresh mushrooms, coarsely
    chopped
½ cup sliced green onions
¼ teaspoon dried thyme leaves,
    crushed

1 cup cooked brown rice
1 can (about 8 ounces) stewed
    tomatoes
1 cup shredded Monterey Jack
    cheese, divided (4 ounces)
¼ cup coarsely chopped toasted
    walnuts

1. Halve squash lengthwise; remove seeds. In 8- by 8-inch baking dish, arrange squash cut-side down. Bake at 375°F. for 30 minutes.

2. Meanwhile, to make stuffing: In 10-inch skillet over medium heat, in hot butter, cook mushrooms, onions and thyme until vegetables are tender and liquid is evaporated, stirring occasionally. Stir in rice and tomatoes. Reduce heat to low. Simmer 5 minutes, stirring often. Stir in ½ cup of the cheese.

3. Turn partially baked squash cut-side up in baking dish. Spoon about 1¼ cups of the stuffing into each squash half. Sprinkle with remaining ½ cup cheese and the walnuts. Bake 15 minutes more or until tender. Makes 4 servings.

Honey-Glazed Squash

GRILLED STUFFED TOMATOES

2 large Campbell's Fresh tomatoes
2 slices bacon, diced
2 tablespoons finely chopped onion
1½ cups coarsely chopped Campbell's
 Fresh mushrooms

½ cup Pepperidge Farm herb
 seasoned stuffing
¼ cup grated Parmesan cheese,
 divided
Chopped fresh parsley for garnish

1. Cut tomatoes in half crosswise. Scoop out pulp; chop and reserve. Lightly season tomato shells with salt; turn upside-down on paper towels to drain.

2. In 8-inch skillet over medium heat, cook bacon and onion until bacon is almost crisp. Add mushrooms; cook until mushrooms are tender and liquid is evaporated, stirring occasionally. Stir in reserved tomato pulp, stuffing and 2 tablespoons of the cheese. Spoon ½ cup of the mixture into each tomato shell.

3. To make bundles: On 12-inch piece of heavy-duty or double-thickness foil, place one stuffed tomato. Bring edges of foil together; seal tightly. Repeat, making 3 more bundles. Place bundles 6 inches above glowing coals. Grill 15 minutes or until heated through. Garnish with parsley and remaining Parmesan. Makes 4 servings.

SHIITAKE-STUFFED TOMATOES

2 Campbell's Fresh tomatoes
1 package (3.5 ounces) Campbell's
 Fresh shiitake mushrooms
2 tablespoons butter or margarine
½ cup finely chopped celery
¼ cup finely chopped onion

2 tablespoons chopped fresh parsley
2 tablespoons Italian-seasoned fine
 dry bread crumbs
½ teaspoon dried basil leaves,
 crushed
⅛ teaspoon salt

1. Preheat oven to 400°F. Cut tomatoes in half crosswise. Scoop out pulp; chop and reserve. Turn tomato shells upside-down on paper towels to drain. Trim woody portions of mushroom stems. Remove and chop stems. Chop mushroom caps.

2. To make filling: In 10-inch skillet over medium heat, in hot butter, cook mushroom stems, celery and onion 1 minute. Add mushroom caps. Cook until tender, stirring occasionally. Remove from heat.

3. Stir in parsley, bread crumbs, basil, salt and reserved tomato pulp. Divide filling among tomato shells. Arrange shells in shallow baking dish. Bake 15 minutes or until heated through. Makes 4 servings.

Grilled Stuffed Tomatoes

SKILLET POTATOES

3 tablespoons butter or margarine
1 cup sliced celery
½ cup chopped onion
2 cloves garlic, minced
1 can (10½ ounces) Campbell's
    condensed chicken broth

¼ cup water
4 cups cubed peeled potatoes
1 cup carrots cut into matchstick-
    thin strips
⅛ teaspoon pepper
Chopped fresh parsley for garnish

1. In 10-inch skillet over medium heat, in hot butter, cook celery, onion and garlic until vegetables are tender, stirring occasionally.

2. Add broth, water, potatoes, carrots and pepper. Heat to boiling. Reduce heat to low. Cover; simmer 15 minutes or until potatoes are tender.

3. Uncover; over medium heat, simmer 5 minutes or until broth is slightly thickened, stirring often. Sprinkle with parsley before serving. Makes 5 cups or 6 servings.

CHEESY ONION BAKED POTATOES

4 large baking potatoes (about
    8 ounces *each*)
¼ cup butter or margarine
¼ cup milk

1 pouch Campbell's dry onion soup
    and recipe mix
¼ teaspoon pepper
½ cup shredded Cheddar cheese
    (2 ounces)

1. Bake potatoes at 400°F. for 1 hour or until fork-tender. Increase heat to 450°F.

2. Cut thin slice horizontally from top of each potato. With spoon, scoop out pulp, leaving ¼-inch shell. In large bowl, mash potato pulp with butter and milk until smooth. Stir in soup mix and pepper; mix well.

3. Spoon filling back into shells; place in shallow baking pan. Bake 15 minutes or until heated through. Sprinkle with cheese; bake 2 minutes more or until cheese is melted. Makes 4 servings.

Skillet Potatoes

VEGETABLES IN CHEESE SAUCE

1 can (11 ounces) Campbell's
    condensed Cheddar cheese
    soup
⅓ cup milk
½ teaspoon dried basil leaves,
    crushed

1 clove garlic, minced
2 cups cauliflowerets
1 small onion, cut into thin wedges
1½ cups diagonally sliced carrots
1 package (10 ounces) frozen peas

1. In 3-quart microwave-safe casserole, stir soup until smooth. Stir in milk, basil and garlic; mix well.

2. Add cauliflowerets, onion, carrots and peas; stir to coat well. Cover with lid; microwave on HIGH 15 minutes or until vegetables are tender, stirring twice during cooking. Let stand, covered, 5 minutes. Makes about 5½ cups or 8 servings.

SCALLOPED POTATOES AND CARROTS

1 tablespoon butter or margarine
½ cup chopped onion
¼ teaspoon dried dill weed, crushed
1 can (10½ ounces) Franco-
    American chicken gravy

1 tablespoon chopped fresh parsley
3 cups thinly sliced peeled potatoes
½ cup *very* thinly sliced carrots

1. Grease 1-quart casserole. In 1-quart saucepan over medium heat, in hot butter, cook onion and dill until onion is tender, stirring occasionally.

2. Stir in gravy and parsley. Heat through. Remove from heat.

3. In prepared casserole, layer ½ of the potatoes and ½ of the carrots. Spoon ½ of the gravy over vegetables. Repeat layers.

4. Cover; bake at 425°F. for 30 minutes. Uncover; bake 15 minutes more or until potatoes and carrots are tender. Let stand 5 minutes before serving. Makes 4 servings.

To microwave: Omit butter. In 1½-quart microwave-safe casserole, combine onion, dill, gravy and parsley. Cover with lid; microwave on HIGH 4 minutes or until onion is tender, stirring once during cooking. Stir in potatoes and carrots. Cover; microwave on HIGH 12 minutes or until potatoes and carrots are tender, stirring twice during cooking. Let stand, covered, 5 minutes.

Vegetables in Cheese Sauce

GRILLED CHEESY VENDOR'S ONIONS

3 medium onions, cut in half
    lengthwise and thinly sliced
    (about 2 cups)

1 cup chopped Vlasic Polish dill
    spears
½ cup pasteurized process cheese
    spread

1. To make bundle: Combine onions and pickles in an even layer on 24- by 18-inch piece of heavy-duty or double-thickness foil. Bring short sides of foil together; fold to center. Fold in ends. Pinch to seal.

2. On grill rack, place bundle, seam-side up, directly above medium coals. Grill 20 minutes or until onions are tender. Remove from grill. Carefully open packet at seam. Add cheese spread; stir until spread is melted and mixture is coated. Makes 2 cups.

To microwave: In 2-quart microwave-safe casserole, combine onions and pickles. Microwave, covered, on HIGH 10 minutes or until onions are tender, stirring twice. Pour off excess liquid. Add cheese spread; stir until spread is melted.

SUCCOTASH AND BEANS

1 tablespoon butter or margarine
½ cup chopped onion
¼ teaspoon dried thyme leaves,
    crushed

1 can (16 ounces) Campbell's pork &
    beans in tomato sauce
1 cup frozen succotash, cooked and
    drained
2 tablespoons chopped fresh parsley

1. In 3-quart saucepan over medium heat, in hot butter, cook onion and thyme until tender, stirring often.

2. Stir in beans, succotash and parsley. Heat through, stirring occasionally. Makes 3 cups or 6 servings.

MUSHROOM ARTICHOKE SAUTE

1 jar (6 ounces) marinated artichoke
    hearts, undrained
1 package (8 ounces) Campbell's
    Fresh mushrooms, sliced

1 tablespoon grated Parmesan
    cheese
Lemon wedges

1. Drain 2 tablespoons of the marinade from artichokes; place in 10-inch skillet. Over medium heat, in hot marinade, cook mushrooms until tender, stirring occasionally.

2. Add artichoke hearts and remaining marinade; heat through. Sprinkle with cheese and serve with lemon wedges. Makes 4 servings.

Tip: Makes a delicious complement to both meat and fish. Also good served chilled.

NUTTY SPINACH CASSEROLE

**2 packages (10 ounces *each*) frozen
    chopped spinach
1 can (10¾ ounces) Campbell's
    condensed cream of mushroom
    soup
2 eggs**

**½ cup shredded Monterey Jack
    cheese (2 ounces)
¼ cup chopped green onions
¼ cup chopped walnuts, toasted
2 tablespoons grated Parmesan
    cheese**

1. Place spinach in 1½-quart microwave-safe casserole. Cover with lid; microwave on HIGH 8 minutes or until spinach is heated through, stirring twice during cooking. Drain well.

2. Stir in soup until smooth; stir in remaining ingredients until well blended. Microwave, uncovered, on HIGH 12 minutes or until set in center, rotating dish twice during cooking. Makes 6 servings.

To toast walnuts: In small microwave-safe bowl, combine ¼ cup chopped walnuts and 1 teaspoon butter or margarine. Microwave, uncovered, on HIGH 2 minutes or until walnuts begin to brown, stirring twice during cooking.

DILLED CARROTS AND PARSNIPS

**1 can (10¾ ounces) Campbell's
    condensed cream of celery soup
½ cup milk**

**¼ teaspoon dried dill weed, crushed
2 cups carrots cut in 1-inch sticks
2 cups parsnips cut in 1-inch sticks**

1. In 3-quart microwave-safe casserole, stir soup until smooth. Add milk and dill weed; stir until well blended. Stir in carrots. Cover with lid; microwave on HIGH 6 minutes.

2. Stir in parsnips. Cover; microwave on HIGH 13 minutes or until vegetables are nearly tender, stirring twice during cooking. Let stand, covered, 5 minutes. Makes 6 servings.

Side Dishes

CRANBERRY-ORANGE SWEET POTATOES

2 packages (12 ounces *each*) Mrs.
  Paul's frozen candied sweet
  potatoes
1 cup whole berry cranberry sauce

1 small orange, sliced, seeded and
  quartered
¼ cup orange juice
2 tablespoons butter or margarine

1. In 3-quart saucepan, combine candied sauce mix from sweet potatoes, cranberry sauce, orange, orange juice and butter. Over medium heat, heat to boiling, stirring often.

2. Add sweet potatoes; return to boiling. Reduce heat to low. Cover; simmer 25 minutes or until sweet potatoes are tender, stirring occasionally. Makes 3½ cups or 7 servings.

SAUCY SWEET POTATOES

3 slices bacon, chopped
1 package (20 ounces) Mrs. Paul's
  frozen candied sweet potatoes,
  thawed

1 can (8 ounces) sliced water
  chestnuts, drained
½ teaspoon grated orange peel
⅓ cup orange juice

1. Place bacon in 2-quart microwave-safe casserole. Cover with plain white paper towel; microwave on HIGH 3 minutes or until crisp, stirring once during cooking. Drain bacon on paper towels, reserving drippings in casserole.

2. Stir candied sauce mix from sweet potatoes into drippings until smooth. Stir in sweet potatoes, water chestnuts, orange peel and orange juice. Cover with lid; microwave on HIGH 9 minutes or until potatoes are tender, stirring once during cooking. Let stand, covered, 5 minutes. Sprinkle bacon over potatoes. Makes 5 servings.

COPPER PENNIES

2 pounds carrots, thinly sliced
¼ cup water
1 can (10¾) ounces Campbell's
  condensed tomato soup
½ cup vinegar
¼ cup vegetable oil

¼ cup sugar
1 teaspoon dry mustard
1 teaspoon Worcestershire sauce
1 cup thinly sliced celery
1 medium onion, thinly sliced

1. In 3-quart microwave-safe casserole, combine carrots and water. Cover with lid; microwave on HIGH 10 minutes or until carrots are tender-crisp, stirring twice during cooking. Drain.

2. In large bowl, combine soup, vinegar, oil, sugar, mustard and Worcestershire. Stir in carrots, celery and onion. Cover; refrigerate until serving time, at least 4 hours. Makes about 7 cups or 12 servings.

ZUCCHINI PANCAKES

1 can (10¾ ounces) Campbell's
  condensed cream of mushroom
  soup, divided
4 cups shredded zucchini
½ cup finely chopped onion
1 egg, beaten
¼ cup all-purpose flour
2 tablespoons vegetable oil
½ cup sour cream
¼ teaspoon curry powder

1. In large bowl, combine ⅓ cup of the soup, the zucchini, onion, egg and flour; stir to mix well. Let stand 15 minutes.

2. In 10-inch skillet over medium-low heat, heat oil. Drop vegetable mixture by rounded tablespoonfuls into skillet, making 4 pancakes at a time; press with spoon to flatten to 2½-inch rounds. Fry until golden brown, turning once. Drain on paper towels; keep warm. Repeat with remaining vegetable mixture, adding more oil to skillet, if needed.

3. In small saucepan, combine remaining soup, the sour cream and curry powder until smooth. Over medium heat, heat through, stirring occasionally. Serve pancakes with curry sauce. Makes 6 servings.

TOMATO-GREEN BEAN SKILLET

2 tablespoons vegetable oil
1 large onion, chopped
1 medium green pepper, cut into
  strips
1 clove garlic, minced
1 can (10¾ ounces) Campbell's
  condensed tomato soup
4 cups fresh or frozen cut green
  beans
½ teaspoon dried thyme leaves,
  crushed
1 tablespoon lemon juice
1 cup shredded Cheddar cheese
  (4 ounces)

1. In 10-inch skillet over medium heat, in hot oil, cook onion, green pepper and garlic until tender, stirring occasionally.

2. Stir in soup, beans, thyme and lemon juice. Heat to boiling. Reduce heat to low. Cover; simmer 5 to 15 minutes until beans are nearly tender, stirring occasionally. Uncover; simmer until sauce is desired consistency.

3. Sprinkle with cheese. Cook 2 minutes more or until cheese is melted. Makes 6 servings.

APPLE THREE-BEAN BAKE

1 tablespoon butter or margarine	1 can (10 ounces) kidney beans,
1 medium apple, chopped	drained
¼ cup finely chopped onion	½ cup cooked butter beans, drained
1 can (16 ounces) Campbell's pork &	1 tablespoon prepared mustard
beans in tomato sauce	Dash pepper
	Apple slices for garnish

1. In 10-inch skillet over medium heat, in hot butter, cook apple and onion until tender, stirring often. Stir in beans, mustard and pepper. Pour mixture into 1½-quart casserole.

2. Bake at 350°F. for 30 minutes or until heated through. Stir before serving. Garnish with apple slices. Makes 4 cups or 6 servings.

To microwave: In 1½-quart microwave-safe casserole, combine butter, apple and onion. Cover; microwave on HIGH 3 minutes or until tender, stirring once during cooking. Stir in beans, mustard and pepper. Cover; microwave on HIGH 7 minutes or until heated through, stirring twice during cooking.

MAPLE BAKED BEANS

2 cans (16 ounces *each*) Campbell's	2 tablespoons maple syrup
pork & beans in tomato sauce	½ teaspoon dry mustard
2 tablespoons finely chopped onion	¼ teaspoon ground ginger

In 1½-quart casserole, combine all ingredients. Bake at 350°F. for 1 hour or until hot and bubbling. Makes 4 cups or 8 servings.

SPICY LIMA BEAN BAKE

4 slices bacon, quartered	1 package (10 ounces) frozen baby
1 small onion, sliced and separated	lima beans, cooked and drained
into rings	½ cup Open Pit original flavor
1 teaspoon chili powder	barbecue sauce
1 can (16 ounces) Campbell's pork &	
beans in tomato sauce	

1. In 10-inch skillet over medium heat, cook bacon until crisp. Drain bacon on paper towels, reserving 1 tablespoon of the drippings in pan.

2. In hot drippings, cook onion and chili powder 5 minutes or until onion is tender, stirring often. Stir in beans and barbecue sauce. Pour mixture into 1-quart casserole; top with bacon.

3. Bake at 350°F. for 30 minutes or until most of sauce is absorbed. Stir before serving. Makes 3½ cups or 6 servings.

Apple Three-Bean Bake

CAJUN-STYLE BEANS

1 tablespoon butter or margarine
½ cup diced cooked ham
½ cup chopped onion
1 stalk celery, chopped
1 medium green pepper, chopped
1 clove garlic, minced

1 can (16 ounces) Campbell's pork &
    beans in tomato sauce
2 tablespoons chopped pimento
¼ teaspoon black pepper
⅛ teaspoon ground red pepper

1. In 10-inch skillet over medium heat, in hot butter, cook ham, onion, celery, green pepper and garlic until vegetables are tender, stirring often.

2. Stir in beans, pimento, black pepper and red pepper. Heat to boiling; reduce heat to low. Simmer 5 minutes, stirring occasionally. Makes 3 cups or 6 servings.

CLASSIC BAKED BEANS

2 cans (16 ounces *each*) Campbell's
    pork & beans in tomato sauce
½ cup finely chopped onion
⅓ cup ketchup

2 tablespoons packed brown sugar
1 tablespoon prepared mustard
4 slices bacon, cut in half and
    partially cooked

1. In 1½-quart casserole, combine beans, onion, ketchup, sugar and mustard. Top with bacon.

2. Bake at 350°F. for 1 hour or until hot and bubbling. Stir before serving. Makes 3½ cups or 6 to 8 servings.

To microwave: Starting with uncooked bacon, in 1½-quart microwave-safe casserole, cover bacon with plain white paper towel; microwave on HIGH 4 minutes or until crisp, stirring once. Drain bacon on paper towels, reserving 1 teaspoon drippings in casserole. Add onion to drippings. Cover with lid; microwave on HIGH 3 minutes, stirring once during cooking. Stir in beans, ketchup, sugar, mustard and bacon. Cover; microwave on HIGH 8 minutes or until heated through, stirring twice during cooking.

Cajun-Style Beans

BROCCOLI AND NOODLES PARMESAN

1 bunch broccoli (about 1½ pounds)
2 tablespoons butter or margarine
½ cup chopped onion
1 clove garlic, minced
1 can (10¾ ounces) Campbell's
    condensed cream of mushroom
    soup

½ teaspoon dried tarragon leaves,
    crushed
1 cup shredded American cheese
    (4 ounces)
½ cup grated Parmesan cheese
1 cup sour cream
6 cups cooked wide noodles
    (8 ounces uncooked)

1. Cut broccoli into bite-size pieces. In covered 4-quart saucepan over medium heat, in 1-inch boiling water, cook broccoli 6 minutes or until tender. Drain in colander.

2. In same saucepan over medium heat, in hot butter, cook onion and garlic until onion is tender, stirring occasionally. Stir in soup and tarragon; mix well.

3. Add cheeses, stirring until melted. Stir in sour cream, broccoli and noodles. Pour into 2-quart casserole. Cover; bake at 350°F. for 30 minutes or until hot and bubbling. Makes 8 servings.

PEANUT NOODLES

1 cup V8 vegetable juice
½ cup chopped green onions
½ cup chopped sweet red pepper
⅓ cup creamy peanut butter
1 clove garlic, minced
1 tablespoon soy sauce

½ teaspoon grated fresh ginger
Dash crushed red pepper
8 ounces spaghetti, cooked and
    drained
Chopped unsalted peanuts for
    garnish

1. In 1-quart saucepan, combine V8 juice, green onions, sweet red pepper, peanut butter, garlic, soy sauce, ginger and crushed red pepper. Over medium heat, heat until hot and smooth, stirring often.

2. In large bowl, combine spaghetti and V8 mixture; toss to coat well. Garnish with peanuts. Makes 5 cups or 8 servings.

Broccoli and Noodles Parmesan

PASTA PRIMAVERA

2 cups V8 vegetable juice
1 tablespoon all-purpose flour
⅛ teaspoon pepper
1 tablespoon olive oil
2 large stalks celery, thinly sliced
1 large onion, thinly sliced
2 cloves garlic, minced
1 teaspoon dried oregano leaves,
   crushed

½ teaspoon dried basil leaves,
   crushed
1 large sweet red pepper, cut into
   strips
1 medium zucchini, cut into quarters
   lengthwise and sliced
6 cups hot cooked linguine
   (8 ounces uncooked)
   Grated Parmesan cheese
   (optional)

1. In small bowl, combine V8 juice, flour and pepper; set aside. In 10-inch skillet over medium heat, in hot oil, cook celery, onion, garlic, oregano and basil until vegetables are tender, stirring occasionally.

2. Add red pepper and zucchini. Cook until tender, stirring occasionally. Stir V8 juice mixture into skillet. Cook until mixture boils and thickens, stirring often. Reduce heat to low. Simmer 3 minutes.

3. Serve over linguine. Top with Parmesan, if desired. Makes 4 cups sauce or 8 side-dish servings.

CHEESY NOODLES

8 ounces wide noodles, uncooked
¼ cup butter or margarine
1 can (10¾ ounces) Campbell's
   condensed cream of mushroom
   soup

¾ cup milk
½ cup grated Parmesan cheese

1. Cook noodles according to package directions. Drain; place in 4-quart saucepan and toss with butter.

2. Meanwhile, in medium bowl, combine soup, milk and Parmesan. Stir into buttered noodles. Over medium heat, heat through, stirring constantly. Pour into serving dish; sprinkle with additional grated Parmesan, if desired. Makes about 5 cups or 8 servings.

Side Dishes

Pasta Primavera

SCALLOPED OYSTERS AND MUSHROOMS

¼ cup butter or margarine
1 package (8 ounces) Campbell's Fresh mushrooms, sliced
1 cup coarsely crushed saltine crackers
1 cup coarsely crumbled stale white bread

½ teaspoon Worcestershire sauce
¼ teaspoon celery salt
⅛ teaspoon pepper
1 pint shucked oysters, undrained
2 tablespoons milk or light cream
Chopped fresh parsley for garnish

1. In 10-inch skillet over medium heat, in hot butter, cook mushrooms until tender and liquid is evaporated, stirring occasionally. Add crackers, bread, Worcestershire, celery salt and pepper; mix well.

2. Drain oysters, reserving ½ cup oyster liquor. In buttered 10- by 6-inch baking dish, layer ½ of the mushroom mixture. Top with oysters and remaining mushroom mixture. Combine reserved oyster liquor and milk; pour over mushroom mixture.

3. Bake at 400°F. for 25 minutes or until hot and bubbling. Garnish with parsley. Makes 6 servings.

LOUISIANA BEANS AND RICE

1 tablespoon vegetable oil
1 cup chopped onions
1 large green pepper, chopped
2 cloves garlic, minced
½ teaspoon dried thyme leaves, crushed
¼ teaspoon dried oregano leaves, crushed

2 cans (16 ounces *each*) red beans or pinto beans, drained
1 can (10¾ ounces) Campbell's condensed tomato soup
1 cup diced cooked ham or smoked sausage
¼ teaspoon ground red pepper
Hot cooked rice

1. In 2-quart microwave-safe casserole, combine oil, onions, green pepper, garlic, thyme and oregano. Cover with lid; microwave on HIGH 5 minutes or until vegetables are tender, stirring once during cooking.

2. Stir in beans, soup, ham and red pepper. Cover; microwave on HIGH 5 minutes or until hot. Stir.

3. Cover; microwave on MEDIUM (50% power) 15 minutes or until flavors are blended. Serve over rice. Makes about 5 cups or 5 servings.

CAJUN DIRTY RICE

¼ cup butter or margarine
½ pound chicken livers, chopped
½ cup chopped green pepper
½ cup chopped celery
1 clove garlic, minced

1 pouch Campbell's dry onion
  mushroom soup and recipe mix
2 cups water
½ teaspoon hot pepper sauce
1 cup regular long-grain rice,
  uncooked

1. In 10-inch skillet over medium-high heat, in hot butter, cook livers, green pepper, celery and garlic until vegetables are tender, stirring often.

2. Stir soup mix, water and hot pepper sauce into skillet. Heat to boiling; stir in rice.

3. Reduce heat to low. Cover; simmer 20 minutes or until rice is tender. Makes 6 servings.

MUSHROOM RISOTTO

1 tablespoon butter or margarine
½ cup finely chopped onion
1 can (10½ ounces) Campbell's
  condensed chicken broth
½ cup water
¼ cup Chablis or other dry white wine

1 cup regular long-grain rice,
  uncooked
1 cup sliced Campbell's Fresh
  mushrooms
½ cup grated Parmesan cheese
Chopped fresh parsley for garnish

1. In 2-quart microwave-safe casserole, combine butter and onion. Cover with lid; microwave on HIGH 3 minutes or until onion is tender, stirring once during cooking.

2. Stir in broth, water and wine. Cover; microwave on HIGH 2 minutes or until hot.

3. Stir in rice. Cover; microwave on HIGH 10 minutes or until bubbling. Stir in mushrooms. Cover; microwave on MEDIUM (50% power) 10 minutes or until rice is nearly done. Stir in Parmesan. Let stand, covered, 5 minutes. Garnish with parsley. Makes about 3 cups or 6 servings.

Side Dishes

SPANISH RICE

5 slices bacon, diced
½ cup chopped onion
½ cup chopped green pepper
1 clove garlic, minced
1 cup regular long-grain rice, uncooked

1 can (10¾ ounces) Campbell's condensed tomato soup
1 soup can water
1 cup salsa

1. In 10-inch skillet over medium heat, cook bacon until lightly browned. Stir in onion, green pepper and garlic; cook until vegetables are tender, stirring occasionally.

2. Stir in rice; cook until rice is slightly browned, stirring often. Stir in soup, water and salsa; mix well.

3. Over high heat, heat to boiling. Reduce heat to low. Cover; simmer 25 minutes, stirring occasionally. Makes 6 servings.

RICE OLE

1 can (10¾ ounces) Campbell's condensed cream of celery soup
1 cup plain yogurt
1 can (4 ounces) chopped green chilies, drained
¼ cup chopped onion

4 cups cooked rice (1⅓ cups uncooked)
1½ cups shredded Monterey Jack cheese (6 ounces)
¼ cup grated Parmesan cheese
Paprika for garnish

1. In large bowl, stir soup until smooth. Add yogurt, chilies and onion; stir until well blended. Stir in rice and Monterey Jack cheese.

2. Spread mixture evenly in 12- by 8-inch microwave-safe dish. Cover with waxed paper; microwave on HIGH 9 minutes or until edges are bubbling and center is hot, rotating dish once during cooking.

3. Sprinkle with Parmesan and paprika. Microwave, uncovered, on HIGH 1 minute. Let stand 5 minutes. Makes 8 servings.

Spanish Rice

BARLEY PILAF

2 tablespoons butter or margarine
¾ cup pearl barley
1 pouch Campbell's dry onion soup and recipe mix

2½ cups water
1½ cups sliced Campbell's Fresh mushrooms

1. In 10-inch skillet over medium heat, in hot butter, cook barley about 5 minutes until browned, stirring constantly.

2. Stir in soup mix and water. Heat to boiling, stirring often. Reduce heat to low. Cover; simmer 45 minutes, stirring occasionally.

3. Stir in mushrooms. Cover; simmer 15 minutes more or until barley is tender. Makes 6 servings.

VEGETABLE COUSCOUS

1 tablespoon olive oil
1½ cups sliced Campbell's Fresh mushrooms
1 cup chopped onions
¼ cup chopped sweet red pepper
4 cloves garlic, minced

¼ teaspoon dried thyme leaves, crushed
⅛ teaspoon pepper
1¼ cups V8 vegetable juice
1 cup shredded zucchini
1 cup quick-cooking couscous, uncooked

1. In 3-quart saucepan over medium heat, in hot oil, cook mushrooms, onions, red pepper, garlic, thyme and pepper until vegetables are tender-crisp, stirring often.

2. Stir in V8 juice and zucchini; heat to boiling. Remove from heat. Stir in couscous. Cover; let stand 5 minutes or until liquid is absorbed. Makes 4½ cups or 9 servings.

Barley Pilaf

BROCCOLI AND CELERY ORIENTAL

1 tablespoon vegetable oil
3 cups broccoli flowerets
1½ cups thinly sliced celery
¼ cup sliced green onions
1 can (10½ ounces) Franco-
American chicken gravy

2 tablespoons chopped pimento
1 tablespoon soy sauce
Hot cooked rice
Cashews or peanuts for
garnish

1. In 2-quart microwave-safe casserole, combine oil, broccoli, celery and onions. Cover with lid; microwave on HIGH 4 minutes or until vegetables are tender-crisp, stirring once during cooking.

2. Stir in gravy, pimento and soy sauce. Cover; microwave on HIGH 3 minutes or until hot and bubbling. Serve with rice. Garnish with cashews. Makes 3 cups or 4 servings.

STIR-FRIED VEGETABLES WITH BULGUR

2 tablespoons vegetable oil
2 cups broccoli flowerets
1 cup thinly sliced carrots
1 cup bulgur wheat
1 clove garlic, minced
1 tablespoon sesame seed
1 teaspoon dried oregano leaves,
crushed

1¾ cups V8 vegetable juice
1 cup thinly sliced zucchini
1 cup sliced Campbell's Fresh
mushrooms
¼ cup sliced green onions
½ cup shredded Swiss cheese
(2 ounces)

1. In 10-inch skillet or wok over medium-high heat, in hot oil, cook broccoli, carrots, bulgur, garlic, sesame seed and oregano, stirring quickly and frequently (stir-frying), about 2 minutes.

2. Add V8 juice, zucchini, mushrooms and onions. Heat to boiling; reduce heat to low. Cover; simmer 15 minutes or until all liquid is absorbed, stirring occasionally.

3. Stir in cheese. Makes 5 cups or 10 servings.

Broccoli and Celery Oriental

BUTTERED VEGETABLE BUNDLES

1 package (12 ounces) Campbell's Fresh mushrooms, sliced
1 medium onion, thinly sliced and separated into rings
2 large carrots, cut into thin diagonal slices
1 medium green pepper, cut into strips
2 tablespoons chopped fresh parsley
¼ teaspoon salt
Generous dash pepper
4 teaspoons butter or margarine

1. To make bundles: Divide vegetables and seasonings among four 12-inch squares of heavy-duty or double-thickness foil. Top each with 1 teaspoon butter. Bring 2 sides of foil together; fold to center. Fold in ends. Pinch to seal.

2. On grill rack, place bundles, seam-side up, directly above medium coals. Grill 20 minutes or until tender, turning occasionally. Makes 4 servings.

GRILLED SHIITAKE MUSHROOMS

¼ cup peanut or vegetable oil
1 teaspoon sesame oil (optional)
2 teaspoons grated fresh ginger
1 clove garlic, minced
2 packages (3.5 ounces *each*) Campbell's Fresh shiitake mushrooms
Finely chopped green onions for garnish
Toasted sesame seed for garnish

1. In small bowl, combine oils, ginger and garlic. Let stand at least 30 minutes.

2. Trim woody portions of mushroom stems and discard. Cut any large mushrooms into quarters. On skewers, thread mushrooms. Generously brush with oil mixture.

3. Place skewers on grill 6 inches above glowing coals. Grill 5 minutes or until mushrooms are tender, turning often and brushing with oil mixture.

4. Garnish with onions and sesame seed. Makes 4 servings.

To broil: Prepare kabobs as in steps 1 and 2. On rack in broiler pan, place skewers. Broil 6 inches from heat 5 minutes or until mushrooms are tender; turning often and brushing with oil mixture.

Buttered Vegetable Bundles

SPICED CRANBERRY-NUT STUFFING

½ cup butter or margarine
2 cups sliced celery
1 package (16 ounces) Pepperidge Farm herb seasoned stuffing mix
1 can (14½ ounces) Swanson clear ready to serve chicken broth
1 cup whole berry cranberry sauce
½ cup coarsely chopped toasted nuts (almonds, pecans or walnuts)
1 egg, beaten
1 teaspoon grated orange peel
¼ teaspoon ground cinnamon

1. In 4-quart saucepan over medium heat, in hot butter, cook celery until tender. Add remaining ingredients; toss to mix well.

2. Spoon into greased 2-quart casserole. Cover; bake at 375°F. for 30 minutes or until hot. Makes 8 cups or 16 servings.

Note: Stuffing can be prepared through step 1 and used to stuff a 14- to 16-pound turkey.

To microwave: In 3-quart microwave-safe casserole, combine butter and celery. Cover with lid; microwave on HIGH 4 minutes or until celery is tender, stirring once during cooking. Add remaining ingredients; toss to mix well. Cover; microwave on HIGH 6 minutes or until hot, stirring twice during cooking.

CORN BREAD STUFFING

½ pound bulk pork sausage
1 cup chopped onions
½ cup chopped celery
¼ cup butter or margarine
2 large apples, chopped
1 cup Swanson clear ready to serve chicken broth
1 package (8 ounces) Pepperidge Farm corn bread stuffing mix
¼ cup chopped pecans
¼ cup chopped fresh parsley

1. Crumble sausage into 3-quart microwave-safe casserole; stir in onions and celery. Cover with lid; microwave on HIGH 5 minutes or until sausage is no longer pink, stirring once during cooking to separate meat.

2. Stir in butter, apples and broth. Cover; microwave on HIGH 5 minutes or until apples are tender and broth is boiling, stirring once during cooking.

3. Stir in stuffing mix, pecans and parsley. Let stand, covered, 5 minutes. Makes about 6½ cups or 10 servings.

Salads & Salad Dressings

Marinated Pepper Salad (page 226)

MARINATED PEPPER SALAD

⅓ cup olive oil
¼ cup lime juice
2 tablespoons chopped fresh cilantro
2 tablespoons Vlasic sweet banana pepper juice
½ teaspoon dried oregano leaves, crushed
½ teaspoon garlic powder
¼ teaspoon salt
¼ teaspoon ground red pepper
2 cups sliced Campbell's Fresh mushrooms

1 cup Vlasic sweet banana pepper rings, drained
1 medium avocado, sliced crosswise
1 Campbell's Fresh tomato, chopped
1 Campbell's Fresh tomato, sliced, for garnish
Curly endive for garnish
Vlasic mild banana peppers for garnish

1. To make dressing: In small bowl, combine oil, lime juice, cilantro, pepper juice, oregano, garlic powder, salt and red pepper.

2. In medium bowl, combine mushrooms, pepper rings, avocado and chopped tomato. Add dressing; toss gently to coat. Cover; refrigerate until serving time, at least 2 hours.

3. To serve: Line plate with tomato slices and endive. With slotted spoon, place salad on plate. Top with whole peppers. Makes 4½ cups or 6 servings.

MARINATED GARDEN SALAD

1 can (10½ ounces) Campbell's condensed chicken broth
⅓ cup red wine vinegar
½ teaspoon dried basil leaves, crushed
¼ teaspoon pepper
3 medium zucchini, thinly sliced

2 medium Campbell's Fresh tomatoes, cut into wedges
1 medium green pepper, cut into strips
1 medium onion, sliced
Lettuce

1. In large bowl, combine chicken broth, vinegar, basil and pepper; mix well.

2. Add zucchini, tomatoes, green pepper and onion; toss gently to mix. Cover; refrigerate until serving time, at least 4 hours, stirring occasionally. Spoon into lettuce-lined bowls. Makes about 4 cups or 6 servings.

Salads & Dressings

ANTIPASTO

2 tablespoons olive oil
2 tablespoons vegetable oil
2 tablespoons red wine vinegar
2 teaspoons anchovy paste or
   2 anchovy fillets, chopped
1 package (8 ounces) Campbell's
   Fresh mushrooms, sliced
½ cup Vlasic medium pitted ripe
   olives

1 cup diced hard salami (about
   4 ounces)
1 cup diced provolone or fontinella
   cheese (4 ounces)
6 cups torn romaine lettuce
6 to 12 Vlasic pepperoncini salad
   peppers for garnish

1. In large bowl, combine oils, vinegar and anchovy paste.

2. Add mushrooms and olives; toss to coat well. Cover; refrigerate until serving time, at least 4 hours, stirring occasionally.

3. Just before serving, add salami and cheese; mix well. Serve over lettuce; garnish with salad peppers. Makes 3½ cups or 6 servings.

MARINATED VEGETABLE SALAD

1 jar (16 ounces) Vlasic mild banana
   pepper rings, undrained
Swanson clear ready to serve
   chicken broth
2 cloves garlic, minced
2 tablespoons chopped fresh parsley

½ teaspoon dried thyme leaves,
   crushed
¼ teaspoon black pepper
4 cups cauliflowerets
2 medium carrots, cut into thin
   diagonal slices

1. Drain pepper rings, reserving liquid. Add enough broth to reserved liquid to equal 2 cups. In 3-quart saucepan, combine broth mixture, garlic, parsley, thyme and black pepper. Over medium heat, heat to boiling. Stir in cauliflower. Reduce heat to low. Cover; simmer 3 minutes. Stir in carrots. Cover; simmer 5 minutes more or until vegetables are tender-crisp.

2. Spoon vegetable mixture into large bowl; stir in pepper rings. Cover; refrigerate until serving time, at least 4 hours. Makes about 6 cups or 12 servings.

To microwave: In 2-quart microwave-safe casserole, combine broth mixture, garlic, parsley, thyme, black pepper and cauliflower. Cover; microwave on HIGH 5 minutes. Stir in carrots. Cover; microwave on HIGH 10 minutes or until tender-crisp, stirring once during cooking. Let stand, covered, 5 minutes before adding pepper rings.

Salads &
Dressings

SPINACH MUSHROOM SALAD

2 cups sliced Campbell's Fresh
   mushrooms
3 cups packed spinach leaves torn
   into bite-size pieces
1 large avocado, cubed
¼ cup chopped red onion

¼ cup vegetable oil
¼ cup red wine vinegar
1 teaspoon sugar
¼ teaspoon salt
   Generous dash pepper

1. In large bowl, toss together mushrooms, spinach, avocado and onion; set aside.

2. To make dressing: In small saucepan, combine remaining ingredients. Over medium heat, heat to boiling. Pour over mushroom mixture; toss to coat. Serve immediately. Makes 3 servings.

To microwave: Proceed as in step 1. To make dressing: In small microwave-safe bowl, combine remaining ingredients. Cover; microwave on HIGH 2 minutes. Stir. Pour dressing over mushroom mixture; toss to coat. Serve immediately.

CRUNCHY CUCUMBER SALAD

1 can (10¾ ounces) Campbell's
   condensed cream of celery soup
½ cup sour cream
1 cup sliced celery
1 cup sliced red onion

2 tablespoons white wine vinegar
1 tablespoon chopped fresh parsley
4 cups thinly sliced cucumbers
   Lettuce

In large bowl, combine soup, sour cream, celery, red onion, vinegar and parsley; stir well. Add cucumbers; stir to mix. Cover; refrigerate until serving time, at least 4 hours. Spoon into lettuce-lined bowl. Makes 4 cups or 8 servings.

Tip: To score cucumbers, pull a fork lengthwise through skin on all sides before slicing.

Spinach Mushroom Salad

LAYERED SPINACH SALAD

10 ounces spinach leaves, torn into bite-size pieces (6 cups)
6 hard-cooked eggs, chopped
1 medium head iceberg lettuce, chopped (8 cups)
2 cans (16 ounces *each*) Campbell's pork & beans in tomato sauce
½ cup sliced green onions
½ cup chopped sweet red pepper
1 cup Marie's refrigerated sour cream and dill salad dressing
Sweet red pepper rings for garnish
Green onion brush for garnish

In 4-quart glass bowl, layer ½ each of the spinach, eggs, lettuce, beans, onions and chopped pepper. Repeat layers. Spread salad dressing evenly over top. Cover; refrigerate until serving time, at least 12 hours. Garnish with pepper rings and green onion brush. Makes 16 cups or 10 servings.

Note: For directions for making green onion brush, see Mexicali Sipper on page 32.

CITRUS-MUSHROOM-SPINACH SALAD

1 package (8 ounces) Campbell's Fresh mushrooms, sliced
2 oranges, peeled and sectioned
½ cup Vlasic pitted ripe olives, halved
2 tablespoons thinly sliced green onion
2 tablespoons olive oil
1 tablespoon wine vinegar
1 tablespoon chopped fresh basil leaves or ½ teaspoon dried basil leaves, crushed
½ teaspoon salt
Dash pepper
2 cups packed torn spinach leaves

1. In medium bowl, combine mushrooms, oranges, olives, onion, oil, vinegar, basil, salt and pepper; toss gently to coat. Cover; refrigerate until serving time, at least 2 hours.

2. To serve: In large serving bowl, combine mushroom mixture and spinach; toss gently to coat. Makes 5 cups or 5 servings.

Layered Spinach Salad

ROASTED PEPPER AND BEAN SALAD

2 large sweet red peppers
¼ cup vinegar
¼ cup vegetable oil
½ teaspoon sugar
¼ teaspoon salt

1 can (about 16 ounces) small white
   beans, rinsed and drained
1 package (8 ounces) Campbell's
   Fresh mushrooms, each cut in
   half
2 tablespoons chopped fresh parsley

1. On rack in broiler pan, arrange peppers. Broil 6 inches from heat until skin is charred on all sides, turning often. Put peppers in paper bag; let stand 10 minutes. Peel, seed and cut peppers into 1-inch strips.

2. In large bowl, combine vinegar, oil, sugar and salt. Add peppers, beans, mushrooms and parsley; toss to coat well.

3. Cover; refrigerate until serving time, at least 4 hours, stirring often. Makes 4 cups or 6 servings.

TANGY BULGUR SALAD

1 can (10½ ounces) Campbell's
   condensed chicken broth
¾ cup bulgur wheat, uncooked
½ cup chopped fresh parsley
1 medium Campbell's Fresh tomato,
   seeded and chopped
¼ cup lemon juice
¼ cup olive or vegetable oil

1 tablespoon chopped fresh mint
   leaves or 1 teaspoon dried mint
   leaves, crushed
¼ teaspoon pepper
   Romaine lettuce leaves for garnish
   Sliced Campbell's Fresh tomatoes
   for garnish
   Fresh mint leaves for garnish

1. In 1½-quart microwave-safe casserole, combine broth and bulgur. Cover with lid; microwave on HIGH 6 minutes or until liquid is absorbed and bulgur is tender, stirring once during cooking.

2. Stir in parsley, chopped tomato, lemon juice, oil, mint and pepper. Cover; refrigerate until serving time, at least 4 hours.

3. Line serving plate with lettuce and tomato slices. Spoon bulgur mixture over tomato slices. Garnish with fresh mint leaves. Makes about 3½ cups or 6 servings.

Roasted Pepper and Bean Salad

BULGUR-BEAN SALAD

¾ cup boiling water
¾ cup bulgur wheat, uncooked
1 can (16 ounces) Campbell's pork &
    beans in tomato sauce
1 medium cucumber, seeded and
    chopped
½ cup finely chopped fresh parsley
¼ cup finely chopped fresh mint
    leaves or 2 teaspoons dried
    mint leaves, crushed

2 green onions, thinly sliced
¼ cup lemon juice
2 tablespoons vegetable oil
½ teaspoon coarse ground pepper
    Campbell's Fresh butterhead
    lettuce leaves for garnish
    Fresh mint leaves for garnish

1. In medium bowl, pour boiling water over bulgur. Let stand, covered, 30 minutes or until water is absorbed, stirring occasionally.

2. In large bowl, combine beans, cucumber, parsley, mint, onions, lemon juice, oil and pepper. Add bulgur; toss gently to coat. Cover; refrigerate until serving time, at least 4 hours.

3. To serve: Spoon into lettuce-lined salad bowl. Garnish with mint. Makes 3½ cups or 7 servings.

VEGETABLE-BULGUR SALAD

⅓ cup bulgur wheat, uncooked
1 cup hot water
1 teaspoon vegetable oil
¼ cup chopped sweet red pepper
¼ cup chopped zucchini
¾ cup V8 vegetable juice

1 teaspoon lemon juice
¼ teaspoon dried basil leaves,
    crushed
    Lettuce leaves for garnish
    Chopped green onion for garnish

1. In 2-cup measure, combine bulgur and hot water. Let stand 5 minutes; drain.

2. Meanwhile, in 1½-quart saucepan over medium heat, in hot oil, cook red pepper and zucchini until tender-crisp, stirring often.

3. Stir in V8 juice, lemon juice, basil and drained bulgur. Heat to boiling; reduce heat to low. Cover; simmer 15 minutes or until liquid is absorbed, stirring occasionally.

4. Serve warm or chilled. To serve chilled: Cover; refrigerate until serving time, at least 2 hours. Spoon into lettuce-lined salad bowl. Garnish with green onion. Makes 1 cup or 2 servings.

Salads & Dressings

Bulgur-Bean Salad

MUSHROOM RICE SALAD

3 cups cooked brown rice
1 package (8 ounces) Campbell's
   Fresh mushrooms, sliced
1 medium cucumber, chopped
10 cherry tomatoes, each cut in half
⅓ cup sliced green onions

½ cup Marie's refrigerated blue
   cheese, ranch or Italian garlic
   salad dressing
2 tablespoons lemon or lime juice
   Toasted sliced almonds for garnish

1. In large bowl, combine rice, mushrooms, cucumber, tomatoes and green onions.

2. In cup, combine dressing and lemon juice; mix well. Pour over rice mixture; toss to mix well. Cover; refrigerate until serving time, at least 2 hours. Garnish with almonds. Makes 6 cups or 6 servings.

SHRIMP-STUFFED AVOCADOS

¾ pound medium shrimp, cooked,
   shelled and deveined
1¼ cups quartered Campbell's Fresh
   mushrooms
½ cup coarsely chopped Vlasic
   pitted ripe olives
¼ cup chopped red onion
⅓ cup mayonnaise

2 tablespoons lime juice
1 teaspoon ground coriander
½ teaspoon ground cumin
⅛ teaspoon ground red pepper
2 large ripe avocados
   Lettuce
   Lime wedges for garnish

1. In bowl, combine shrimp, mushrooms, olives, onion, mayonnaise, lime juice, coriander, cumin and red pepper; mix lightly but well. Cover; refrigerate until serving time, at least 2 hours.

2. Cut avocados in half lengthwise; remove pits and peel. Cut into lengthwise slices. Arrange avocado slices on four lettuce-lined plates. Spoon shrimp mixture over each; garnish with lime wedges. Makes 4 servings.

VEGETABLE-RICE SALAD

½ cup Marie's refrigerated regular
   Italian garlic salad dressing
1 tablespoon lemon juice
   Generous dash pepper

2 cups cooked rice
½ cup broccoli flowerets, cooked
½ cup sliced carrot, cooked
½ cup quartered cherry tomatoes

In medium bowl, combine salad dressing, lemon juice and pepper. Add rice, broccoli, carrot and tomatoes; toss gently to coat. Cover; refrigerate until serving time, at least 4 hours. Makes 4½ cups or 8 servings.

CUCUMBER BEAN SALAD

1 can (16 ounces) Campbell's pork & beans in tomato sauce
1 medium cucumber, cut in half lengthwise, seeded and sliced
⅓ cup Vlasic mild banana pepper rings, drained

2 tablespoons Vlasic pitted ripe olives cut into quarters
2 tablespoons chopped onion
2 tablespoons diced pimento
2 tablespoons Vlasic mild banana pepper juice
⅛ teaspoon black pepper

In medium bowl, combine all ingredients; stir gently to mix. Cover; refrigerate until serving time, at least 2 hours, stirring occasionally. Makes 2 ½ cups or 4 servings.

PENNSYLVANIA DUTCH CHOW CHOW

1 cup cauliflowerets
1 cup whole kernel corn
1 cup green beans cut into 1½-inch pieces

1 jar (10 ounces) Vlasic country classic sweet chunky relish
½ cup cooked or canned kidney beans, drained
¼ cup thinly sliced celery

1. In 2-quart saucepan over medium heat, in boiling water, cook cauliflower, corn and green beans 4 minutes or until tender-crisp. Drain.

2. In medium bowl, combine cooked vegetables, relish, kidney beans and celery. Cover; refrigerate until serving time, at least 4 hours, stirring occasionally. Makes 5 cups or 10 servings.

To microwave: In 1-quart microwave-safe casserole, combine cauliflower, corn, green beans and 2 tablespoons water. Cover; microwave on HIGH 5 minutes or until vegetables are tender-crisp, stirring twice. Proceed as in step 2.

Salads & Dressings

SUMMERTIME SAUERKRAUT SALAD

1 jar (16 ounces) Vlasic old
   fashioned sauerkraut, rinsed
   and drained
1 cup shredded carrots
1 large sweet red or yellow pepper,
   chopped
½ cup thinly sliced green onions

¼ cup chopped fresh parsley
¼ cup Vlasic country classic sweet
   chunky relish
2 tablespoons cider vinegar
½ teaspoon celery seed
1 to 4 tablespoons Vlasic country
   classic sweet chunky relish juice

In medium bowl, combine all ingredients except relish juice. Add just
enough relish juice to moisten. Cover; refrigerate until serving time, at least
2 hours, stirring occasionally. Makes 4½ cups or 6 servings.

SOUTHERN-STYLE SLAW

1 cup Marie's refrigerated buttermilk
   spice ranch style salad dressing
3 tablespoons cider vinegar
2 tablespoons sugar
1 teaspoon prepared mustard

¼ teaspoon celery seed
¼ teaspoon pepper
6 cups shredded cabbage
1 cup shredded carrots

In medium bowl, combine salad dressing, vinegar, sugar, mustard, celery
seed and pepper. Add cabbage and carrots; toss gently to coat. Cover;
refrigerate until serving time, at least 2 hours. Makes 5½ cups or 6 servings.

GARDEN PASTA SALAD

⅓ cup Marie's refrigerated buttermilk
   spice ranch style salad dressing
2 tablespoons cider vinegar
1 tablespoon chopped fresh basil
   leaves or 1 teaspoon dried basil
   leaves, crushed
1 can (16 ounces) Campbell's pork &
   beans in tomato sauce

7 ounces pasta ruffles, cooked and
   drained (3 cups)
1 Campbell's Fresh tomato, seeded
   and chopped
1 medium zucchini, halved
   lengthwise and thinly sliced
2 tablespoons Vlasic pitted ripe
   olives coarsely chopped

In large bowl, combine salad dressing, vinegar and basil. Add beans, pasta,
tomato, zucchini and olives; toss gently to coat. Cover; refrigerate until
serving time, at least 2 hours. Makes 6 cups or 8 servings.

Summertime Sauerkraut Salad

FOUR-BEAN SALAD

¾ cup wine vinegar
¼ cup vegetable oil
1 tablespoon sugar
¼ teaspoon pepper
1 can (20¾ ounces) Campbell's
    pork & beans in tomato sauce
1 can (16 ounces) black beans,
    drained

1 can (16 ounces) red kidney beans,
    drained
1½ cups cut green beans, cooked
1 medium red onion, cut in half
    lengthwise and sliced
Cucumber slices for garnish

In large bowl, combine vinegar, oil, sugar and pepper. Add beans and onion; toss gently to coat. Cover; refrigerate until serving time, at least 4 hours. Serve in cucumber-lined salad bowl. Makes 8 cups or 16 servings.

BLUE RIBBON CARROT SALAD

2 pounds carrots, cut into 2- by
    ¼-inch sticks
1 can (10¾ ounces) Campbell's
    condensed tomato soup
½ cup vinegar
¼ cup sugar

¼ cup vegetable oil
1 teaspoon prepared mustard
1 teaspoon Worcestershire sauce
1 cup sliced celery
1 cup fresh snow peas, cut in half
    crosswise, cooked and drained

1. In 4-quart saucepan over medium heat, in 1-inch boiling water, cook carrots until tender. Drain; cool slightly.

2. In large bowl, combine soup, vinegar, sugar, oil, mustard and Worcestershire.

3. Add cooked carrots, celery and snow peas; toss to coat well. Cover; refrigerate until serving time, at least 4 hours. Makes about 6 cups or 8 servings.

To microwave: In 2-quart microwave-safe casserole, combine carrots and ¼ cup water. Cover; microwave on HIGH 8 to 12 minutes until tender, stirring twice during cooking. Let stand, covered, 2 minutes. Drain; cool slightly. Proceed as in steps 2 and 3.

Tip: The dressing on this salad also makes a delicious marinade for broiled or grilled meats.

Four-Bean Salad

TORTELLINI SALAD

⅓ cup vegetable oil
2 tablespoons wine vinegar
2 teaspoons Dijon-style mustard
½ teaspoon dried basil leaves, crushed
3 cups cooked cheese-filled tortellini
2 cups broccoli flowerets, cooked

1½ cups sliced Campbell's Fresh mushrooms
1½ cups halved cherry tomatoes
1 cup chopped Vlasic zesty dill spears
Fresh basil for garnish

1. To make dressing: In small bowl, combine oil, vinegar, mustard and basil.

2. In large bowl, combine tortellini, broccoli, mushrooms, tomatoes and pickles. Add dressing; toss gently to coat. Cover; refrigerate until serving time, at least 4 hours.

3. With slotted spoon, place salad on plate. Garnish with basil. Makes 9 cups or 9 servings.

SESAME-PASTA SALAD

1½ cups V8 vegetable juice
1 tablespoon sesame seed, toasted
1 tablespoon soy sauce
1 tablespoon vinegar
2 teaspoons honey
¼ teaspoon grated fresh ginger

1¼ cups small shell macaroni, cooked and drained (3 cups cooked)
1 cup diagonally sliced carrots
1 cup sweet red pepper squares
½ cup sliced water chestnuts
¼ cup sliced green onions

1. In medium bowl, combine V8 juice, sesame seed, soy sauce, vinegar, honey and ginger.

2. Add macaroni, carrots, red pepper, water chestnuts and onions; toss to coat. Cover; refrigerate until serving time, at least 4 hours. Makes 6 cups or 8 servings.

OLIVE MEDLEY MEDITERRANEAN

1 jar (5 ounces) Vlasic pimento stuffed Spanish olives, drained
1 can (6 ounces) Vlasic pitted ripe olives, drained
½ cup drained Vlasic cocktail onions
2 tablespoons olive oil

2 tablespoons red wine vinegar
3 cloves garlic, minced
½ teaspoon crushed red pepper
½ teaspoon ground allspice
¼ teaspoon dried oregano leaves, crushed

1. In large glass bowl, combine all ingredients; toss to mix well. Cover; refrigerate at least 4 hours before serving, stirring occasionally.

2. Serve chilled or at room temperature with decorative toothpicks. Makes 3 cups or 12 appetizer servings.

Tortellini Salad

LOUISIANA-STYLE POTATO SALAD

2 pounds small new potatoes, sliced ¼ inch thick (6 cups)
5 slices bacon
¾ cup Marie's refrigerated regular or lite sour cream and dill salad dressing
1 to 2 tablespoons Louisiana-style hot sauce
¼ teaspoon black pepper
1 medium green pepper, diced
½ cup sliced green onions
½ cup Vlasic country classic sweet chunky relish
Lettuce leaves for garnish

1. In 4-quart saucepan over medium heat, cook potatoes in boiling water to cover 10 minutes or until tender. Drain.

2. In 8-inch skillet over medium heat, cook bacon until crisp. Drain bacon on paper towels, reserving 1 tablespoon drippings. Crumble bacon.

3. To make dressing: In small bowl, combine salad dressing, hot sauce, black pepper, bacon and reserved drippings.

4. In large bowl, combine potatoes, green pepper, onions and relish. Add dressing; toss gently to coat. Cover; refrigerate until serving time, at least 4 hours.

5. Spoon into lettuce-lined salad bowl. Makes 8 cups or 8 servings.

OLD-FASHIONED POTATO SALAD

2 pounds small new potatoes, cut up (6 cups)
1 cup Marie's refrigerated buttermilk spice ranch style salad dressing
2 teaspoons prepared mustard
⅛ teaspoon pepper
1 cup sliced celery
⅓ cup chopped Vlasic sweet pickles
2 hard-cooked eggs, chopped

1. In 4-quart saucepan over medium heat, cook potatoes in boiling water to cover 10 minutes or until tender. Drain.

2. In large bowl, combine salad dressing, mustard and pepper. Add potatoes, celery, pickles and eggs; toss gently to coat. Cover; refrigerate until serving time, at least 4 hours. Makes 8 cups or 8 servings.

Louisiana-Style Potato Salad

SPRINGTIME POTATO SALAD

5 new potatoes, cut into 1-inch
   pieces (about 1 pound)
2 cups green beans cut into 1-inch
   pieces (about ½ pound)
1 package (8 ounces) Campbell's
   Fresh mushrooms, quartered

½ cup vegetable oil
3 tablespoons vinegar
½ teaspoon salt
2 tablespoons chopped fresh or
   frozen chives
¼ teaspoon dry mustard

1. In 2-quart saucepan over medium heat, cook potatoes in boiling water to cover 5 minutes. Add beans; cook 5 minutes more or until vegetables are tender-crisp. Drain.

2. In large bowl, combine remaining ingredients; mix well.

3. Add potatoes and beans; toss to coat well. Cover; refrigerate until serving time, at least 4 hours, stirring occasionally. Makes 6½ cups or 8 servings.

To microwave: Pierce whole potatoes with fork. Arrange on plain white paper towel in microwave oven. Microwave on HIGH 7 minutes or until almost tender. Let stand 5 minutes. Cut potatoes into 1-inch pieces. In 1-quart microwave-safe casserole, place beans and ½ cup water. Cover with lid; microwave on HIGH 2 minutes or until beans are tender-crisp. Let stand 5 minutes; drain. Proceed as in steps 2 and 3.

CREAMY POTATO SALAD

3 pounds small new potatoes
1 can (10¾ ounces) Campbell's
   condensed cream of celery soup
¾ cup mayonnaise
2 tablespoons red wine vinegar

⅛ teaspoon pepper
1 cup chopped celery
¾ cup cooked peas
½ cup sliced radishes
2 hard-cooked eggs, chopped

1. In 4-quart saucepan over high heat, cook potatoes in boiling water to cover 5 minutes. Over high heat, heat to boiling. Reduce heat to low. Cover; simmer 20 to 30 minutes until fork-tender; drain. Cool slightly. Peel potatoes; cut potatoes into ½-inch cubes.

2. In large bowl, combine soup, mayonnaise, vinegar and pepper until well blended.

3. Add potatoes, celery, peas, radishes and eggs; toss gently to coat. Cover; refrigerate until serving time, at least 4 hours. Makes about 7 cups or 8 servings.

Springtime Potato Salad

GERMAN-STYLE RED POTATO SALAD

2 pounds small new potatoes, sliced
  ¼ inch thick (6 cups)
6 slices bacon
1 medium onion, thinly sliced and
  separated into rings
1 large sweet red pepper, coarsely
  chopped
½ teaspoon black pepper

1 tablespoon all-purpose flour
½ cup cider vinegar
½ cup water
2 tablespoons Vlasic mild banana
  pepper juice
½ cup Vlasic mild banana pepper
  rings

1. In 4-quart saucepan over medium heat, cook potatoes in boiling water to cover 10 minutes or until tender. Drain.

2. In 10-inch skillet over medium heat, cook bacon until crisp. Drain bacon on paper towels, reserving 2 tablespoons drippings in pan. Crumble bacon.

3. In same skillet over medium heat, in reserved drippings, cook onion, red pepper and black pepper until vegetables are tender, stirring often. Stir in flour; cook 1 minute, stirring constantly. Stir in vinegar, water and pepper juice. Cook until mixture boils and thickens, stirring constantly. Stir in potatoes, pepper rings and bacon. Makes 7 cups or 7 servings.

COUNTRY RELISH SLAW

1 jar (16 ounces) Vlasic country
  classic sweet chunky relish
3 cups shredded cabbage

½ cup sliced celery
⅓ cup shredded carrot

In medium bowl, combine all ingredients. Cover; refrigerate until serving time, at least 2 hours, stirring occasionally. Makes 5 cups or 6 servings.

OLIVE-ORANGE SALAD

6 large oranges, peeled, sliced and
  seeded
¾ cup Vlasic pitted ripe olives
  halved lengthwise
1 large red onion, sliced and
  separated into rings

¼ cup orange juice
¼ cup olive oil
⅛ teaspoon ground red pepper
  Campbell's Fresh butterhead
  lettuce leaves for garnish

1. In large bowl, combine oranges, olives, onion, orange juice, oil and red pepper; toss gently to coat. Cover; refrigerate at least 2 hours before serving.

2. To serve: Arrange chilled fruit mixture on lettuce-lined platter. Makes 6 cups or 6 servings.

Salads &
Dressings

ONION VINAIGRETTE DRESSING

1 cup olive or vegetable oil
½ cup wine vinegar
¼ cup water
1 clove garlic, minced

1 teaspoon paprika
1 pouch Campbell's dry onion soup
  and recipe mix

In covered jar or shaker, combine all ingredients. Shake until well blended. Cover; refrigerate until serving time, at least 2 hours. Shake well before using. Serve over tossed greens or an arranged salad of cucumbers, tomatoes, avocados and green onions. Makes 2 cups.

TOMATO FRENCH DRESSING

1 can (10¾ ounces) Campbell's
  condensed tomato soup
½ cup vegetable oil
¼ cup cider vinegar

4 slices bacon, crisp-cooked and
  crumbled
½ teaspoon dry mustard

In covered jar or shaker, combine all ingredients. Shake until well blended. Cover; refrigerate until serving time, at least 2 hours. Shake well before using. Serve over mixed salad greens or fruit salads. Makes about 2 cups.

LOW-CALORIE SALAD DRESSING

1 can (10½ ounces) Campbell's
  condensed chicken broth
⅓ cup vinegar
2 tablespoons vegetable oil
⅓ cup finely chopped Campbell's
  Fresh tomato

1 tablespoon chopped fresh parsley
1 clove garlic, minced
Generous dash pepper

In covered jar or shaker, combine all ingredients. Shake until well blended. Cover; refrigerate until serving time, at least 2 hours. Shake well before using. Serve over salad greens. Makes about 2 cups.

CREAMY V8 DRESSING

1 package (8 ounces) reduced-
    calorie cream cheese, softened
1 cup reduced-calorie mayonnaise

1 cup V8 vegetable juice
3 cloves garlic, minced
1 teaspoon lemon juice

1. In medium bowl, blend cream cheese until smooth. Gradually stir in mayonnaise until well blended.

2. Stir in V8 juice, garlic and lemon juice. Cover; refrigerate until serving time, at least 2 hours. Use as a salad dressing, for dipping or as a sandwich spread. Makes 2½ cups.

GINGER-SOY DRESSING

¾ cup V8 vegetable juice
⅓ cup vegetable oil
2 tablespoons soy sauce
2 tablespoons red wine vinegar

1 tablespoon sugar
1 tablespoon grated fresh ginger
1 tablespoon dry sherry

In covered jar or shaker, combine all ingredients. Shake until well blended. Cover; refrigerate until serving time, at least 2 hours. Shake well before using. Serve over salad greens or pasta salads. Makes 1½ cups.

ROSY BLUE CHEESE DRESSING

¾ cup V8 vegetable juice
3 tablespoons vegetable oil
2 tablespoons crumbled blue cheese

1 tablespoon lemon juice
1 tablespoon finely chopped onion
1 clove garlic, minced

In covered jar or shaker, combine all ingredients. Shake until well blended. Cover; refrigerate until serving time, at least 2 hours. Shake well before using. Serve over salad greens or vegetable salads. Makes 1 cup.

DIJON-PARMESAN DRESSING

1 can (14½ ounces) Swanson clear
    ready to serve chicken broth
1 package (8 ounces) cream cheese
½ cup grated Parmesan cheese

3 tablespoons Dijon-style mustard
2 tablespoons vinegar
1 clove garlic, minced

In covered blender or food processor, combine all ingredients. Blend until smooth. Cover; refrigerate at least 2 hours before serving. Serve over torn salad greens. Makes 3⅓ cups.

Clockwise from top: Creamy V8 Dressing,
Ginger-Soy Dressing and Rosy Blue Cheese Dressing

TOMATO-CUCUMBER DRESSING

1 can (10¾ ounces) Campbell's
  condensed cream of celery soup
1 cup mayonnaise
½ cup milk
1 cup chopped Campbell's Fresh
  tomato, drained

½ cup chopped seeded cucumber
¼ cup chopped fresh chives
1 tablespoon grated onion
⅛ teaspoon pepper

1. In medium bowl, combine soup and mayonnaise, stirring until well blended. Gradually stir in milk. Add remaining ingredients; mix well. Refrigerate until serving time, at least 4 hours.

2. Serve over mixed salad greens. Makes about 3 cups.

Tip: This dressing also makes a flavorful dip for crackers or vegetables.

ONION GREEN GODDESS DRESSING

1 pouch Campbell's dry onion soup
  and recipe mix
1½ cups mayonnaise
¾ cup chopped fresh parsley
⅓ cup milk
1 tablespoon lemon juice

1 tablespoon anchovy paste
2 teaspoons dried basil leaves,
  crushed
½ teaspoon dried tarragon leaves,
  crushed

In medium bowl, combine all ingredients. Stir until well blended. Cover; refrigerate until serving time, at least 2 hours. Thin with additional milk to desired consistency. Serve over salad greens or as a dip for raw vegetables. Makes 2 cups.

CREAMY SALAD DRESSING

1 can (10¾ ounces) Campbell's
  condensed cream of asparagus
  soup
½ cup mayonnaise
⅓ cup chopped fresh parsley

¼ cup tarragon vinegar
3 green onions, thinly sliced
2 tablespoons finely chopped
  anchovies
⅛ teaspoon pepper

In small bowl, combine soup and mayonnaise; mix until smooth. Add remaining ingredients; mix well. Cover; refrigerate until serving time, at least 4 hours. Serve over mixed salad greens. Makes about 2 cups.

Salads &
Dressings

Sauces & Gravies

From top to bottom: Sweet and Sour Sauce I, Sweet and Sour Sauce II and Sweet and Sour Sauce III (page 254)

SWEET AND SOUR SAUCE I

⅓ cup apple jelly
2 tablespoons cornstarch
1 stick cinnamon
1 clove garlic, minced
1 can (10½ ounces) Campbell's
    condensed chicken broth

⅓ cup cider vinegar
1 to 2 teaspoons soy sauce
¼ cup zucchini cut into matchstick-
    thin strips
½ cup halved cherry tomatoes

1. In 2-quart saucepan over medium-high heat, combine apple jelly, cornstarch, cinnamon stick and garlic. Gradually stir in broth, vinegar and soy sauce. Over medium-high heat, heat to boiling, stirring constantly; boil 1 minute.

2. Stir in zucchini and cherry tomatoes; heat through. Discard cinnamon stick. Serve over fish, poultry and meat. Makes about 2 cups.

SWEET AND SOUR SAUCE II

⅓ cup sugar
2 tablespoons cornstarch
¼ teaspoon ground nutmeg
1 clove garlic, minced
1 can (10½ ounces) Campbell's
    condensed chicken broth

⅓ cup cider vinegar
1 to 2 teaspoons soy sauce
¼ cup sliced water chestnuts
1 can (8 ounces) mandarin orange
    segments, drained

1. In 2-quart saucepan, combine sugar, cornstarch, nutmeg and garlic. Gradually stir in broth, vinegar and soy sauce. Over medium-high heat, heat to boiling, stirring constantly; boil 1 minute.

2. Stir in water chestnuts and mandarin oranges; heat through. Serve over fish, poultry or meat. Makes about 2 cups.

SWEET AND SOUR SAUCE III

⅓ cup honey
2 tablespoons cornstarch
6 whole cloves
1 clove garlic, minced
1 can (10½ ounces) Campbell's
    condensed chicken broth

⅓ cup cider vinegar
1 to 2 teaspoons soy sauce
¼ cup green onions cut into 1-inch
    lengths
1 cup drained pineapple chunks

1. In 2-quart saucepan, combine honey, cornstarch, cloves and garlic. Gradually stir in broth, vinegar and soy sauce. Over medium-high heat, heat to boiling, stirring constantly; boil 1 minute.

2. Stir in green onions and pineapple; heat through. Discard cloves. Serve over fish, poultry or meat. Makes about 2 cups.

Sauces &
Gravies

SAUCE AMANDINE

1 teaspoon butter or margarine
¼ cup finely chopped onion
¼ cup sliced almonds

1 can (10¾ ounces) Campbell's
condensed cream of mushroom
soup
⅓ cup milk

1. In 1-quart microwave-safe casserole, combine butter, onion and almonds. Microwave, uncovered, on HIGH 3 minutes or until onion is tender and almonds are lightly browned, stirring once during cooking.

2. Stir in soup until smooth. Stir in milk until blended. Cover with lid; microwave on HIGH 3 minutes or until hot and bubbling, stirring once during cooking. Serve with fish, chicken or vegetables. Makes about 1½ cups.

SOUPER CREAM SAUCE

1 can (10¾ ounces) Campbell's
condensed cream of celery soup
½ cup half-and-half

1 tablespoon prepared mustard
⅛ teaspoon paprika

In 2-quart saucepan, combine all ingredients. Over medium heat, heat through, stirring often. Serve over vegetables, meat or fish. Makes about 1½ cups.

CHEESE SAUCE

1 can (10¾ ounces) Campbell's
condensed cream of celery soup
⅓ cup milk

1½ cups shredded sharp Cheddar
cheese (6 ounces)
½ teaspoon dry mustard

In 2-quart saucepan, combine all ingredients. Over medium heat, heat through, stirring frequently. Serve over vegetables, hamburgers or pasta. Makes about 2 cups.

To microwave: In 1-quart microwave-safe casserole, combine all ingredients; stir to blend well. Cover; microwave on HIGH 4 to 6 minutes until hot, stirring occasionally during cooking.

Sauces & Gravies

ORIENTAL DIPPING SAUCE

¾ cup V8 vegetable juice
¼ cup packed light brown sugar
2 tablespoons rice wine vinegar or
dry sherry

1 tablespoon soy sauce
1 tablespoon cornstarch
¼ teaspoon grated fresh ginger

In medium microwave-safe bowl, combine all ingredients. Cover with waxed paper; microwave on HIGH 3 minutes or until hot and bubbling, stirring once during cooking. Serve as a dipping sauce for Swanson chicken nuggets, Mrs. Paul's fish sticks, onion rings or Oriental Turkey Puffs (page 15) for dipping. Makes 1 cup.

CHILI CON QUESO SAUCE

1 can (11 ounces) Campbell's
condensed nacho cheese
soup/dip
½ cup water
1 tablespoon chopped fresh parsley
or cilantro

¼ teaspoon ground cumin
½ cup chopped Campbell's Fresh
tomato

In 1-quart microwave-safe casserole, stir soup until smooth. Stir in water, parsley and cumin; mix well. Microwave, uncovered, on HIGH 3 minutes or until hot and bubbling. Stir in tomato. Serve with hamburgers, potatoes or vegetables. Makes about 2 cups.

CURRY SAUCE

2 tablespoons butter or margarine
¼ cup chopped onion
2 teaspoons curry powder
1 can (10¾ ounces) Campbell's
condensed cream of celery soup

½ cup apple juice
½ cup chopped apple
Salted peanuts for garnish

1. In 2-quart saucepan over medium heat, in hot butter, cook onion and curry powder until onion is tender, stirring occasionally.

2. Stir in soup and juice until well blended. Add apple; heat through, stirring occasionally. Garnish with peanuts. Serve over meat, poultry or rice. Makes about 2 cups.

To microwave: In 1-quart microwave-safe casserole, combine butter, onion and curry powder. Cover; microwave on HIGH 2 to 3 minutes until onion is tender. Stir in soup and juice until well blended. Add apple. Cover; microwave on HIGH 3 to 5 minutes until heated through, stirring occasionally during cooking. Garnish with peanuts.

Oriental Dipping Sauce

SOUR CREAM SAUCE

2 tablespoons butter or margarine
⅓ cup chopped onion
¼ teaspoon paprika
1 can (10¾ ounces) Campbell's
    condensed golden mushroom
    soup

⅓ cup sour cream
⅓ cup milk

1. In 2-quart saucepan over medium heat, in hot butter, cook onion and paprika until onion is tender, stirring occasionally.

2. Stir in soup, sour cream and milk. Heat through, stirring occasionally. Thin to desired consistency with additional milk, if desired. Serve over meat, vegetables, pasta or rice. Makes about 2 cups.

To microwave: In 1-quart microwave-safe casserole, combine butter, onion and paprika. Cover; microwave on HIGH 2 to 4 minutes until onion is tender. Stir in soup, sour cream and milk. Microwave, uncovered, on HIGH 3 to 5 minutes until heated through, stirring occasionally during cooking.

BORDELAISE SAUCE

2 tablespoons butter or margarine
1 tablespoon finely chopped onion
¼ teaspoon dried tarragon leaves,
    crushed
2 tablespoons all-purpose flour
1 can (10½ ounces) Campbell's
    condensed beef broth (bouillon)

1 tablespoon Burgundy or other dry
    red wine
1 teaspoon finely chopped fresh
    parsley
1 teaspoon lemon juice

1. In 1-quart microwave-safe casserole, combine butter, onion and tarragon. Cover with lid; microwave on HIGH 2 minutes or until onion is tender.

2. Stir in flour. Gradually stir in broth. Add wine, parsley and lemon juice. Cover; microwave on HIGH 4 minutes or until mixture boils, stirring twice during cooking. Serve with beef or liver. Makes about 1½ cups.

APRICOT SAUCE

1 pouch Campbell's dry onion
    mushroom soup and recipe mix

¾ cup apricot preserves
½ cup orange juice

In 1-quart saucepan, combine all ingredients. Over medium heat, heat to boiling, stirring constantly. Reduce heat to low. Simmer 8 minutes, stirring occasionally. Use to glaze poultry, turkey or ham. Makes 1 cup.

Sauces &
Gravies

HOMEMADE GRAVY

Drippings from roast meat or poultry
1 can (10½ ounces) Campbell's condensed French onion soup
½ soup can water

2 tablespoons cornstarch
1 teaspoon Worcestershire sauce
¼ teaspoon dried thyme leaves, crushed

1. Remove roast from pan. Pour off pan drippings, reserving 2 tablespoons in pan. Pour soup into roasting pan; stir well to loosen brown bits.

2. In cup, combine water and cornstarch; stir into roasting pan along with Worcestershire and thyme. Over medium heat, heat to boiling, stirring constantly; cook 1 minute more. Serve with meat or poultry. Makes about 2 cups.

MUSHROOM GRAVY

3 to 4 tablespoons poultry drippings
1 package (8 ounces) Campbell's Fresh mushrooms, sliced
¼ cup all-purpose flour

2 cups Swanson clear ready to serve chicken broth
1 cup milk
Salt
Pepper

1. In 10-inch skillet or roasting pan over medium heat, in hot drippings, cook mushrooms until tender and liquid is evaporated, stirring occasionally.

2. Stir in flour until blended; cook 1 minute, stirring constantly. Gradually stir in broth and milk. Cook until mixture boils and thickens, stirring often. Season with salt and pepper. Makes about 3 cups.

MADEIRA-MUSHROOM GRAVY

1 tablespoon butter or margarine
1 cup sliced Campbell's Fresh mushrooms
1 tablespoon chopped green onion
1 can (10¾ ounces) Franco-American beef gravy

2 tablespoons tomato paste
1 tablespoon Madeira wine
½ teaspoon chopped fresh thyme leaves or ¼ teaspoon dried thyme leaves, crushed

1. In 1-quart microwave-safe casserole, combine butter, mushrooms and onion. Cover with lid; microwave on HIGH 3 minutes or until mushrooms are tender, stirring once during cooking.

2. Stir in remaining ingredients. Cover; microwave on HIGH 3 minutes or until hot and bubbling. Serve with beef or pork. Makes about 2 cups.

Sauces & Gravies

NO-COOK SPICY BARBECUE SAUCE

1 can (10¾ ounces) Campbell's
   condensed tomato soup
¼ cup cider vinegar
2 tablespoons packed brown sugar

2 tablespoons Worcestershire sauce
2 teaspoons chili sauce
1 teaspoon dry mustard

In medium bowl, combine all ingredients; stir well. Use to baste chicken, spareribs, lamb, hamburgers or turkey. Makes about 1½ cups.

FRUITED BARBECUE SAUCE

2 tablespoons vegetable oil
½ cup chopped onion
1 clove garlic, minced
1 can (10½ ounces) Campbell's
   condensed beef broth (bouillon)

1 cup apricot preserves
¼ cup lemon juice
1 tablespoon soy sauce

In 2-quart saucepan over medium heat, in hot oil, cook onion and garlic until tender, stirring occasionally. Stir in remaining ingredients. Reduce heat to low. Simmer 15 minutes, stirring occasionally. Use to baste chicken or ribs during last 15 minutes of barbecuing. Heat remaining sauce; serve with meat. Makes 2 cups.

WESTERN BARBECUE SAUCE

1 pouch Campbell's dry onion soup
   and recipe mix
½ cup ketchup
1 cup water

¼ cup packed brown sugar
2 tablespoons vinegar
1 teaspoon chili powder
¼ teaspoon hot pepper sauce

In 1-quart saucepan, combine all ingredients. Over medium heat, heat to boiling, stirring constantly. Reduce heat to low. Simmer 8 minutes, stirring occasionally. Use to baste poultry, ribs or sausages during last 15 minutes of barbecuing or broiling. Makes 1½ cups.

No-Cook Spicy Barbecue Sauce

PEANUT DIPPING SAUCE

1 cup Swanson clear ready to serve chicken broth
¼ cup dry roasted peanuts
1 tablespoon lime juice

1 teaspoon grated fresh ginger
¼ teaspoon ground cumin
¼ cup half-and-half

1. In covered blender or food processor, combine broth, peanuts, lime juice, ginger and cumin. Blend until smooth. Pour into small saucepan.

2. Over low heat, heat to boiling. Simmer 10 minutes or until thickened, stirring frequently. Stir in half-and-half. Serve with Beef and Mushroom Sate (page 88) and your favorite kabobs. Makes ½ cup.

CHASSEUR SAUCE

1 package (3.5 ounces) Campbell's Fresh shiitake mushrooms
3 tablespoons butter or margarine
3 tablespoons chopped shallots
¼ teaspoon dried tarragon leaves, crushed

¼ cup Chablis or other dry white wine
1 can (10¼ ounces) Franco-American beef gravy
½ cup tomato sauce
2 tablespoons chopped fresh parsley

1. Trim woody portions of mushroom stems and discard. Chop mushrooms. In 10-inch skillet over medium heat, in hot butter, cook mushrooms, shallots and tarragon until vegetables are tender, stirring occasionally.

2. Add wine; cook until most of liquid is evaporated. Add gravy and tomato sauce. Heat through, stirring occasionally.

3. Stir in parsley just before serving. Serve with Beef en Croute with Duxelles (page 82), roast beef or grilled steak. Makes 1¾ cups.

CHUNKY MUSHROOM TOMATO SAUCE

2 tablespoons olive or vegetable oil
2 packages (8 ounces *each*) Campbell's Fresh mushrooms, sliced
1 large onion, chopped
1 medium carrot, shredded
2 cloves garlic, minced
2 cans (15 ounces *each*) tomato sauce

1 can (6 ounces) tomato paste
¼ cup chopped fresh parsley
1 tablespoon chopped fresh basil leaves or 1 teaspoon dried basil leaves, crushed
1 teaspoon dried oregano leaves, crushed
⅛ teaspoon pepper

1. In 3-quart saucepan over medium heat, in hot oil, cook mushrooms, onion, carrot and garlic until mushrooms are tender and liquid is evaporated, stirring occasionally.

2. Add remaining ingredients; heat to boiling. Reduce to low. Simmer 30 minutes or until sauce thickens, stirring occasionally. Serve over hot cooked pasta. Makes 6 cups.

Desserts & Breads

Cheesecake Pie (page 264)

CHEESECAKE PIE

6 tablespoons butter or margarine	½ cup sugar
1½ cups graham cracker crumbs	2 teaspoons grated lemon peel
2 packages (8 ounces *each*) cream cheese	2 tablespoons lemon juice
	1 teaspoon vanilla extract
1 can (11 ounces) Campbell's condensed Cheddar cheese soup	½ cup sour cream
	Chocolate Leaves for garnish (recipe follows)
3 eggs	Raspberries for garnish

1. To make crust: Place butter in 10-inch microwave-safe pie plate. Cover; microwave on HIGH 45 seconds or until melted. Stir in cracker crumbs; mix well. Press mixture on bottom and side of pie plate. Microwave, uncovered, on HIGH 1½ minutes, rotating plate once during cooking. Set aside.

2. To make filling: Place cream cheese in large microwave-safe bowl. Microwave, uncovered, on HIGH 1 minute or until softened. With electric mixer, beat cream cheese until smooth. Add soup, eggs, sugar, lemon peel, lemon juice and vanilla; beat until smooth. Microwave, uncovered, on HIGH 7 minutes or until mixture is hot and very thick, stirring often during cooking.

3. Pour filling into prepared crust. Microwave, uncovered, on MEDIUM (50% power) 5 minutes or until almost set in center, rotating dish once during cooking. Let stand directly on countertop until completely cooled. Refrigerate until serving time, at least 4 hours.

4. Spread sour cream evenly over cheesecake. Garnish with Chocolate Leaves and raspberries. Makes 4 servings.

CHOCOLATE LEAVES: In small microwave-safe bowl, combine 2 squares (1 ounce *each*) semisweet chocolate and 1 teaspoon shortening. Microwave, uncovered, on MEDIUM (50% power) 2½ minutes or until chocolate is melted, stirring twice during heating. Brush a thin layer of melted chocolate on veined side of a nontoxic leaf such as an orange or rose leaf. Place, chocolate-side up, on cookie sheet lined with waxed paper. Refrigerate until chocolate is firm, then carefully peel chocolate from leaf.

Or, spread chocolate in a thin layer on waxed paper and refrigerate until firm but not hard. Use a sharp knife or cookie cutters to cut leaves or other decorative shapes.

TOMATO SOUP SPICE CAKE

1 tablespoon granulated sugar	2 eggs
1 package (about 18 ounces) spice cake mix	2 tablespoons water
	1 cup sour cream
1 can (10¾ ounces) Campbell's condensed tomato soup	¼ cup packed brown sugar
	1 teaspoon vanilla extract

1. Generously grease 14-cup microwave-safe Bundt® pan. Sprinkle pan with granulated sugar.

2. In large bowl, combine cake mix, soup, eggs and water. With electric mixer at medium speed, beat 2 minutes or until well mixed, constantly scraping side and bottom of bowl.

3. Pour into prepared pan. Microwave, uncovered, on MEDIUM (50% power) 9 minutes, rotating pan once during cooking.

4. Microwave, uncovered, on HIGH 5 minutes or until wooden toothpick inserted into cake comes out clean. Let stand directly on countertop 15 minutes. Invert onto serving plate; cool completely.

5. In small bowl, combine sour cream, brown sugar and vanilla until sugar dissolves. Spoon evenly over cooled cake. Makes 12 servings.

SPICY CARROT CAKE

2 cups all-purpose flour	1 can (10¾ ounces) Campbell's condensed tomato soup
1⅓ cups packed brown sugar	
2 teaspoons baking powder	½ cup shortening
1 teaspoon baking soda	2 eggs
1 teaspoon ground cinnamon	¼ cup molasses
1 teaspoon ground nutmeg	1 cup shredded carrots
1 teaspoon ground allspice	½ cup raisins

1. Preheat oven to 350°F. Grease 10-inch tube pan.

2. In large bowl, combine flour, brown sugar, baking powder, baking soda, cinnamon, nutmeg and allspice. Add soup and shortening. With mixer at medium speed, beat 2 minutes, constantly scraping side and bottom of bowl.

3. Add eggs and molasses; beat 2 minutes more. Fold in carrots and raisins. Pour into prepared pan; bake about 1 hour or until wooden toothpick inserted in cake comes out clean. Cool in pan on wire rack 10 minutes. Remove from pan; cool completely. Serve plain or topped with whipped cream. Makes 16 servings.

FRUITED CHEESE MOLD

2 packages (10 ounces *each*) frozen
  raspberries, thawed
2 tablespoons sugar
2 envelopes unflavored gelatin
1 can (10¾ ounces) Campbell's
  condensed cream of celery soup

1 container (8 ounces) cream-style
  cottage cheese
1½ cups sour cream
½ cup chopped celery
Raspberries for garnish
Celery leaves for garnish

1. Drain raspberries, reserving liquid. Add enough water to liquid to make 1 cup. Pour liquid into 1-quart saucepan; add sugar. Sprinkle gelatin over liquid. Let stand 5 minutes. Over low heat, heat until gelatin is dissolved, stirring constantly.

2. In large bowl, combine gelatin mixture, drained raspberries and soup. Refrigerate 1 to 1½ hours until almost set.

3. Fold in cottage cheese, sour cream and celery. Pour into 7-cup mold. Refrigerate until set, at least 4 hours or overnight.

4. Unmold onto serving plate. Garnish with raspberries and celery leaves. Makes 8 servings.

CHOCOLATE SAUCEPAN BROWNIES

½ cup butter or margarine
1 package (12 ounces) semi-sweet
  chocolate pieces
1 can (11 ounces) Campbell's
  condensed Cheddar cheese
  soup

½ cup sugar
2 eggs, beaten
1½ cups all-purpose flour
2 teaspoons baking powder
1 cup chopped pecans, divided

1. Preheat oven to 350°F. Grease 13- by 9-inch baking pan.

2. In 3-quart saucepan over medium heat, melt butter. Reduce heat to low. Add chocolate pieces; stir until melted. Remove from heat.

3. With spoon, beat in soup, sugar and eggs. Add flour and baking powder; stir until blended. Stir in ¾ cup of the pecans. Spread batter in prepared pan. Sprinkle with remaining ¼ cup pecans.

4. Bake 25 to 35 minutes or until top springs back when lightly touched. Cool in pan on wire rack. Makes 24.

Fruited Cheese Mold

APPLE CRUMB

4 cups thinly sliced peeled apples
¼ cup packed brown sugar
1 teaspoon lemon juice
¼ teaspoon ground cinnamon
2 tablespoons butter or margarine

½ package (5- to 8-ounce size)
Pepperidge Farm Irish oatmeal,
hazelnut or lemon nut cookies,
coarsely crumbled (about 1 cup)
½ cup chopped walnuts (optional)

1. In large bowl, toss together apples, brown sugar, lemon juice and
cinnamon. Spoon mixture into 9-inch microwave-safe pie plate; set aside.

2. Place butter in medium microwave-safe bowl. Cover; microwave on HIGH
30 seconds or until melted. Stir in cookies and walnuts, if desired.

3. Sprinkle over apple mixture. Microwave, uncovered, on HIGH 7 minutes
or until apples are tender, rotating dish twice during cooking. Let stand,
uncovered, 5 minutes. Makes 6 servings.

Tip: A 21-ounce can of apple or cherry pie filling may be substituted for
apples; omit brown sugar. Proceed as in steps 1 through 3.

AMARETTI CUPCAKES

¼ cup butter or margarine, softened
½ cup sugar
1 egg
½ cup milk
1 teaspoon vanilla extract
1 cup all-purpose flour

1 teaspoon baking powder
1 cup (12 pairs) finely crushed
Lazzaroni amaretti disaronno
biscuits, divided
1 teaspoon ground cinnamon
3 tablespoons butter or margarine

1. In medium bowl, with electric mixer at medium speed, beat ¼ cup butter
and the sugar until smooth. Beat in egg, milk and vanilla. Fold in flour,
baking powder and ½ cup of the biscuit crumbs.

2. Place 2 paper liners in each cup of microwave-safe muffin ring or
6 custard cups. Spoon batter into cups, filling ½ full. Microwave, 6 at a
time, uncovered, on HIGH 2½ minutes or until wooden toothpick inserted
in centers comes out clean, rotating or rearranging once during cooking.
Repeat step 2 with remaining batter.

3. In small bowl, combine remaining ½ cup biscuit crumbs and the
cinnamon. Place 3 tablespoons butter in small microwave-safe bowl. Cover;
microwave on HIGH 40 seconds or until melted. Dip top of each cupcake
into butter, then into crumb mixture. Makes 12 cupcakes.

COOKIE ICE CREAM SUPREME

½ gallon vanilla ice cream
1 package (6½ ounces) Pepperidge
    Farm capri brownie creme
    cookies, coarsely crumbled

½ cup raspberry preserves
1 tablespoon lemon juice
1 tablespoon orange-flavored
    liqueur

1. Place ice cream in large microwave-safe bowl. Microwave, uncovered, on MEDIUM (50% power) 2 minutes or until softened, stirring once during heating.

2. Stir in cookies until well blended. Spoon into 10-inch pie plate. Cover; freeze 3 hours or until firm. Just before serving, make sauce.

3. To make sauce: In small microwave-safe bowl, combine preserves, lemon juice and liqueur. Microwave, uncovered, on HIGH 1½ minutes or until preserves are melted, stirring once during heating.

4. To serve: Let dessert stand at room temperature 5 minutes; cut into wedges. Serve with warm sauce. Makes 10 servings.

CINNAMON-RAISIN BREAD PUDDING

4 cups cubed Pepperidge Farm
    cinnamon bread
½ cup raisins
1½ cups milk
2 eggs, beaten

½ cup packed brown sugar
1 tablespoon brandy (optional)
½ teaspoon ground nutmeg
    Brandied Sauce (recipe follows)

1. In 1½-quart microwave-safe casserole, toss together bread cubes and raisins; set aside.

2. Pour milk into 4-cup glass measure. Microwave, uncovered, on HIGH 2 minutes or until warm. Stir eggs, brown sugar, brandy and nutmeg into milk until sugar dissolves.

3. Microwave, uncovered, on MEDIUM (50% power) 2 minutes or until heated through. Pour over bread cubes.

4. Cover with waxed paper; microwave on MEDIUM (50% power) 8 minutes or until custard is set, rotating dish every 2 minutes. Let stand 5 minutes. Serve with Brandied Sauce. Makes 6 servings.

BRANDIED SAUCE: In 2-cup glass measure, combine ¼ cup butter or margarine, ½ cup packed brown sugar, 3 tablespoons brandy and ⅛ teaspoon ground nutmeg. Microwave, uncovered, on HIGH 2½ minutes or until hot and bubbling, stirring twice during cooking.

GIANT ZUCCHINI MUFFINS

2½ cups all-purpose flour
½ cup cornmeal
⅓ cup sugar
1 tablespoon baking powder
1 teaspoon dried oregano leaves,
   crushed

1 can (11 ounces) Campbell's
   condensed nacho cheese
   soup/dip
½ cup milk
2 eggs
¼ cup vegetable oil
1 cup shredded zucchini

1. Preheat oven to 400°F. Grease twelve 3-inch muffin-pan cups.

2. In large bowl, combine flour, cornmeal, sugar, baking powder and oregano.

3. In medium bowl, combine soup, milk, eggs, oil and zucchini; mix well. Add to dry ingredients, stirring just to moisten. (Batter will be lumpy.)

4. Spoon batter into muffin cups, filling almost full. Bake 25 minutes or until wooden toothpick inserted in center of muffin comes out clean. Serve warm. Makes 12 muffins.

DILL-ONION MUFFINS

1 pouch Campbell's dry onion soup
   and recipe mix
2 cups all-purpose flour
¼ cup sugar
1 tablespoon baking powder

3 eggs
1 cup milk
⅓ cup vegetable oil
¼ cup chopped fresh parsley
2 teaspoons dried dill weed, crushed

1. Preheat oven to 375°F. Grease twelve 2½-inch muffin-pan cups or line with paper liners.

2. In large bowl, combine soup mix, flour, sugar and baking powder.

3. In small bowl, beat eggs; stir in milk, oil, parsley and dill. Add to dry ingredients, stirring just enough to moisten.

4. Spoon batter into prepared muffin cups. Bake 20 minutes or until muffins are golden. Cool in pan a few minutes; serve warm. Makes 12 muffins.

Giant Zucchini Muffins

NO-KNEAD ONION BREAD

3 cups all-purpose flour, divided
2 tablespoons sugar
2 packages active dry yeast
1 can (10½ ounces) Campbell's
    condensed French onion soup

¼ cup butter or margarine
1 egg
1 cup grated Romano cheese
1 tablespoon water
2 teaspoons sesame seed

1. In large bowl, combine 1 cup of the flour, the sugar and yeast.

2. In small saucepan over medium heat, heat soup and butter until very warm (120° to 130°F.). Butter does not need to melt completely.

3. With mixer at low speed, gradually pour soup mixture into dry ingredients, mixing well. At medium speed, beat 3 minutes or until smooth. Add egg, cheese and 1 cup of the flour; beat 2 minutes more.

4. With spoon, stir in enough remaining flour to make a stiff batter. Cover; let rise in warm place until doubled, about 1½ hours.

5. Grease 1½-quart casserole. Stir down batter. Turn into prepared casserole. Cover; let rise until doubled, about 45 minutes. Preheat oven to 325°F.

6. Brush with water and sprinkle with sesame seed. Bake 50 minutes or until bread sounds hollow when tapped with finger. Remove from pan; cool on wire rack before slicing. Makes 1 loaf or 16 servings.

NACHO CORN BREAD

1 cup plus 1 tablespoon yellow
    cornmeal, divided
1 cup all-purpose flour
¼ cup sugar
1 tablespoon baking powder
1 can (11 ounces) Campbell's
    condensed nacho cheese
    soup/dip

1 egg, beaten
½ cup milk
1 tablespoon vegetable oil
½ cup chopped onion

1. Grease 9-inch microwave-safe ring pan. Dust with 1 tablespoon cornmeal.

2. In medium bowl, combine remaining 1 cup cornmeal, the flour, sugar and baking powder.

3. In small bowl, stir soup until smooth. Add egg, milk, oil and onion; stir until well blended. Pour all at once into dry ingredients; stir just until flour is moistened. (Batter will be stiff.)

4. Spread evenly in prepared pan. Microwave, uncovered, on MEDIUM (50% power) 6 minutes, rotating pan once during cooking.

5. Microwave, uncovered, on HIGH, 4 minutes or until wooden toothpick inserted in bread comes out clean, rotating dish once during cooking. Let stand on countertop 5 minutes. Invert onto serving plate. Makes 8 servings.

No-Knead Onion Bread

CHEESY PEPPER CORN BREAD

1 package (8½ to 12 ounces) corn muffin mix
1 cup shredded Monterey Jack cheese (4 ounces)

2 to 3 teaspoons seeded and chopped Vlasic hot jalapeno or chili peppers

Prepare and bake corn muffin mix according to package directions, but stir cheese and peppers into batter. Cut into wedges or squares. Makes 8 servings.

DOUBLE CHEESE RING

2 cups all-purpose flour
1 cup whole-wheat flour
2 tablespoons sugar
4 teaspoons baking powder
¾ cup shortening
1 can (11 ounces) Campbell's condensed Cheddar cheese soup

¼ cup milk
4 (1-ounce) slices American cheese, each cut into 4 triangles
1 egg yolk
2 teaspoons water
Poppy seed

1. Preheat oven to 425°F. Grease large cookie sheet.

2. In large bowl, combine flours, sugar and baking powder. With pastry blender, cut in shortening until mixture resembles coarse crumbs.

3. In small bowl, combine soup and milk; mix well. Add to flour mixture, stirring with fork just until dough forms. Turn out onto lightly floured surface. Knead dough 10 times. Divide dough in half.

4. Roll out each dough half to 12-inch circle. Cut each into 8 wedges. Place 1 piece of cheese on each dough wedge. Roll up, jelly-roll fashion, from wide end. On prepared cookie sheet, arrange rolls side-by-side to form a ring.

5. In small bowl, combine egg yolk and water; brush on ring. Sprinkle with poppy seed.

6. Bake 25 to 30 minutes or until browned. Serve warm. Makes 16 servings.

POTATO DOUGHNUTS

6 to 6½ cups all-purpose flour,
    divided
1 cup sugar
2 packages active dry yeast
1 can (10¾ ounces) Campbell's
    condensed cream of potato soup
1 soup can water

¼ cup butter or margarine
¼ teaspoon ground nutmeg
1 egg
Vegetable oil
Cinnamon sugar

1. In large bowl, combine 3 cups of the flour, the sugar and yeast. In blender or food processor, blend soup until smooth. In 2-quart saucepan over low heat, heat soup, water, butter and nutmeg until mixture is very warm (120° to 130°F.). Butter does not need to melt completely.

2. With mixer at low speed, gradually pour soup mixture into dry ingredients. At medium speed, beat 2 minutes, scraping bowl with rubber spatula. Beat in egg and ½ cup of the flour; beat 2 minutes more, scraping bowl occasionally. With spoon, stir in enough additional flour (about 2½ cups) to make a soft dough. On floured surface, knead until smooth and elastic, about 10 minutes.

3. Shape dough into ball; place in greased large bowl, turning dough over to grease top. Cover; let rise in warm place until doubled, about 1 hour.

4. Punch dough down. On floured surface, roll out dough to ¼ inch thickness; cut with floured 3-inch doughnut cutter. Cover; let rise in warm place until doubled, about 30 minutes.

5. In skillet or Dutch oven, heat 1-inch oil to 375°F. Fry doughnuts, a few at a time, in hot oil until browned, about 1 minute on each side. Drain on paper towels. Cover warm doughnuts with cinnamon sugar mixture. Makes about 30 doughnuts.

Tip: To make glaze, in medium bowl, combine 1 pound confectioners' sugar, 6 tablespoons water or orange juice and 1 teaspoon vanilla. Dip doughnuts in glaze to coat on both sides.

PARMESAN BREAD DELUXE

¾ cup grated Parmesan cheese
⅓ cup Marie's refrigerated regular
    ranch, blue cheese, sour cream
    and dill, Italian garlic or
    buttermilk spice ranch style
    salad dressing

3 tablespoons finely chopped onion
1 loaf (8 ounces) Italian bread, cut
    into ½-inch-thick slices

In small bowl, combine Parmesan, salad dressing and onion. Spread a generous teaspoon of the dressing mixture onto one side of each bread slice. Arrange bread, spread side up, on cookie sheets. Broil 4 inches from heat 2 minutes or until golden brown. Makes about 24 slices.

Desserts & Breads

V8 CHEESE BREAD

5½ to 6 cups all-purpose flour, divided
2 packages active dry yeast
1½ teaspoons salt
1 cup V8 vegetable juice
¾ cup water

3 tablespoons butter or margarine
1½ cups shredded Cheddar cheese
(6 ounces)
1 egg

1. In large bowl, combine 2 cups of the flour, the yeast and salt; set aside. In small saucepan over medium heat, heat V8 juice, water and butter until warm (115° to 120°F.).

2. Stir V8 juice mixture into flour mixture. With mixer at low speed, beat 30 seconds. Add cheese and egg. With mixer at high speed, beat 3 minutes. Stir in 2½ cups of the flour.

3. Place dough on lightly floured surface; knead until smooth and elastic, about 6 minutes, adding remaining flour while kneading. Shape dough into ball; place in large greased bowl, turning dough to grease top. Cover; let rise in warm place until doubled, about 1 hour.

4. Spray two 8- by 4-inch loaf pans with vegetable cooking spray. Punch dough down; divide in half. Shape into 2 loaves. Place in prepared pans. Cover; let rise in warm place until doubled, about 45 minutes.

5. Preheat oven to 375°F. Bake 35 minutes or until golden and loaves sound hollow when lightly tapped with finger. Remove from pans; cool on wire racks. Makes 2 loaves.

CRANBERRY-ORANGE TEA BREAD

1 can (11 ounces) Campbell's
condensed Cheddar cheese
soup
½ cup granulated sugar
¼ cup packed brown sugar
2 tablespoons vegetable oil

1 egg, beaten
2 cups all-purpose flour
2 teaspoons baking powder
2 teaspoons grated orange peel
1 cup chopped cranberries
½ cup chopped walnuts

1. Preheat oven to 350°F. Grease 9- by 5-inch loaf pan.

2. In medium bowl, combine soup, granulated sugar, brown sugar, oil and egg; mix until blended.

3. Add flour, baking powder and orange peel; stir just until moistened. Stir in cranberries and walnuts.

4. Pour batter into prepared pan. Bake 1 hour 10 minutes or until wooden toothpick inserted in center comes out clean. Cool in pan on wire rack 10 minutes. Remove from pan; cool on rack. Makes 1 loaf.

V8 Cheese Bread; Harvest Bowl Soup

GERMAN CHEESE FRUIT KUCHEN

3½ to 3¾ cups all-purpose flour,
    divided
¼ cup sugar
2 packages active dry yeast
1 can (11 ounces) Campbell's
    condensed Cheddar cheese
    soup, divided
½ cup water
¼ cup butter or margarine

4 eggs, divided
1 can (21 ounces) cherry pie filling
1 package (8 ounces) cream
    cheese, softened
⅓ cup sugar
2 tablespoons orange juice
1 tablespoon grated orange peel
    Ground nutmeg

1. In large bowl, combine 1½ cups of the flour, ¼ cup sugar and the yeast. In 1-quart saucepan over low heat, heat ½ cup of the soup, the water and butter until mixture is very warm (120° to 130°F.). Butter does not need to melt completely.

2. With mixer at low speed, gradually pour soup mixture into dry ingredients. At medium speed, beat 2 minutes, scraping bowl with rubber spatula. Beat in 2 of the eggs and ½ cup of the flour; beat 2 minutes more, scraping bowl occasionally. With spoon, stir in enough additional flour (about 1½ cups) to make a soft dough. On floured surface, knead until smooth and elastic, about 5 minutes. Shape dough into ball; place in greased large bowl, turning to grease top. Cover; let rise in warm place until doubled, about 45 minutes.

3. Grease 13- by 9-inch baking pan. Press dough into prepared pan, making 1-inch rim on edges. Top with cherry pie filling. Cover and let rise in warm place until doubled, about 30 minutes. Preheat oven to 350°F.

4. Meanwhile, in small bowl with mixer at medium speed, beat cream cheese and remaining soup until smooth. Beat in remaining 2 eggs and the ⅓ cup sugar. Stir in orange juice and peel; pour over filling. Sprinkle with ground nutmeg.

5. Bake 45 to 55 minutes or until crust is golden brown and cheese is set. Cool slightly in pan on wire rack. Serve warm. Makes 12 servings.

Index

(continued)

(continued)